Richard Ballantine

Richard's bicycle book

new revised and expanded edition
Pan Books London and Sydney

1 quick release hub
2 rear brake
3 seat stay
4 seat post
5 saddle
6 seat tube
7 top tube
8 front changer
9 stem

10 expander bolt
11 handle bars
12 headset
13 brake lever
14 head tube
15 front brake
16 front fork
17 chrome fork tips
18 quick release hub

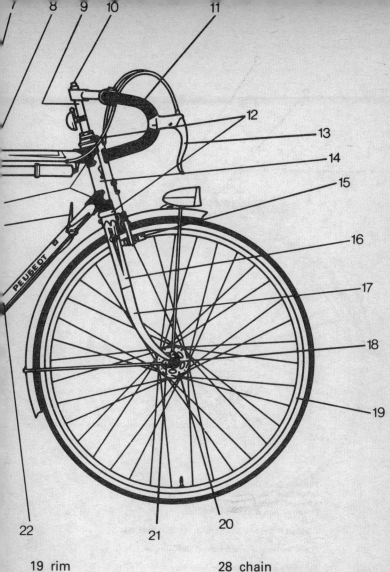

19 rim
20 front hub
21 fork rake
22 down tube
23 chain guard and chain-wheels
24 bottom bracket
25 crank
26 pedal
27 chain stay

28 chain
29 guide wheels of the rear changer
30 rear changer (derailleur)
31 rear sprockets (freewheel)
32 lugs
33 gear change
34 cotter pin

This book is
dedicated to
Samuel Joseph Melville,
Hero.

First published in Great Britain 1975 by Pan Books Ltd,
Cavaye Place, London SW10 9PG
Revised editions 1976, 1977, 1984
Revised and expanded editions 1979, 1983
19 18
© Richard Ballantine 1972, 1975, 1976, 1977, 1979, 1983, 1984
ISBN 0 330 26766 3
Printed and bound in Great Britain by Collins, Glasgow

Mechanical illustrations by John Batchelor and courtesy
Ron Kitching Organisation,
old bicycles and cycling scenes from the author's library,
with contributions from Heywood Hill and Sherry Rubin.
Cover bicycle by F. W. Evans Ltd, London

BOOK 1

BOOK 2

Foreword

Fair notice: I am an American and, despite Scottish and English
grandparents and an English mother, some of my notions
differ from those of the British,
just as Italians can be
distinguished from Swedes.

A daring and foolhardy feat was performed by a bicyclist the other afternoon at Cabin John Bridge. The place is a general pleasure resort about twelve miles from town, over the military road built by Jefferson Davis while Secretary of War. The bridge is said to be the largest single span of masonry in the world. It is 125 feet high, and about 200 feet long, a single magnificent arch spanning a deep and rocky gorge. A good many people go out there to see the bridge, and the man who keeps the little hotel known as Cabin John, just at the end and across the bridge, does a good business, especially on Sunday. Every nice Sunday the sheds about the place are crowded with vehicles of every description, and sporting men, family parties, wheelmen, and gentlemen of leisure, are loafing about the house, getting country dinners or picnicking in the wild gorge below the bridge. As at all such places, there are always a few wheelmen lounging in and out, and a number of machines were stacked in the yard that afternoon, and a lively party within could be heard telling stories and boasting of their personal skill on the road. In the midst of the hilarity one young man suddenly came out alone, and, singling out his machine, mounted, and without a word rode towards the bridge. There is a brownstone coping on the three-foot wall on either side of the roadway. This coping is about a foot broad, and is bevelled on the two upper edges for an inch or two. On the inside of these walls is the solid roadway above the duct. On the outside is a perpendicular descent of about 125 feet in the centre of the bridge, and no less than 75 feet at either abutment. The young man stopped and dismounted at the end of the bridge and lifted his machine upon the coping. The act was noticed by a couple of gentlemen smoking under the trees, but it was looked upon as a freak, and no particular attention was paid to it. The next moment there was an exclamation of horror, for the young man was seen mounted upon his bicycle deliberately riding along the narrow coping. The sight froze the blood of the ladies and children picnicking in the gorge below, and was enough to appeal to the stoutest heart. The gentlemen in front of the hotel started to their feet and called to the other wheelmen within. It was too late. The young man was already in the centre of the bridge. He never swerved a hair's breadth from his seat. From the end of the bridge he seemed a toy machine running by mechanism, so erect and motionless he sat, and so evenly he rode. 'Let him alone,' cried one of his companions, 'he could ride it if it was a rope.' Nevertheless, the fear that interference might hasten the horror that all wished to prevent left the party rooted to the spot. In two places the coping makes a zigzag by the widening of the roadway, and at these places the rider must steer his wheel through a very narrow space at nearly right-angles with his course. The daring fellow had passed the first of these ticklish spots, and, when he carefully wore round the second, not a single one of the horrified spectators could draw a breath for fear. From thence to the end was a short and straight run, and in another moment the young man had completed his dangerous ride, dismounted, and was waving his hand laughingly at the frightened men and women and children who had witnessed it. The young fellow calmly remounted his wheel and rode on towards the city as if he done a very common thing not worth mentioning. He was induced to undertake the feat because someone had doubted whether he had the requisite ability and nerve to perform it.

Bicycling News, 10 October 1886

Book One

1 Get a Bike!

Zowie! The world will pedal into the twenty-first century on billions of bicycles. From remote semi-arid high plains to teeming cities the bicycle has emerged as the most efficient, convenient and pleasant form of personal transport. Global production of cycles, nearly 80 million units in 1981, is steadily increasing by about 10 per cent annually.

World-wide, one person in ten owns a bicycle, but the proportion varies considerably in different countries. Bicycles outsell cars in Western Europe, the United States and Japan. Over 100 million Americans – half the population – ride on two wheels. In Japan, over 50 million bikes are in use, and congestion is so severe that if one parked bike in a line falls, the resulting chain-reaction of falling bikes can last for several minutes, and travel a block. In the Netherlands 80 per cent of the population own bicycles. And in China, where one quarter of all the people in the world live and private cars are virtually non-existent, 80 per cent of personal travel is by bike. The bicycle, as Stuart S. Wilson of Oxford University says, is the most important modern invention (*Scientific American,* March 1973). It was not always thought to be so.

In America, for example, the typical pre-World War II bike was sturdy but cumbersome. Equipped with a single pedal-operated coaster brake and one low, slow gear, these 'balloon tyre bombers' hit the scales at about 5 stone plus. Used primarily by youngsters not old enough to drive, they were wonderful work-horse machines tough enough to withstand jolting rides over kerbs and through fields, frequent nights out in the rain, and a generally high level of abuse. Fond nostalgia permeates memories of these bikes, but for the most part only people who had no other alternative used them. Pre-World War II sales could not have exceeded 500,000 per annum. In contrast, in much smaller Great Britain, 1935 was the heyday of the bicycle, with a record sale of 1.6 million. The bicycle was then a transportation staple in widespread use. The basic design established by 1910 had been subject to a long evolutionary series of minor improvements. Most machines were middleweights with lightened frames, roller lever rim brakes, and 1½ inch tyres,

Rover Safety – 1885

and fancier models had calliper cable-actuated rim brakes, gears, and $1\frac{1}{4}$ inch or $1\frac{1}{2}$ inch tyres. Tipping the scales at 45 to 50 pounds, they were dubbed 'English Racers' by the Americans because of their startlingly better performance over the domestic product. Here, they were just the ordinary ride-around bike for local use, to and from work, shopping, mail delivery, police work, light touring, and the like.

The bottom dropped out of the market after the war. Although in America the 'English Racer' provided the foundation for the growth of cycling as an adult sport and means of transport, after World War II sales in Great Britain dropped below 500,000 per annum. Britain went car-crazy, and the bicycle went the way of the Dodo bird. Roads, car parks, petrol stations, motorways, and cars, cars, cars proliferated, so that now Britain is a world leader in number of cars per mile of road, and many of her towns and villages have been transformed into mazes of one-way motordromes.

Re-enter our Dodo bird, the bicycle. In 1972 sales were 700,000. In 1980 they were 1.6 million, a match for the halcyon record set in 1935. The important fact behind these figures is that where once the majority of bikes sold were children's models, adult models now account for around 80 per cent of all bikes sold. Of these, fully half are adult sport bikes – drop handlebar, derailleur gear 'racers' weighing between 19 and 32 pounds and almost incomparably faster and easier to ride than other bikes. Another model popular with commuters and shoppers is the unisex mini bike with 20 inch wheels. The faithful old 3-speed roadster is now a lightweight at about 35 pounds. There are folding bikes weighing as little as 20 pounds that will fit into a suitcase. And just entering the market-place are HPVs – human powered vehicles with full aerodynamic body shells that give protection from the elements and an impressive turn of speed.

The boom in bikes has done wonders for technology, quality and value. You can buy a better bike today, for less money, than ever before.

Economics

With even moderate use a bike will pay for itself. Suppose you use a bike to get to work and back instead of public transportation or a car. Figure public transport costs at £1.20 a day. Say it rains once a week* and you use an alternative form of transport. That is 4 days X 48 weeks X £1.20 or £230 which buys a very handsome bike. On a 10-mile round trip (the national commuting average) at 25p a mile, a car costs £2.50 a day, or £600 a year. For that kind of money you could ride a different colour bicycle each day of the week.

Travelling to and from work is just one application. If you are a car owner, try this exercise: total all your car-related expenses (for 6000 miles annually it will easily exceed £1000) for the year. Add in the total annual expenditure on all other transport.

Next, add and total:

●A bike and accessories for each family member at a generous £300 each;

*A generous allowance. There is no measureable rainfall twenty days a month. In the time between 8-9 a.m. and 5-6 p.m. it rains only twelve days a year. You will get wet sometimes, but not as often as you might imagine. In towns such as Stevenage where cycles are a popular form of transport, the variation in use is at most 5 per cent, and is not related to the weather.

• The cost of renting cars for weekends, holidays, and so on;
• The revised cost for all other transport, including a generous allowance for taxi-cabs.

Unless you motor a high number of miles per year, or regularly cart about a large family, the bike/rental car combination will probably produce a saving within a year, and certainly within two years. Think about the fact that you will still have a rental car or taxi-cab whenever required, but more money to spend however you fancy.

Whether you're a car owner or not, bikes are just dandy for visiting friends, light shopping, nipping down to the cinema, delivering the kids to school, and so on. You save money every time and it can add up to an impressive amount. Besides easing many of your chores and tasks, bikes are worthwhile in themselves, so that a bike easily 'pays for itself' in rides taken just for fun and pleasure.

Convenience and Reliability

In metropolitan areas for a distance of up to five miles, a bike is faster than a train, bus or car. In heavy traffic you can expect to average 10 mph, and in lighter traffic 15 mph. In London, I used to ride from my home in Primrose Hill to Covent Garden in 15 minutes or less. The same journey by tube took a minimum of 30 minutes, if it transpired at all. When I lived in New York City it used to be my delight to race subway-travelling friends from 120th street to Greenwich Village – about 6 or 7 miles – and beat them. The story is the same everywhere. There have been bike versus bus, tube and car contests in many cities, and in each case I know about, the bike has always won.

One reason why a bike is so fast is that it can wiggle through the traffic jams that now typify cities and towns. A car or bus may have a higher peak speed, but is often completely immobile. A bike can just keep on moving, posting a higher average speed. Another advantage of travelling by bike is that the journey is door-to-door. Use of public transportation involves walking to the local stop, waiting around for the bus or train, possibly incurring a change with another wait, and then a walk from the final stop to your destination. Cars have to be parked. With a bike, you simply step out the door and take off. No waiting, no parking problems.

The bike's capabilities make it a real freedom machine. Your lunch hour: tired of the same company cafeteria slop or local sandwich bar? Cycling to a new and interesting cafe a mile or so away is a matter of minutes. Or how about a picnic in the park? Lots of errands to do? A bike can nip from one place to another much faster than you can hoof it, and has a car beat all hollow in traffic and for parking. What might ordinarily take an hour or more is only 15 minutes on the bike. And if there is a lot to lug around, it is the bike and not you that does the work. Last-minute decision to catch a film or visit friends? Boom! Ten minutes and you're there before the tube even gets going. If, like me, you are at all nocturnal, a bike is a tremendous advantage. Trains and buses tend to become elusive as the wee hours approach. There is also a powerful contrast between a journey on a noisy and often dirty train or bus, and a graceful rhythmic ride in which you glide through calm and silent streets or through the stillness of a country night under the moon and stars.

The reliability of a bike does a lot for peace of mind. Worrying questions such as 'Will the car start?', 'Is there a train strike today?' or 'Do I have enough money for a taxi?' need never arise.

Bikes are little affected by general traffic conditions. The going may be a little slower during the morning and evening rush hours, but only a little experience is necessary to make the timing of most journeys predictable to within a minute or two. Best of all, the whole enterprise is under your direct control. If you are late you can pedal faster, and if you have time in hand you can dawdle for a while in an interesting shop or pause for a quick snooze in the park.

Medical

All right, you say. So it takes less time than the tube. But I've got to work for a living and the tube is easier, takes less out of me. You expect me to get up in the morning and crack off 5 miles? Finish a day of hard work and do another 5? I'd never make it.

Get this. Even a moderate amount of exercise makes life *easier*. It gives your body tone and bounce which makes daily work and chores a breeze. Simply put, this is because exercise increases your range of possible effort, putting daily activities towards the centre

14

rather than the peak of your capabilities. So as you go through the day you are just cruising. It's something like the difference between a 25-and 100-horsepower automobile engine. At 60 mph the 25 horse is working hard but the 100 is just loafing. It is important to realize that you can get this increased bounce, verve, and good feeling with relatively little time and effort. Bicycling will make your work and day easier, not harder.

Are you familiar with 'cleaning out' a motor vehicle? Cars today often operate in stop-and-go traffic for long periods of time. The engine becomes clogged with carbon and other residue. The car stumbles and staggers, it works harder than it needs to, and petrol consumption goes up. The best thing for any such car is to be taken out on a motorway and run fast, for at higher speeds the engine cleans itself out. Your body is a machine with exactly similar characteristics, and you will literally become more fagged out and tired just sitting still than if you run around the block a few times.

According to Eugene Sloane in his *Complete Book of Bicycling*, if you get some sort of regular exercise you can expect to:
- live for up to five years longer;
- think better (more blood to the brain – and if you think this is crazy, go out and run around for a while and then think it through again);
- sleep better, and in general be more relaxed;
- be stronger and more resistant to injury;
- reduce the incidence of degenerative vascular diseases responsible for or associated with heart attacks, strokes, and high blood pressure.

As cardiovascular problems account for over 50 per cent of all deaths each year, this last point is worth some elaboration. The basic deal with the cardiovascular system is movement, the flow of blood through your heart, veins, arteries, and so forth. The heart normally pumps about 5 quarts per minute and, during exercise, up to 30 quarts per minute. If this flow is sluggish and slow, the system clogs up. In arteriosclerosis, for example, the walls of the system become hardened and calcified. This decreases the bore of the arteries and veins, resulting in a diminished capacity to carry blood. The heart must therefore pump harder and higher blood pressure results. High blood pressure is a cause of stroke or rupture of brain blood vessels. Arteriosclerosis happens to everybody, but extent is governed by the rate of flow of the blood. Exercise stimulates the blood flow, and does not permit calcification to occur as rapidly.

Atherosclerosis is a related malady. This is when fatty substances are deposited on the lining of the blood vessels. Clots in the blood may be formed as a result, and these can jam up the system at critical points, such as the brain or heart, causing a stroke or heart attack. Again, exercise by stimulating the blood flow helps prevent fatty deposits.

So, the main benefits of regular exercise are first, that it will help keep your blood circulatory system cleaned out; secondly, the heart muscle, like any other, reponds to exercise by becoming larger and more efficient, so that each heartbeat delivers more oxygen to the body; and thirdly, lung-filled capacity is restored or enlarged. In short, you can do more, and recover more quickly from doing it.

Bicycling, in particular, is a complete exercise. Not only are the legs, the body's largest accessory blood-pumping mechanism, used extensively, but also arm, shoulder, back, abdominal and diaphragmatic muscles. At the same time there is enough flexibility so that muscle groups can be worked individually, and of course pace can be set to suit the rider.

A word about weight control. Bicycling or other exercise will help your body's tone and figure. But for weight loss, eat less food. A brisk ride does not entitle you to apple pie and ice cream. Regular cycling burns about 300 calories per hour and hill climbing or racing about 600 per hour. Your body uses up about 150 calories per hour anyway, and so in the case of regular cycling this means a burn-up of an extra 150 calories per hour. At 3,600 calories per pound, it would take 24 hours of riding to lose this amount. It's much simpler just to eat less. Curiously enough, cycling may help you to do this. Regular exercise can change the metabolic balance of the body and restore normal automatic appetite control so that you eat no more than you actually need.

A serious health hazard for the urban cyclist is the breathing of highly polluted air. (See 7, Fast is safe).

Ecology

Great Britain is literally drowning in pollutants and many of them come from transportation machinery. In cities the internal combustion engine is a prime offender, contributing up to 85 per cent of all air pollution,* and of an especially noxious quality. The effluents from petroleum engines hang in the air and chemically interact with other substances and sunlight to form even deadlier poisons. Living in a major city is the same thing as smoking two packs of cigarettes a day.†

All city transportation contributes to pollution. Trains run on electricity generated in plants fired by fossil fuels or deadly atomic reactors. But as anyone who has been lucky enough to live through a taxicab strike or vehicle ban knows, cars and buses are the real problem. I shall never forget a winter many years ago when a friend and I came driving into New York City late at night after a holiday in Canada. To my amazement, the lights of the city shone like jewels and each building was clear and distinct. From the west bank of the Hudson river I could for the first (and perhaps only) time in my life see Manhattan and the Bronx in perfect detail from beginning to end, and even beyond to Brooklyn and her bridges. As we crossed the George Washington Bridge the air was clean and fresh, and the city, usually an object of horror and revulsion, was astoundingly beautiful and iridescent. The explanation was simple: enough snow had fallen to effectively eliminate vehicle traffic for a couple of days. No vehicles, no junk in the air. A better world.

Arguments against motorized transport are usually dismissed as idealistic and impractical and on the grounds that the time-saving characteristics of such vehicles are essential. The fact is that even

*Reinow, L. & L., *Moment in the Sun* (Ballantine, New York).
†Commoner, Barry, *The Closing Circle* (Jonathan Cape, London).

pedestrians are easily able to drone past most traffic, and of course bicycles can do even better. A saving in physical effort is realized, but few of us are healthy enough to need this, or dismiss inhaling the poisons (equivalent to two packs of cigarettes a day) which necessarily accompany the internal combustion engine.

Walking, roller-skating, or riding a bicycle is an efficient use of energy and reduces wastage. Professor Rice in *Technology Review* has calculated that a cyclist can do 1,000 miles on the food energy equivalent of a gallon of petrol, which will move a car only some 20 or 30 miles. His figures are based on a 40 pound bicycle, and could probably be doubled for a 20 pound lightweight. Facts and figures be as they may, utilizing a 100-horsepower, 3,000 pound behemoth to move one single 150 pound person a few miles is like using an atomic bomb to kill a canary. Great Britain runs neck and neck with the United States in its ability to consume and waste, and in relation to the size of her population utilizes a disproportionately large proportion of the world's resources. For example, we import fish meal from African countries where people are starving, to feed beef herds, and then wonder why people down there don't like us. Great Britain's dependence on imports needs no documentation. The point is, many of the commodities we take for granted are gained at considerable expense to a world hurting badly for food and other necessities. Using a bicycle is a starting antidote to the horrors of consumerism.

Which brings us to the most positive series of reasons for trying to use bicycles at every opportunity. Basically, this is that it will enhance your life, bringing to it an increase in quality of experience which will find its reflection in everything you do.

Well! You have to expect that I would believe bicycling is a good idea, but how do I get off expressing the notion that bicycling is philosophically and morally sound? Because it is something that *you do,* not something that is done to you. Need I chronicle the oft-cited concept of increasing alienation in our lives? The mechanization of work and daily activities, the hardships our industrial society places in the way of loving and fulfilling relationships and family life, the tremendous difficulties individuals experience trying to influence political and economic decisions which affect them and others?

The most important effect of mechanical contraptions is that they defeat consciousness. Consciousness, self-awareness, and development are the prerequisites for a life worth living. Now look at what happens to you on a bicycle. It's immediate and direct. *You* pedal. *You* make decisions. *You* experience the tang of the air and the surge of power as you bite into the road. You're vitalized. As you hum along you fully and gloriously experience the day, the sunshine, the clouds, the breezes. You're alive! You are going some place, and it is *you* who are doing it. Awareness increases, and each day becomes a little more important to you. With increased awareness you see and notice more, and this further reinforces awareness.

Each time you insert *you* into a situation, each time *you* experience, you fight against alienation and impersonality, you build consciousness and identity. You try to understand things in the ways that are important to you. And these qualities carry over into everything you do.

An increased value on one's own life is the first step in social conscience and politics. Because to you life is dear and important and fun, you are much more easily able to understand why this is also true for a Vietnamese, an Eskimo, or a Tobago islander. Believe it. The salvation of the world is the development of personality and identity for everybody in it. Much work, many lifetimes. But a good start for you is to *get a bicycle!*

S.T.DADD /94

2   Choosing Mounts

What kind of cycle for you? The main points are covered in this chapter, but read also the sections on riding, fitting and touring for additional information on the capabilities of various types of machines and what your particular needs may be before arriving at a final selection.

This chapter is broken down into five sections: nomenclature; full size safety bicycles; recumbent cycles; other cycles (tandems, tricycles, folding bikes, mini bikes, et al); and children's cycles. The basic technical information given with safety bicycles applies to any cycle and is not repeated in subsequent sections.

Nomenclature

Conventional full size bicycles are called 'safety' bicycles, and owe the term to an unendearing characteristic of an earlier design, the Ordinary. In the early 1870s chain technology was too crude for ready use on bicycles. Pedals and cranks were attached directly to the front wheel. The only way to make such a machine go faster was to increase the diameter of the front wheel – in extreme cases, up to 60 inches. The rider, perched above the wheel just abaft the centre of gravity, was lofted up to between $4\frac{1}{2}$ and $5\frac{1}{2}$ feet above the ground. The Ordinary was magnificently elegant, and even rather fast, but any slight obstacle to forward progress, such as the then oft-encountered stone, would cause the bike to cartwheel, catapulting the rider over the handlebars to 'come a cropper'.

Singer 'Xtraordinary

To move the rider's weight back toward the rear wheel and thereby improve stability, some designers utilised a treadle drive, as in the Singer 'Xtraordinary.

Other designers elected for a chain drive and gearing. The first such machine to gain widespread attention was the Lawson Bicyclette of 1879.

The *Cyclist* of 21 April 1880 commented on the Lawson Bicyclette: 'Here, indeed, is safety guaranteed, and the cyclist may ride rough-shod over hedges, ditches and similar obstacles without fear of going over the handles . . .' Such machines were advertised as 'safety bicycles', and the conventional high wheeler came to be called an 'Ordinary'. Although the latter had firm adherents, the safety offered incomparably better handling, braking and speed and the type flourished rapidly; by 1885, with the advent of the second model Rover Safety, the bicycle was recognisably in the form we know today.

The safety bicycle has since reigned supreme for nearly one hundred years. Now the apple-cart is being upset yet again by a new generation of cycles called recumbents. In these, the rider is positioned as if in a beach chair lounge, with the legs and feet pointing forward and the back slightly inclined or even – in racing models – fully supine. (Prone positions, with the rider on his/her stomach and the legs pointing to the rear, are also used, but have been found to constrict breathing and are therefore unlikely to see immediate development.)

At speeds past 12mph aerodynamic drag is the main retarding force for a bike. Because a recumbent has a reduced frontal area it is subject to less aerodynamic drag, and maintaining a given speed takes less effort than with a safety bike. The addition of a streamlined body shell or fairing to further improve aerodynamic efficiency can yield speeds in excess of 50 mph. Happily, most recumbents have a low centre of gravity and commensurately improved braking power!

As in the early days of the safety bicycle, the development of recumbent cycles is at an embryonic stage and commercial production is limited to individual builders and small firms. There is no doubt that recumbents will soon gain widespread popularity, and their substantial benefits are discussed in detail later in this chapter. For the moment, the important point to note is that the recumbent design compliments rather than supersedes the safety bicycle; each type has advantages and disadvantages and it is the individual priorities of the rider and the conditions of use which will determine a choice between the two. Unlike the Ordinary, the safety bicycle will keep on rolling for millennia to come.

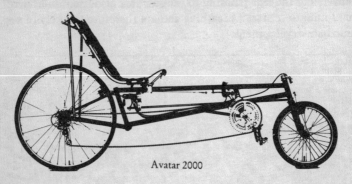

Avatar 2000

Full size safety bicycles

Bicycle categories by function break down into ten overlapping groups.

1. Cruisers. The two basic types are beach cruisers and BMX cruisers.

Beach cruisers are a modern reincarnation of the classic American 'paperboy' bike. Built entirely of steel, with a heavy robust frame, wide 2 inch tyres, and a 1- or 2-speed rear hub equipped with a pedal-operated coaster brake, these are simple, laid back, comfortable machines for casual fun (such as beach riding) needing little to no mechanical care.

BMX cruisers are a derivative of BMX dirt track racing bikes, and generally feature knobby tyres and multi-range gearing suitable for off-road use. Certain models are made specifically for short sprint dirt track racing. Generally, BMX cruisers use a straight front fork with welded plates to provide mounting holes for the front wheel axle; beach cruisers use a conventional raked (curved) fork.

Most cruiser bikes look flash when parked outside the local pizza parlour, but at a weight of 50 pounds and up are hard pedalling on anything but flat terrain.

2. Mountain bikes. Superficially these resemble a beach cruiser, but otherwise there is no comparison. Made of light alloys and fairly bristling with the latest bicycle technology in components, mountain bikes weigh in at about 24 to 28 pounds, which is less than some road racing bikes. They are nimble but comfortable over rough ground, and have very strong brakes. These characteristics make them also excellently suited for town riding. A mountain bike is not as swift as a proper road bike, but on the other hand will fare better on the jagged surfaces typical of urban streets.

Off-road riding and touring is tremendous fun. A decided advantage is that there are no cars to worry about – an especial boon if you have youngsters. If you need a durable and exciting town bike, and/or have the yen to get away from it all with a vengeance, then a mountain bike is one to consider. However, a good mountain bike is a first class machine that will cost around £300 and up. Ensure that this is exactly the type of bike you want before plunking down the cash. It cannot be done on the cheap.

THE AMERICAN STAR MACHINE

3. The heavy roadster, built entirely of steel, with wide 1½ inch tyres, roller lever rim brakes, and 1- or 3-speed hub gears. Weight about 50 pounds. This garden variety European work-horse has been around at least since the 1920s. It is sometimes called an

'Africa' model because of its popularity in developing countries for transporting heavy loads, bouncing across deserts and through jungles and the like. They were used extensively by the North Vietnamese for transporting supplies during their last war with the Americans. A frame and forks designed for taking the sting out of bumps make them particularly steady and graceful, and for this reason they are also popular with Dutch housewives. The Netherlands are mostly flat, however, and pedalling a heavy roadster where there are any kind of hills is hard work.

4. The sports roadster, also called a 'tourist' model or English Racer, with lighter steel frame and mudguards, $1\frac{3}{8}$ inch wide tyres, calliper rim brakes, and 1- or 3-speed hub gears. This is the bike for utility use such as local errands, shopping, lots of stop-and-go riding, short trips, and gives good durability with minimal maintenance. Weight about 35 pounds.

5. The town bike (also called 'lightweight tourist' or 'commuter') can be as the sports roadster above, but with 5- to 10-speed derailleur gears, or it can be as the sports bike below, with a truly lightweight frame, $1\frac{1}{4}$ inch tyres, and steel or alloy components. In either case it usually features flat handlebars and a wide mattress saddle. Weight from 25 to 35 pounds. It is a hybrid intended to give the light weight and gear range of the sports bike with the riding position of the sports roadster, and is suitable for local errands, commuting and short tours up to 25-35 miles.

6. The sports bicycle features a lightweight frame, steel or alloy components depending on model, $1\frac{1}{4}$ inch wide tyres, calliper rim brakes, multi-speed derailleur gears, narrow 'racing' saddle and drop handlebars. Weight from 25 to 35 pounds. These bikes are intended for general use, moderately hilly terrain, commuting and touring up to 40-50 miles. These bikes can vary considerably in quality. At one end of the spectrum the machine may simply be a sports roadster glossed over with drop handlebars and a narrow saddle. At the other end, the machine may have a truly lightweight frame designed to be lively and responsive, but still directionally stable and comfortable to ride over rough ground.

7. The touring bicycle will follow the general outlines of the sports bicycle above, but is specifically designed for a comfortable ride and predictable handling when carrying heavy loads. There is provision for fitting mudguards and carrier racks for panniers, and the gearing is low for easier hill climbing. These machines are for

Bicycle made by T. & H. King, blacksmiths,
Wimborne, Dorset, 1872

day after day touring in the 50-100 mile range, and will also cope
well with regular commuting and local utility use.

8. The fast road bike comes in two versions. One is essentially a
racing machine that has been slightly detuned by the use of narrow
section wire-on tyres in place of the high performance tubular tyres
used in competition. The frame is designed for quick handling and
rapid translation of pedalling effort into forward motion, and has a
stiff ride over rough surfaces. Such bikes are used primarily as
training machines for competition, and do not gladly suffer touring
loads or bumpy urban streets.

The second version of a fast road bike is a tweaked touring
machine with narrow section wire-on tyres in place of conventional
$1\frac{1}{4}$ inch wide tyres, and a moderately stiff frame – say 73° parallel.
The gearing range is typically wider than for a training bike, and
results in a machine that is quick, but that can manage reasonable
touring loads. This 'best of both worlds' approach is popular with
urban riders who want an exciting ride over a regular commuting
journey, and a mount that will serve for weekend touring and the
odd two-week holiday. A definite level of riding skill is required,
however, to prevent rapid wheel wear over bumpy urban streets or
rough roads.

9. The racing bike is a machine pared to the essentials and
designed for all-out performance. The frame is a tight, stiff design
for realising maximum power and very quick handling. There are

no mudguards and the tyres are of the sew-up tubular type – narrow, fast and more expensive and fragile than the conventional wire-on type. Such bikes are intended for competition, but on smooth roads in the hands of an experienced rider can be both comfortable and exceptionally swift. The design is also favoured by aggressive and fast urban riders (who will, however, usually substitute narrow section 1 inch conventional wire-on tyres). Weight can be as little as 19 pounds.

10. The track bicycle is made for racing on wooden tracks and is an utterly stark greyhound with a single fixed gear, no brakes, and a weight of 16 to 17 pounds. A very exciting machine but only the most expert of riders can use these on public roads.

Summary
Very broadly, there are three basic types of safety bikes:

1. Heavy, wide tyre cruiser bikes, with the mountain bike model similar in appearance but made of lightweight materials giving considerably livelier performance;

2. Medium weight, mattress saddle, flat handlebar roadster bikes, usually equipped with hub gears in the strictly utility models and derailleur gears in the lighter, more performance orientated models;

3. Lightweight, narrow saddle, drop handlebar, derailleur gear sport bikes. These can be general use machines (sports bikes), or more refined touring or racing models.

For the sake of simplicity I am going to speak of 3-speed bicycles, by which I mean roadster bikes with 3- to 5-speed internal hub gears, and 10-speed bicycles, meaning lightweight mountain or sport bikes with 5- to 21-speed derailleur gears. If this is Greek to you, hold on for just a bit.

Selection

In the vast majority of cases, if you are going to own just one bicycle it should be a 10-speed. These can be set up to suit nearly any rider, job, or purpose; they are dynamic, responsive, and vibrant and also the most comfortable, giving the most speed for the least effort so that you will get more out of riding and will be encouraged to do even more. They are also the easiest to service. Experience has shown that most people who start with a heavyweight or sports roadster soon find themselves desiring (and acquiring) a 10-speed bike. It takes no longer than the first time such a machine sweeps by them going up a hill. My advice is to save money by buying a 10-speed bike in the first place. You get the most fun and turn-on for your money, and you get it right away.

Assigning utility functions to a 3-speed bike, and touring and racing functions to a 10-speed bike, is only broadly accurate. Actually, a 10-speed can be set up for almost any job or purpose except beach riding. The same machine, with minor modifications, can compete in a race, go on a camping tour, be ridden cross-country through streams and muddy fields, and haul groceries or newspapers. It can even pull a trailer. The only crucial difference between the 3- and 10-speed is the method of operation for the gears: the 3-speed can be shifted to the correct gear at any time, but the 10-speed must be shifted while the bicycle is in motion. It's easy once you get the knack, and the 10-speed's efficiency outweighs the disadvantage of initial unfamiliarity. If you get stopped in a 'wrong' (inefficient) gear, it is easy to shift once you are under way again.

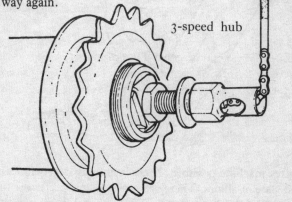

3-speed hub

The choice between a 3-speed and a 10-speed bike rests largely with the kind of person you are and how heavily you want to get into cycling, and the strength of your wallet. Consider a 3-speed if: you are not terribly interested in cycling and just want something you can stick in the shed or basement to use for local jaunts once or twice a month; you or the prospective rider are not at all mechanically inclined and never will be; you need a knock-around bike for use by several different people; or you just want the most

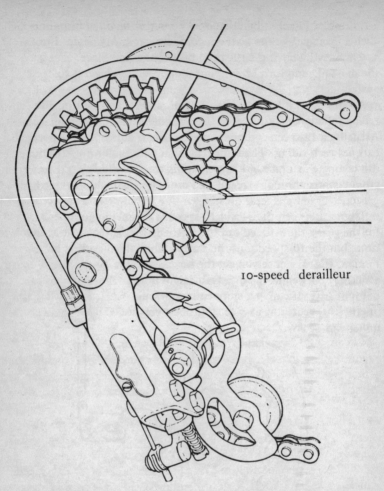

10-speed derailleur

worry-free machine possible. There is nothing degenerate about this last state of affairs. There are times when I prefer the totally casual spirit of the 3-speed, where one can just drop it on the spot, bash it around, loan it to casual friends, and in general not think about what is going on. But this is the exception rather than the rule. Over the long haul, the 10-speed is just so much better, so much more rewarding, that it will surely overcome any diffidence you feel about cycling and make you an enthusiast.

If your wallet can stand it, the ultimate worry-free machine is the 10-speed mountain bike, a machine that is both extremely tough and extremely exciting to ride.

Expense is a consideration only if your absolute maximum is £35, which restricts you to a serviceable second hand 3-speed. For £40 to £50 you can buy a basic but usable 10-speed. More on this later.

Durability is a function of bicycle model rather than type of gearing. For example, a 10-speed mountain bike is both lightweight and very nearly bomb-proof. An ultra-lightweight racing machine also has extraordinary strength and resilience, but can be damaged by casual abuse or rough off-road riding. A heavyweight roadster is definitely a contender in the durability sweepstakes, but the more common 3-speed sports roadsters are often poorly constructed and flimsy.

Rider sense and skill also affect durability. Cyclo-cross racing bikes equipped with lightweight tubular tyres are used over very rough terrain. It is just a question of watching where you go and not over-stressing the machine. A rider who sits on the saddle like a sack of oats when the bike hits a bump needs a machine that can absorb punishment; a rider who moves with the bike, allowing it to pivot underneath him or her over the bumps, can use a lighter more responsive machine.

The classic drop handlebars of the 10-speed are not a requirement; you can equip or buy such a bike with flat handlebars (more on this later). With the exception of the very cheapest and nasty models, 10-speed bikes have better brakes than 3-speed bikes.

Comfort is sometimes cited in favour of the 3-speed. This made sense in the days when most 10-speed bikes were stiff riding, quick handling racing machines. Now that general use and touring models predominate, the comfort advantage lies with the 10-speed. Such a bike has a wider variety of riding positions, which allows you to utilize more muscles to greater advantage; the 10-speed also transmits more pedal effort to the rear wheel. All in all, it is much less tiring than a 3-speed. Professor David Gordon Wilson of the Massachusetts Institute of Technology has calculated that the energy requirement for maintaining an even 12 mph on a lightweight sports (10-speed) bike is half that for the same speed on a roadster (3-speed) bike.

This energy difference is particularly evident when climbing hills. If the terrain you will be encountering is hilly, get a 10-speed no matter what.

Bicycle weight will also turn out to be a significant factor if you intend to carry the machine up and down stairs, at your home, for example, or at work. The two sensible answers are a 10-speed or a lightweight folding bike. 3-speed roadsters and mini-bikes run 35 to 40 pounds and are a clumsy nuisance to manage in a confined space.

RUSHING A RISE.

Using a car or public transportation to get to a departure point for a trip is also part of carrying. Any 10-speed is easier to take apart than a 3-speed, and a good quality 10-speed will have quick-release wheels that come off at the flick of a lever. The only thing handier is a compact folding bike, and this is an option worth considering if your storage space is very limited. Next in line is the 10-speed. With the wheels off it can be hung in a closet. It is light enough to be hung from the ceiling or a wall via brackets or pulleys. It can be kept in the bathtub or shower stall. Under any circumstances it will be easier to deal with than a 3-speed.

For frequency of repair the 3-speed has it all over the 10-speed. All the 3-speed hub will need in years is a monthly shot of oil. Once it does go however, it is complicated to fix, and most bicycle shops will simply replace it. The 10-speed, while more efficient, requires more frequent adjustment and servicing. However, because the parts are all quite simple and out in the open where they are easy to get at, this is easy to do., In fact, it is part of the fun of riding. The vitality and responsiveness of the 10-speed is such that you come to enjoy fine-tuning your bike.

Perhaps now you have started to form a notion of the kind of bike you would like to have. But the array of available machines is still bewildering, with prices ranging from £39.50 for a 'mail order special' to over £1000 for a really fancy one-off 'superbike'. Here is some technical information to guide you through the maze and help you to get your money's worth.

The significant components of a bicycle are the frame; rims, tyres and hubs; brakes; gears and gear changing hardware, crankset and pedals; and stem, handlebars and saddle. According to the grade of frame and components selected by the manufacturer, the price of a 3-speed will range from £80 to £150, from £80 to £300 for production line 10-speeds, and £300 and up for custom-made bikes. Manufacturers tend to assemble rather than manufacture bicycles, obtaining the components from specialist companies. Hence, two bikes in the same price category from two different brand name 'manufacturers' sometimes have exactly the same parts.

The two main factors to consider when assessing a frame and/or components are design and materials. The interface of these two elements determines the intrinsic suitability, quality and value of a product. For example, a racing design frame built of heavy, mild steel is utterly pointless; the material does not have the performance characteristics to fulfill the design. Similarly, an alloy chainset of single piece construction at a remarkably modest price is not necessarily the best value. When it is time to replace the chainrings the whole unit will have to be replaced. A more expensive chainset with detachable chainrings would allow only the relevant part to be replaced, and give the ability to alter gear ratios.

Taken as a whole, a good bike is balanced; design and materials for both frame and specification are in harmony with the intended purpose and price range. We'll return to this subject after some information on frames and specification components.

The frame

The frame is the heart and soul of a bicycle. It is the determining factor of bicycle weight, and the more you pay the lighter the weight for the same or even greater strength. Frames are not meant to be rigid or unyielding, but rather to combine absorption of shock from the road surface, and translation of pedalling effort into forward motion. Called resilience or twang or flex, this is a function of quality of materials and manufacturing methods, and gives better bikes more springiness and vitality. There is no way to improve a cheap frame. Other components can be modified or changed but the frame endures, and it should be the first focus of your attention when considering a prospective bike.

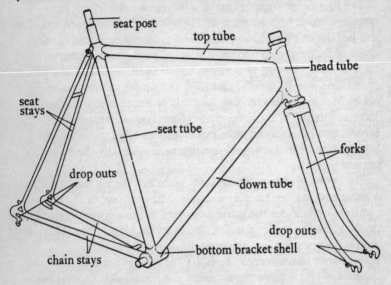

Inexpensive coaster brake, 3-speed, and cheap 10-speed bikes use seamed tubing, made by wrapping a long, flat strip of low carbon mild (1010) steel into a tube and then welding it together (electrically) at high temperature. Despite manufacturers' designations such as 'high tension' or 'high tensile' steel, frames made of this material are heavy and inflexible, giving a very 'dead' feel to the rider. Better frames feature seamless tubing of alloy steel with more carbon and small quantities of nickel (1020 and 1030), and are lighter in weight and livelier to ride. Next up the list is 4130 chromium molybdenum (chrome-moly) alloy steel, which gives a light and very responsive frame. This, or the near equivalent, is the material of proprietary alloys such as Columbus, Vitus, Tange and Ishiwata. The finest tubings available are Reynolds 531 and Reynolds 753, which are a specially heat treated manganese-molybdenum steel. Some people may regard a different

34

make as 'finest'; but historically, frames of Reynolds 531 or 753 hold the highest resale values.

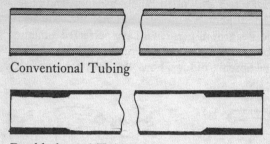

Conventional Tubing

Double-butted Tubing

Superior bicycle frames use double-butted tubing. This has a uniform external diameter; on the inside, though, the tubing is thin in the middle sections and thicker at the tube ends (the joining points) where greater strength is needed. Double-butted tubing for a frame in place of plain gauge tubing will give an average one pound saving in weight, and is standard for any serious racing bike. Until recently, many mid-range production touring and commuting bikes used plain gauge tubing rather than double-butted. Such bikes often carry extra weight in the form of baggage and saving a pound on the frame then makes little difference. More importantly, the economic advantage of using plain gauge tubing could be invested in better quality components. But manufacturers have now introduced new types of inexpensive double-butted tubing with characteristics suitable for the production methods used in making mid-range bikes.

Herein lies the second major element of frame quality: construction. Inexpensive frames of seamed tubing are usually just stuck together and electrically welded by machine, leaving a smooth joint. Although low carbon high-tensile steel can withstand high welding temperatures without losing strength, this is the weakest type of assembly. Better quality steels with a high carbon content became brittle and subject to fatigue when heated to a high temperature. Frames of this material are brazed, a joining method that uses lower temperatures than welding. As an aid to accurate assembly, lugs (see illustrations) are used to position the tubes. Strictly speaking, lugs do not need to be neat and tidy for a strong joint. However, clean lugwork is a sign of care and thoroughness, and bodes well for the rest of the bike. Tandems, mountain bikes, recumbents and other machines with odd size tubing or special requirements in frame geometry often cannot use lugs, and have bronze welded (filleted) joints. Some conventional bikes are also made this way, and Peugeot in particular have perfected a method of lugless frame construction. In general, quality orthodox bike frames use lugs; the absence of lugs, however, does not necessarily indicate an El Cheapo.

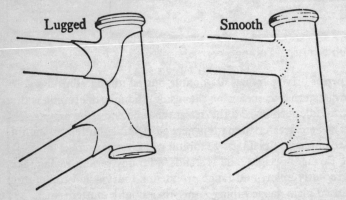

Machine brazing of good quality frames has now been made much more feasible by the introduction of high manganese chrome molybdenum steels such as Ishiwata Magny-V and Reynolds 501. These will withstand higher temperatures without damage, but are quality butted tubings with strength and weight characteristics that are very close to those of the more expensive top line tubings such as Reynolds 531. This amounts to something of a revolution in bicycle manufacturing, and will lead to an increasing number of mid-range price bikes with butted frame tubing.

Indeed, quality frame tubing comes in many grades and weights. The tubing used in ultra-lightweight frames for a kind of racing called time-trialling, for example, would not readily accommodate the rigours of regular urban commuting or heavily laden touring. Tubing of significant quality is usually attested by a small transfer affixed to the top of the seat tube. There are many variations, so always read the transfer carefully to see what you are getting. The main thing to watch is whether the transfer refers to the frame main tubes only (top, seat and down tubes), or also includes the stays and forks. Generally, it is better for the complete frame to be of consistent quality throughout. Here is a selection of transfers from the Reynolds range:

In the current Reynolds range, 501 is intended for mid-range utility, sports (or 'look alike') and touring bikes. 531ST (Special Tourist) and 531C (Competition) are respectively designed for quality touring and racing bikes. 531 Professional replaces the old 531SL (Special Lightweight) and is intended purely for competition, as are the even lighter 753 Race and 753 Track. There is no point in using these materials unless you spend the money to equip the frame with ultra-lightweight components – a total of £500 or more. These tubings are so fine that tolerances in frame assembly and brazing temperatures are absolutely critical. The slightest error can result in a pile of junk. Do not buy a frame of these materials unless it is from a master builder. This applies double to 531SL Speedstream, an aerodynamic tubing which looks extremely flash (and may thereby daunt the competition), but has only a small performance advantage.

With the exception of Ishiwata Magny V and Reynolds 501, chances are you will not find double-butted tubing in a bike unless you spend upwards of £200. However, at the very least you should get seamless high carbon steel tubing, which is used even on low-cost quality bikes. Here are three tests for frame quality. Differences between price ranges should be evident.

1. Weight. Pick the bike up. Cheap bikes with electrically welded tubing and joints will nudge 35 pounds, mid-range bikes with good tubing will be at the 30 pound mark or slightly less, and top quality bikes will be at around 27-29 pounds in touring models and as little as 20 pounds in racing models.

2. Lift the bike a few inches and bounce it on the wheels. Better frames have more twang and bounce.

3. Stand to one side of the bike. Hold nearest handlebar with one hand and saddle with the other and tilt bike away from you. Place one foot on end of bottom bracket axle and give a definite but restrained push. A good frame will flex and then spring right back. Try several different bikes to get the feel of it and be careful – the idea is to find frames that will give with a gentle push, not bend anything you may encounter. If enough force is applied cheap frames will bend – permanently.

Bicycle frames are also available in aluminium, aluminium and graphite, and titanium. These frames are very light and very, very expensive. I do not advise buying such a frame until you have owned at least a couple of bikes, and know exactly what you are getting into.

The design and geometry of a bicycle frame varies according to its intended purpose and weight and type of rider. The commonest design for touring and general use is 72° parallel. This means that the angle to the top tube formed by the seat and head tubes is 72°.

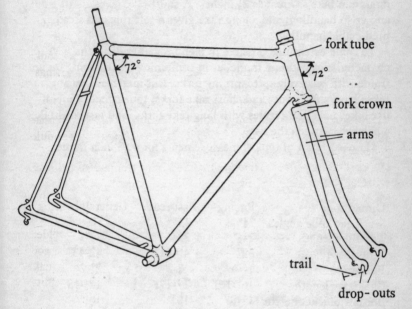

This is the classic design for good shock absorption, steady handling with baggage, and even power transmission. It is good for bumpy urban streets. Many variations are possible. The frame built by Jack Taylor for his Superlight Tourist model uses a 73° seat and 71° head. It is designed for stability and comfort with heavy touring loads.

Fast road bikes generally have frames with the angles at around 73° parallel. This gives a brisker response to power input and quicker handling, at the cost of a slightly stiffer ride over rough surfaces.

In a racing bike, a $73\frac{1}{2}°$ or $74°$ parallel frame is regarded as stiff, although seat angles can be as steep as $76°$. The frame will be more compact throughout, with a shorter fork rake, seat stays and chainstays. This brings the wheels in closer together, shortening the wheelbase. Usually, there is not enough room between the rear tyre and seat tube to fit a mudguard.

Fork rake refers to the distance between the front wheel axle and a line formed by extending the head tube downwards. The fork rake on a racing bike may be as little as 1 inch and on a touring or mountain bike as great as $2\frac{1}{2}$ inches. A short rake gives a stiff ride and crisp handling, and a long rake gives a soft ride and steady, predictable handling.

To some extent it is possible to blend together different characteristics within a frame, as in combining a stiff racing design frame with relatively soft, springy forks. But in general, racing bikes have stiff frames and short rake forks, touring and general use bikes have soft frames with long rake forks, and fast road bikes a balance between the two.

Here is a chart of typical measurements for a 23 inch frame:

Dimensions	Racing	Fast road	General/Touring
Seat/head tube angles	$74°$	$73°$	$72°$
Top tube length	$21\frac{1}{2}''$	$22\frac{1}{2}''$	$23''$
Wheelbase	$39''$	$40\text{-}41''$	$42\text{-}43''$
Fork rake	$1\text{-}1\frac{1}{2}$	$1\frac{3}{4}\text{-}2''$	$2\frac{1}{4}\text{-}2\frac{1}{2}$
Chainstay length	$16\frac{1}{4}\text{-}16\frac{3}{4}''$	$17\text{-}17\frac{1}{4}''$	$17\frac{1}{2}\text{-}18''$
Bottom bracket height	$11''$	$10\frac{3}{4}''$	$10\frac{1}{2}''$

These figures are only a general guide. For example, a short person might require a relatively short top tube, and one way to achieve this is by steepening the angle of the seat tube. In balance, and despite the 'stiffness' of the seat tube angle, the frame will give a comfortable ride. Materials also play a role. Forks made of Reynolds 531 tubing are springier than forks made of ordinary tubing, and can stand a shorter rake for better handling without sacrificing ride comfort.

Another factor to take into account is rider weight. A frame and forks that are stiff for a person weighing 10 stone may be soft for a person weighing 13 stone. Frame design is a complicated subject, well covered by Albert Eisentraut in 'The Frame', a chapter in Tom Cuthbertson's *Bike Tripping* (Ten Speed Press, Box 4310, Berkeley, CA 94704 USA), and by Joe Kossak in *Bicycle Frames* (obtainable from Selpress Books, Dept RB, 35 High Street, Wendover, Bucks HP22 6DU, and the Cyclists' Touring Club, 69 Meadrow, Godalming, Surrey GU7 3HS).

Summary

One of the most satisfying and important features of a good bike is responsiveness and vitality that you can feel with your whole body. The main determinants of this quality are the frame materials and construction method.

Under £120 – Seamed, smooth-joint frame of mild, low carbon steel.

£120 to £175 – Seamless, lugged-joint frame of low nickel alloy steel.

£175 to £200 – Seamless, lugged-joint frame of 4130 chrome moly steel or equivalent.

Over £200 – Seamless, lugged-joint, low temperature brazed frame of double-butted proprietary alloy steel.

The brakes

There are three basic types of brakes: hub, disc and calliper.

Hub brakes may be hand or pedal operated. They are easy to apply but hard to control and can cause a skid by locking up the wheel. They do not have much actual stopping power. It's a skid or next to nothing. Skidding to a stop takes too long, is excessively exciting at high speeds and wears out tyres very quickly. Most hub brakes have poor heat dissipating qualities, and can burn out in the middle of a long downhill descent. Hub brakes remain effective in wet weather, and this used to be their sole advantage over other types of brakes. The development of new brake block materials, however, now gives the other types a comparable performance in wet conditions.

Disc brakes are powerful, and effective in wet weather. They are often fitted to tandems and tricycles. They are heavy, though, and are not commonly used on lightweight solo bicycles.

Calliper brakes come in two types: centre-pull and side-pull.

Side-pull brakes come in two versions: inexpensive, for use on 3-speed and cheap 10-speed bikes, and expensive, for use on quality racing and touring bikes. The inexpensive side-pull brake is strictly from hunger, and cannot be compared in performance to a good quality side-pull or centre-pull brake. It works, but only just, and requires constant adjustment.

The centre-pull brake operates via a pull on a yoke cable connecting the two brake arms, and thus works in balance for even, powerful performance. The good quality side-pull brake is built to a rigid design which affords precise control at high speeds. The softer and less rigid centre-pull requires less brake lever pressure for a complete stop than a quality side-pull, but at high speeds can 'snatch' and exert more deceleration than necessary or safe. Both types stop equally well, but the quality side-pull is better for speed control and is therefore favoured for racing bikes.

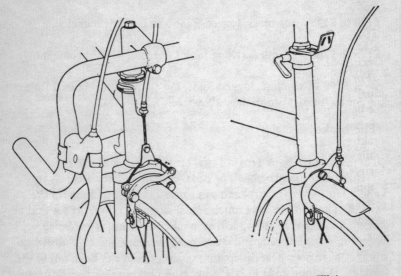

On production bikes costing up to around £250, the Weinmann 605 side-pull (about £20) and 999 centre-pull (about £16) dominate the market.

Other good brand names are Campagnolo, Sun Tour, Shimano, Weinmann, Dia-Compe, Modolo, Galli, Zeus, Universal and Mafac. Be sure that the levers on the brand you select fit your grip, as some makes are only suitable for large hands.

On some bikes the brakes are fitted with a second 'touring' or 'safety' lever positioned underneath and in line with the straight section of the handlebars:

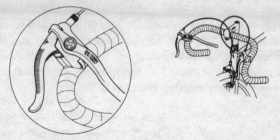

These were originally developed for use on touring bikes, to increase the number of riding positions from which the brakes can be operated and thereby aid rider comfort when making long descents. This is fine for a touring bike running along in the wide open spaces. But then marketing people decided to promote the device as a 'safety' lever, implying that in an emergency it would increase the chances of avoiding an accident. The actual case is precisely the opposite.

For one thing, 'safety' levers (or, as they are more aptly called, 'dual' levers) require a greater length of travel in order to actuate the brake mechanism than do conventional levers. If the brake mechanism itself is not closely adjusted, it is possible under hard braking for the 'safety' lever to bang uselessly against the handlebar while you carry on to destruction. For another thing, even when correctly adjusted, dual levers show inferior performance. In stopping power tests on several different makes of brakes with dual levers we first established an average stopping distance using the standard levers from a given speed, and marked it with a chalk line. Then we repeated the test using the dual levers. The bikes sailed over the line every time, increasing the distance for a stop in some cases by as much as 30 per cent.

Dual levers are operated from a top of the bars riding position. This is fine when there is plenty of road room, but steering control is poorer and the rider's centre of gravity is higher, further reducing manoeuvrability. This can be disastrous in an emergency situation. Finally, the use of dual levers makes uncomfortable the favoured position for raising the head and being able to see when riding in traffic, i.e. hands over the brake hoods.

Not surprisingly, dual levers are rarely, if ever, seen on top quality bikes. Unfortunately, they are the rule rather than the exception on bikes costing up to around £175. What you do about this is simple. At the time of bike purchase, insist that the dual levers be removed, or that a substitute unit without dual levers be installed. A modest charge for this service is in order, but if the shop becomes balky, or tries to convince you that dual levers are a good idea, then buy elsewhere – the shop is only interested in selling, not in properly meeting your needs.

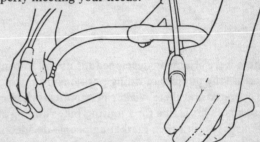

One periodic bit of fluff for boosting sales of bikes are self-adjusting brake levers and mechanisms. Such units are heavy and mechanically complex, and more trouble than they are worth.

An important point about calliper brakes is that their performance in wet conditions depends strongly on the right mix of brake block and rim materials. Brake blocks come in rubber, leather or synthetic material, rims in chrome steel or aluminium alloy. Rubber blocks work well on alloy or steel rims in the dry; on alloy in the wet stopping distance increases about 200 per cent, and on steel in the wet the increase is between 300 and 400 per cent. Leather blocks are designed only for use with steel rims and will chew an alloy rim to bits. Their performance in wet conditions is first rate, but useless in dry conditions. Synthetic blocks outperform all others on alloy or steel rims in the dry, and are in the top performance class in the wet.

The single drawback of synthetic blocks is that they can be too effective. A novice rider who panics and clamps the front wheel brake too hard could cartwheel the bike. However, at this writing the vast majority of new bikes are fitted with rubber blocks. These are more even-tempered in performance and will suffice for the novice rider until he or she is familiar with braking technique (see Riding), but their potential for disaster in wet conditions and/or on a long descent makes graduation to synthetic blocks an early priority.

An important variation on the centre-pull calliper brake is the cantilever brake, which pivots on a boss brazed to the fork blades and seat stays.

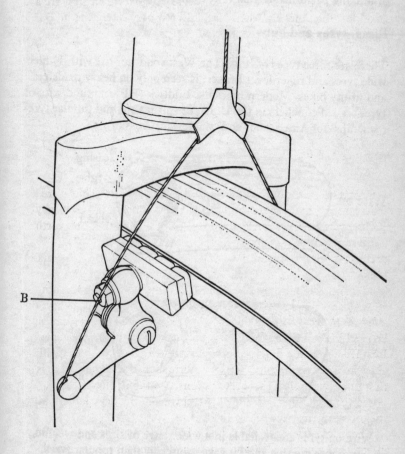

Very powerful, and less likely to 'whip' (where the stress of braking makes the whole brake assembly judder back and forth), cantilever brakes are good for the heavily laden tourist, and are fairly standard for cyclo-cross, tandems, tricycles and mountain bikes. There is also a saving of six ounces in weight over the conventional centre-pull. However, only custom-made touring frames are likely to have the requisite brazed on bosses necessary to mount cantilevers. This is a pity. Mountain bikes, for example, use 'oversize' tandem cantilever brakes and blocks and offer a level of braking performance that few, if any, other bikes can match.

Rims, tyres and hubs

There are three types of rims. The Westwood, for use with $1\frac{1}{2}$ inch wide tyres and roller lever brakes, is seen only on heavy roadsters and utility bikes. Modern bikes use Endrick (HP) rims and wire-on tyres (called clinchers in the U.S.), or sprint rims and tubular tyres ('sew-ups' for Americanos and 'singles' for Aussies).

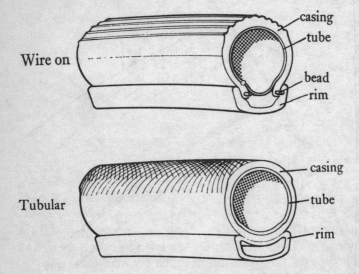

Wire-on tyres are available in a wide range of sizes and weights, and are more durable and far easier to repair than tubular tyres. Tubulars offer the ultimate in light weight and minimal rolling resistance, but are expensive and puncture easily. Because the tube is sewn into the tyre it is impractical to repair on the road, necessitating the carrying of a spare tyre wherever you go, as it cannot be left on the bike when locking up on the street.

Wire-on tyres are available in a range of models from $2\frac{1}{4}$ inch wide heavy-duty knobby variety through to the 1 inch narrow profile high pressure (100 psi) tyre. These latter will match the performance of a heavy tubular, so only the lightest tubulars are worth using, and then only for racing and ultra-fast day rides. Wire-on tyres are the sensible choice for any other use.

The traditional system for indicating tyre size is in inches: 27 X $1\frac{1}{4}$ means a tyre diameter of 27 inches and a cross section or width of $1\frac{1}{4}$ inches. A more precise metric system of European origin is now coming into international use. This consists of a two-figure number, a dash and a three-figure number, as in 32-620. The first figure gives the tyre width, and the second the diameter of the rim it fits. Both are in millimetres.

Tyre sizes

Commonly Known As	Standard Designation
27 X $1\frac{1}{4}$	32-630
27 X $1\frac{1}{8}$ (or 1)	25 or 28-630
700C	28-622
700C Narrow	25 or 28-622
26 X $1\frac{1}{4}$	32-597
26 X $1\frac{3}{8}$	37-590
26 X $1\frac{1}{2}$ or 650B	37 or 40-584

The 700C has the braking surface of the rim in the same position as the sprint rims used for tubular tyres, and is often used when both wire-on and tubular tyres need to be interchangeable on the same bike. It is also the common Continental size – a point to note if you are touring in Europe. The 650B is a sturdy tyre mainly used on French tandems, and to a lesser extent on French solo touring bikes.

In general, wide tyres give a more comfortable ride, better traction on loose surfaces such as gravel and in wet conditions, and the best durability. Narrow tyres have a stiffer ride, less traction, and are more vulnerable to punctures and bruising – but are a good deal faster than wide tyres. Hence, a stout wide tyre is typically used for general riding, commuting and heavily laden touring bikes; in this category the Michelin Sports and Speed models are well regarded for performance and durability. Fast road and light touring bikes typically use a light, narrow tyre; here, the Nutrak and Specialized ranges offer exceptional performance and very long life. Other good brands are Michelin and Worthy. Light, high performance tyres are susceptible to punctures and bruising. One viable route to increased protection against punctures is the Wolber Invulnerable tyre, available in both wire-on and tubular models. These have a closely woven mesh of stainless steel inserted between the tyre tread and casing that reduces punctures, on average, by 30 per cent. Performance is equivalent to an ordinary tyre, but cost is about double.   (See Accessories for a detailed discussion of anti-puncture products.)

Rims are made either of aluminium alloy or steel, and form a dividing line between basic quality bikes and good to best quality bikes. This is because rim and tyre weight are compounded by the gyroscopic force of a rotating wheel. In practical terms this means that a bike with steel rims accelerates and handles much more slowly than a bike with alloy rims. Another important consideration is that in the wet, alloy rims have a much better braking power than steel rims.

In wire-on rims, Super Champion is widely regarded as the best. Other good brands are Rigida, Mavic and Weinmann. In sprint rims Mavic SSC are the strongest – as well they should be at over £100 per pair! Still exceptional in quality and strength but far more reasonable in price is the Mavic GP4. Good value strong sprint rims are Super Champion and AVA.

Hubs also come in steel or aluminium alloy. As with rims, steel hubs will be found only on bikes of basic quality grade or less. The hubs may attach to the bike using conventional bolts, or via quick-release levers which work instantly.

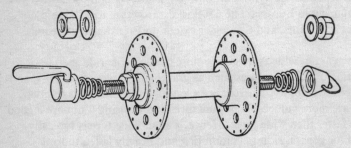

Quick-release hubs are by far the most convenient if you often use mixed mode transport (car-bus-train) and for maximum security when locking up on the street (the front wheel is removed and locked together with the frame and back wheel to a substantial, immobile object).

The hub illustrated is a large-flange design used for racing and sport riding. The flange is the part with all the holes where the spokes are attached. According to theory, the stiffness of a wheel is proportional to the flange diameter squared. Hence, commuting and touring bikes often use small-flange hubs for a softer, less stiff ride. Opinion as to which type is stronger is divided. A large-flange hub reduces the torque loads on the spokes, but increases the angle from the perpendicular where the spokes join the rim, in effect trading one problem for another. Tandems require large-flange hubs to allow room for additional spokes. For solo bikes the size of the flange is less important than the overall quality of wheel-building.

Inexpensive alloy hubs such as Maillard Normandy or Maillard Atom – often seen on mid-range production bikes – can deform at the spoke holes, thereby promoting spoke breakage. The top line brands are Campagnolo, Sun Tour, Shimano and Zeus, followed at an interval by Ofmega and Miche. Most of these manufacturers offer models in several different price ranges. A popular standby for quality and value is the Campagnolo Nuovo Tipo (about £20).

Hubs with sealed bearings to keep out grit and water have become increasingly popular. One of the most famous (and expensive) is the American Phil Wood hub. An almost standard specification on top quality mountain bikes, this hub is extremely robust and reliable. It is also completely sealed, cannot be adjusted, and requires special tools for dismantling. If it does pack up out in the great blue beyond, you're stuck.

The French Maxi-car sealed bearing hub, at about £55, is adjustable and can be taken apart for cleaning. It is an extremely good and reliable hub well suited to touring and the rigours of urban commuting. A recent British offering is the Balance hub. This is a massive unit (in size, not weight) with oversize bearings, and can be dismantled. The rear block side bearing is of the roller rather than ordinary ball type, for additional strength. The Balance hub has not been in use long enough for accurate reliability data.

However, the samples I have examined appear very promising on quality.

The American Bullseye is a well-regarded sealed bearing hub that is particularly easy to service. The Sun Tour Superbe is a top-line hub with sealed bearing units that can be removed and replaced with standard ball bearings. This would be a very desirable feature in the event of a breakdown in a remote location.

The most highly stressed part of a wheel is the spoke. In materials, there is a choice of rustless stainless steel, and chrome- or nickel-plated steel; the latter are prettier but more inclined to rust. In design, there is plain gauge, the same diameter throughout, and double-butted, with the stressed areas at the ends of the spoke thicker, and the mid-section thinner. Plain gauge spokes are easier to work with, and build a stiff wheel that can carry on for a while even if a spoke breaks. Double-butted spokes are more elastic and supple, and if correctly tensioned will in theory give an even stronger wheel. In practice, for strength, most manufacturers and wheel builders prefer plain 14 gauge spokes.

After the frame, the wheels – hubs, spokes, rims and tyres – are the most important component of a bike. The frame is the vitality, the wheels are the point of translation into motion.

It is possible to spend £80-£100 on a set of good wheels – as much as some people might spend on a bike. This buys superior performance and strength, and value for money reliability exceeding that of half a dozen sets of wheels at £25-£30. Very obviously, you are not going to find £100 wheels on production bikes priced under £275. In fact, wheels of only average quality (i.e. not really good enough) predominate down to around the £200 mark. Wheel quality on many bikes priced under £200 is fearsome.

Which is one reason why many people who start with a £150-£200 bike upgrade within 1-2 years to a bike costing £300 or more. Throughout the bike, but particularly with the wheels, they get performance and value for money reliability and durability. They can ride bumpy urban streets or a heavily laden tour without undue worry about bearing failure or a broken spoke. The wheels on most £150 bikes will not stand more than six months to a year of regular urban commuting, and just one long, heavily laden tour can spell cataclasmic doom.

The good news about this state of affairs is that only an extra £20 or so is required to equip a £150 bike with creditable wheels, if the substitution is done at the time of bike purchase. Not every shop will welcome making this arrangement as a heaven-sent opportunity. Persevere – you will never get a better return on investment.

For the scoop on wheels, read an engaging book called *The Bicycle Wheel* by Jobst Brandt (from Selpress Books, Dept. RB, 35 High Street, Wendover, Bucks HP22 6DU). Brandt uses engineering principles in a precise and clear analysis of wheel design and materials. Beautifully balanced in text and graphics, the book is a landmark of technical literary excellence and is a treat to read. It has the best D.I.Y section on wheelbuilding I have ever seen. Street Science have just produced a video guide to wheelbuilding, an interesting development. (Details from them at 5-6 Alvanley Terrace, Edinburgh.)

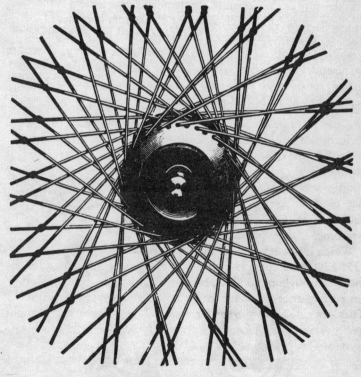

NEW RAPID TANGENT WHEEL.

Gear changing mechanisms, cranksets and pedals

Most hub gear bikes in Britain use Sturmey-Archer gears. The AW 3-speed hub was first introduced in 1901 and has changed very little over the years. High and low gears are, respectively, 25 per cent greater and lower than the middle or 2nd gear, a range that is adequate for ordinary utility use over moderate terrain. There is also an SA 5-speed hub with a slightly increased range of 33 per cent higher or lower than the middle gear, but availability of this unit is extremely limited.

Hub gears are mechanically quite complex and sophisticated, but are extremely reliable and simple to operate. Their primary disadvantage is a power loss of up to 33 per cent through the gear mechanism. In contrast, derailleur gear systems can be up to 99 per cent efficient in transmitting power to the rear wheel.

At the core of the design of the derailleur gear system is the derailleur (or mech), which shifts the chain from sprocket to sprocket. Differences between brands are to be found in weight, durability, smoothness, precision and pattern of shifting. There are two essential types: competition, for use with close-ratio gears, and touring, for use with wide-ratio gears. The touring mech is easily identified by an elongated jockey arm:

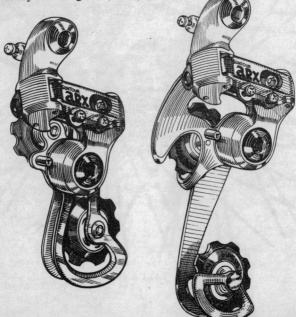

The jockey arm maintains chain tension. Wide-ratio gearing requires a longer chain than close-ratio gearing, and a correspondingly longer jockey arm.

Derailleurs come in different price grades, and brand name alone is not a quality guide. For example, a long revered name in competition derailleurs is the Campagnolo Nuovo Record. The budget Campagnolo 980 model is not even remotely in the same class, and while the unit works well enough, there are others which offer better for the same money or less. Sometimes differences are rather esoteric. For example, the Huret Duopar is an excellent touring mech with a price in excess of £40 owing to the use of titanium parts. The Huret Duopar Eco is identical in design and performance, but steel parts and a less attractive finish more than halve the cost. It weighs a little more, but this is of marginal consequence on a touring bike.

Sun Tour is a popular brand, giving both excellent performance and value for money. The top-line Sun Tour Superbe Pro for example, costs rather less than the comparable Campagnolo Record and Shimano Dura-Ace AX models, but differences in performance are very slight. The middle range Sun Tour Cyclone II in both competition and touring models is an excellent performer, and the Sun Tour BL and VX series deliver very good performance at rock bottom prices. The new Sun Tour AG series gives ultra-wide gear ratio capacity, again at remarkably modest cost.

Shimano is another Japanese brand giving both performance and value. The top line Dura-Ace AX competition mech abounds with technical innovations and may well be the most precise unit going. The middle range 600 series are very reasonably priced and noted for smooth, silent shifting. The inexpensive Shimano Altus series features a self-centring mechanism that helps align the chain over the sprocket. This is a useful feature for novice riders. Even easier to use is the semi-automatic Positron, though it tends to wear out quickly.

The Huret Jubilee, at this writing, is the lightest competition mech available and a nippy performer. The Huret Duopar models are extremely precise over wide-ratio gears even when under load, and are the first choice of many tourists.

Simplex is another well-established French make that is garnering an increasing share of the market. The 5500 series are smooth and reliable top-line touring and competition mechs, and the 810GT and 410T are budget priced functional copies. The new Simplex Selematic uses a unique two position lever to give a positive selection of the next highest or lowest gear, even by a complete novice.

Many racing cyclists regard the Campagnolo Record series as the best available, and in many ways they are right. The finish and assembly of the Record units is arguably the finest. The design may be conservative, but it is race proven for dependability and efficiency. The Record is perhaps the strongest competition mech available. When it does become worn the unit can be rebuilt to perform like new. Spare parts, even for Campagnolo units that are many, many years old, are readily available. The design of other makes usually precludes rebuilding, and in any case the availability of spares is often poor.

Gearing is a major factor to consider in the choice of derailleurs, and this subject is covered under Fitting. Read this chapter before purchasing a bike.

There are four different places on a bicycle commonly used to mount the levers for shifting derailleur gears:

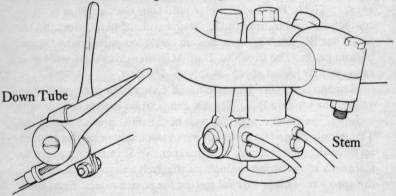

Down Tube

Stem

Each method has advantages and disadvantages. In my own opinion, simplest is best. Down-tube mounting allows the use of short cables giving maximum feel and quick response when shifting. Stem and top-tube mounts are more convenient when flat or all-rounder handlebars are used, but in a crash can dig you nastily in the gut or crotch. Handlebar-end mounting requires long cables which give a sloppier response. It also requires the drilling of holes in the handlebar, and I know of instances where this led to

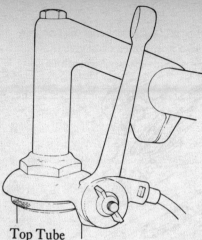
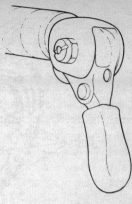

Handlebar

Top Tube

corrosion and a complete snapping apart of the handlebar while the rider was under way. Down-tube mounting is simplest and safest.

The exception is when the hands must remain on the handlebars and brake levers, as with a mountain bike. These have flat bars and use thumb-actuated shift levers mounted on the bars just inboard of the handgrips. Thumb shifters are very handy to use and would be perfect for a town bike with flat bars. At this writing, thumb shifters are unobtainable in Britain. However, their virtues are such that by the time this reaches print, thumb shifters should be available from better shops.

In almost every case, the make of shift lever will be matched to the make and grade of derailleur and so performance will be commensurate. One noteworthy model is the Sun Tour Powershift. This uses a ratchet and leaf spring in place of the conventional pressure washer and gives a frictionless, extremely positive gear change that is a boon for novices and a pleasure for experts.

Cranks and chainwheels are made of aluminium alloy or steel. Design varies in the method of fastening to the bottom bracket axle:

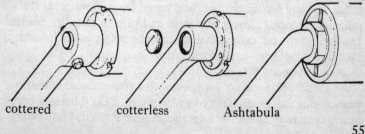

cottered   cotterless   Ashtabula

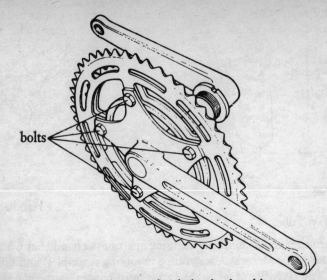

bolts

The Ashtabula is a one-piece crank, chainwheel and bottom bracket axle design, and is most often seen on BMX bikes. Roadster bikes typically use steel cottered cranks, as do the cheapest 10-speed bikes. Low-price quality bikes and up use alloy cotterless cranks. The type and quality of these can very considerably.

Bottom line on many low-price quality bikes is the Sugino single, with a fixed chainring. When the chainring wears out, the entire unit will have to be replaced. The SR Silstar is often seen on mid-range production bikes and has replaceable chainrings, if you can find them. Availability of parts is often a problem with Japanese components. This does not apply to the SR Custom, which is a popular value for money chainset often found on high quality production bikes. The chainrings are compatible with other makes and so there is no spares difficulty. The top quality chainsets are Campagnolo, Shimano, Sun Tour, TA and Stronglight. Of these, TA and Stronglight are best suited for the tourist, as the range of chainring sizes is very large and parts availability excellent. Lesser known and less expensive but nonetheless viable brands include Miche (parts interchange with Campagnolo), Galli, Ofmega, Zeus and Nervar.

As a rule, chainsets are supplied with a conventional bottom bracket that can be dismantled and serviced. Sealed bearing bottom brackets include Sun Tour Superbe, Nadax-Favorit, Phil Wood,

56

Bullseye, OMAS, Mavic and Stronglight. Some of these can be got apart, others cannot – a definite minus if you are in the Far Provinces. Take the advice of a good bike shop on the selection and installation of a sealed bearing bottom bracket unit.

One interesting type of chainwheel uses an elliptical or oval configuration:

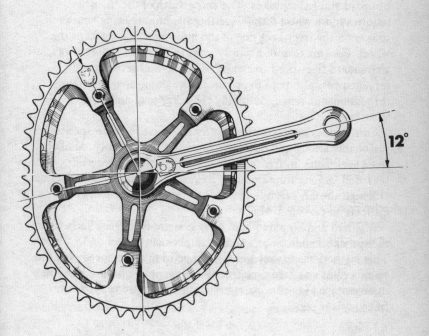

These vary the gear ratio, making it higher on the downstroke and lower when the crank passes through the vertical. Elliptical chainwheels have no history of success in racing. However, at low speeds and under load, as when hill climbing or frequent stop-and-go traffic riding, they can have a power advantage. Enthusiasts claim that over long distances the lowered cadence rate (crank revolutions per minute) is less fatiguing. Other cyclists disagree. There seems to be no hard and fast rule. It is something you have to try for yourself.

The freewheel threads onto the rear wheel hub and holds the gear sprockets. These are available to take five, six, or seven sprockets. The six-speed freewheels may be slightly wider than a five-speed freewheel, or use a narrower chain to squeeze six sprockets into the width of a conventional 5-speed freewheel. Seven speed freewheels use a narrow chain and are the same width as a six-speed freewheel.

In general, six- and seven-speed freewheels are best limited to fast road and racing bikes. The extra width of the freewheel requires more wheel dish – insetting the hub by using shorter spokes on the freewheel side of the hub – and this weakens the wheel. For this reason, a sturdy touring bike will almost always use a strandard five-speed freewheel. The six- and seven-speed arrangements also tend to produce more duplicated gear ratios throughout the range, nullifying the purpose of additional sprockets.

Sun Tour system freewheels offer from five to seven speeds, are reasonably strong and have very good parts availability. Maillard freewheels come in five- and six-speed models and are well regarded. A long time standby, Regina, has come upon hard times, although the CX series is of good quality. Shimano freewheels are difficult on parts availability.

Maillard and Shimano both offer cassette type freewheels where the sprockets slide on to a spline, rather than thread on to a block. This method has advantages for competition when speed is of the essence. But standard type freewheels cannot be used – a double disadvantage as, again, parts availability for cassette system freewheels is poor.

In chains, the Shimano Uniglide and Sun Tour Ultraglide both work well, but tend to wear quickly. The Regina Oro is often seen on production bikes, but is not of the first water. Number one for performance and durability is Sedisport, followed by DID. You'll find, that transmission systems usually follow a brand theme – Shimano mechs and Uniglide chain, Sun Tour mechs and Ultraglide chain, and so on. These are fine for a start, but try to eventually wind up with Sedisport.

Pedals come in three basic types: (1) the classic rubber tread platform; (2) cage design; and (3) metal platform.

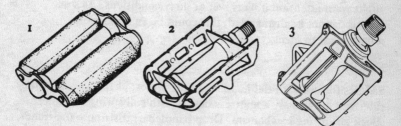

Cage type and metal platform pedals can be used with toe clips, straps and cleats, rubber platform pedals cannot. Cage type pedals presuppose the use of cycling shoes with stiff soles for supporting the foot; used with ordinary shoes they can induce foot cramps on long tours. Platform pedals give good weight distribution. Both metal platform and quill cage pedals are specifically intended for use with toe clips and straps; only one side of these is 'right way up'. Rubber platform and parallel cage pedals are useable from either side.

Pedals may have no ball bearings, adjustable bearings, or sealed bearings. Pedals with no ball bearings signify a chintzy bike and are a complete waste. Adjustable ball bearing pedals are to be found on low cost quality bikes through to superbikes, and range in price from £5 for a basic model through to £80 for the Campagnolo Super Record with titanium spindles.

Expensive pedals are good-looking and cheaper in the long run. With regular maintenance the Campagnolo Strada XL (about £40) will do 100,000 miles. Cheap pedals will pack up after 5-6,000 miles. However, if you ground and damage the pedal on a corner, then the El Cheapo suddenly becomes the more economic proposition.

The parallel cage Lyotard at around £6 is an excellent value inexpensive pedal, and one of the most convenient to use with regular shoes. The Lyotard metal platform model is also utterly reasonable in price, and noted for smooth running. The SR rubber platform at around £6 and with an alloy body is the best of its type. In quill pedals Campagnolo offer models ranging from under £20 to £80. All are excellent. There are also a host of special designs from Ofmega, Cinelli, Sun Tour, Shimano, Lafont and others. Choice of these is largely a matter of personal preference.

Sealed bearing pedals include Sun Tour, Phil Wood, Cinelli and Shimano. These are maintenance-free in ordinary service, but might want attention in very wet or dirty conditions. As some models cannot be dismantled, this could be an impossible requirement to meet.

Saddle

Saddles for use with flat handlebars carry most of the weight of the rider and are usually a mattress design with coil springs or other shock absorbing mechanism. Drop handlebars distribute the rider's weight more evenly and allow the use of a longer, narrower, saddle to minimise friction between the legs.

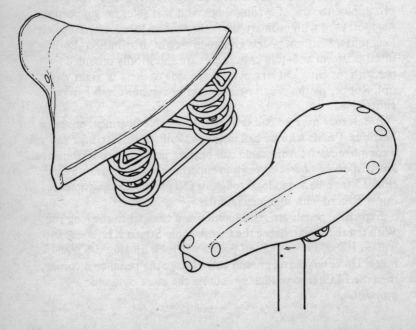

Like shoes, saddles are a personal affair. What suits one individual can be torture for another. There are three essential types: leather, plastic, and plastic covered with a layer of foam and wrapped in leather or plastic.

Leather saddles want a minimum of 500 miles of riding to become supple and broken in, but can then fit so well that you will keep the saddle from one bike to another. Unless regularly treated with neatsfoot oil or Proofide, rain can ruin a leather saddle. If you opt for leather, buy the best – Brooks.

Plastic saddles need no breaking in, are impervious to weather, and run about half the weight of a leather saddle. They can be a good choice for utility bikes that will often be left out in the rain, and are odds-on for short distance races where weight is a decisive factor. However, in warm weather a plastic saddle will leave you slipping about in your own sweat, and few people consider the type comfortable.

Plastic base saddles with a layer of foam and a leather cover need no breaking in and rate high for comfort. Cinelli, Milremo and Sella Italia are all good brands. Special 'anatomic' models are produced by Madison and Sella Italia. These have a thinner plastic base and extra padding where the pelvic bones meet the saddle, and are a gift from heaven for many cyclists. Be sure to give one a try if you find an ordinary saddle uncomfortable.

Women have wider pelvic bones than men, but this fact is ignored on most production bikes (although Brooks, Madison and Sella Italia make wider saddles specifically for women). Perhaps an even greater problem for many women is comfort in the pubic region. There are no saddles currently on the market which take into account the shallower female pubic arch. One drastic but apparently effective method of dealing with the problem is to simply cut away those portions of the saddle which cause discomfort. Perhaps it is these sorts of difficulties which cause so many women to opt for the upright bike with mattress saddle.

Man or woman, if you buy a bike and the saddle is of questionable quality, exchange it immediately for a better one and pay the price difference. You will spend many, many miles and hours on your saddle, and if you pinch pennies on this item you will be so oftimes reminded, for truth, by a sore behind and inflamed crotch.

Handlebars

Handlebars come in four standard designs:

The Maes pattern is the most common downswept version, and is suitable for either touring or racing. The Randonneur and Pista patterns are more specialised, and respectively are for touring and racing. On inexpensive bikes the bars are of steel, and on better bikes of aluminium alloy. The virtues of downswept bars as opposed to flat bars are discussed in Fitting.

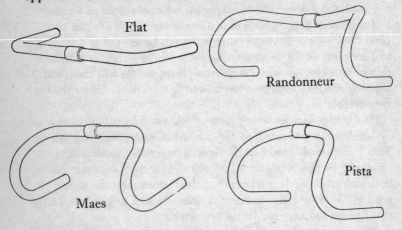

General Summary

There are many different brands of bicycle, and each manufacturer usually produces a range of models in different price grades. As you move from the under £100, all steel bike with seamed tubing and smooth joint frame, to the £500 and over superbikes, you find an increasing use of aluminium alloy for all parts of the bicycle (except the frame, which in quality machines is of specially treated alloy steel) and increasing sophistication of manufacture, such as lugged and brazed frame joints, double-butted frame tubing and cotterless cranks.

A 'good' bicycle is one where design and materials work in harmony to fulfill the intended function of the machine. Design categories include:

Hub gear, flat bars, mattress saddle
1. **Cruiser** – Soft frame, very wide tyres, hub or calliper brakes.
2. **Heavy roadster** – Soft frame, wide tyres, roller lever brakes.

3. Sport roadster – Soft frame, 1 inch wide tyres, calliper brakes. Derailleur gear, drop bars, narrow saddle

1. Racing – Stiff frame, sprint wheels with narrow tubular tyres, closely spaced high gears, no mudguards or carrier rack; very quick handling.

2. Fast road (also 'fast tourer' and 'training' or 'club') – Less stiff frame than racing, HP wheels with narrow 1 to $1\frac{1}{8}$ inch wide tyres, closely spaced middle to high gears, mudguards and carrier optional; quick handling.

3. Touring – Soft frame, HP wheels with standard $1\frac{1}{4}$ inch wide tyres, closely spaced low gears, mudguards and carrier rack, predictable handling even with heavy loads.

4. Sport or general – Soft to medium frame, HP wheels with standard $1\frac{1}{4}$ inch wide tyres, widely spaced gears, mudguards and carrier rack optional, predictable handling.

5. Town (also 'commuter' and 'lightweight tourist') – As sport bike above, but with flat bars and anatomic or mattress saddle.

6. Mountain bike – Soft frame, HP wheels with $1\frac{3}{4}$ to $2\frac{1}{4}$ inch wide tyres, closely spaced low to medium gears, mudguards and carrier rack optional, flat bars and anatomic saddle, predictable handling over rough ground.

Materials divide into four grades:

1. Cheap – Frame of low carbon seamed steel, steel components.

2. Basic – Frame of high carbon, low alloy seamless steel, steel wheels, alloy components thereafter.

3. Medium – Frame of chrome-moly steel or equivalent for at least the three main (top, down and seat) tubes, alloy components throughout.

4. High – Frame of name brand double-butted alloy steel, quality alloy components throughout.

The points of harmony and discord are:

Design	Materials
Cruiser, Heavy roadster, Sport roadster	Cheap to basic. Anything better is a waste.
Racing	High. Anything less will not fulfill design. A 'racing' bike of cheap or basic quality materials is known in the trade as a 'look-alike' and is a lie.
Fast road	Medium to high.
Touring	Basic to high. Extent of touring function limited by quality grade, i.e., basic quality OK for weekend touring but not a tour of Europe.
Sport	Cheap to medium. Anything better will be more specific in design.
Town	Basic to medium.
Mountain	High. Anything less will break.

Selection

Obviously you'll want to pick a bike suitable for your needs and budget. In both cases it is usually wise to buy a little 'upmarket' so that your bike has some open potential. Suppose, for example, that fitness is a priority, and you would like to get in some vigorous exercise over a regular 5 mile commute to and from work, and on occasional day rides. A town bike would be fine for the commute but slow for fast riding. A sports or touring bike would also manage the commute, and be better for speed. But so long as you rode carefully while commuting (bumpy urban streets are hard on bikes), a fast road bike would be the most vital and rewarding when you chose to bend the cranks. Now change the script just slightly: you want a commuting bike, and are interested in touring, possibly even cycle-camping. In such an instance a proper touring bike is the odds-on choice.

Novice riders often either under- or over-buy with respect to their needs. They are interested in cycling, but 'don't need all that fancy stuff'. So they buy an all-steel machine which turns out to be good enough for local use, but just gives a taste of what is possible when touring or going for a turn of speed. A year or so later they are back at the shop laying down the money for a better quality machine.

Alternatively, a prospective cyclist wants 'the best money can buy'. He or she purchases a lightweight racing bike for regular commuting and quickly tires of a sore behind, endless punctures and buckled rims. The bike goes off to moulder in a shed.

Evaluate and understand your own needs carefully, and then try to buy a bike that has some potential in reserve. Biking – be it commuting, racing, touring, hauling the groceries and laundry, or off-road bashing – is an experience. If your machine is a drudge, a non-starter that cannot explore the new experience, you are plain deprived. Conversely, do not buy more machine than is comfortable. Own the bicycle, not the other way round. Expensive, fine-tuned machines require a commensurate level of mechanical attention and riding ability. If your first requirement is a thrasho utility bike to get you from here to there, then buy that sort of machine. A bike should be used, not be an object of deification and worry about investment.

In fact, any serious 'bikie' owns at least two bikes – one for basic transport and often doubling as a training or touring machine, and one purely for fun, whatever the specific function.

THE HUMBER TANDEM.

Recommended Bicycles

My purpose in recommending bicycles by category is largely to set standards for comparison. The bikes listed are prime in their grade and fair value for money at this writing, but diligent shopping may well net you a better buy. Apply and use the technical information given in this chapter. There are many, many other fine bicycles that are not listed here, and you may do yourself a disservice if you pass them by.

Do not be put off if the bike you find in a shop has a slightly different specification than as listed here. The availability of components can change rapidly, but in making alterations most manufacturers will maintain the same quality level.

Without being tiresome, seek as many opinions as possible. Like people, bicycle manufacturing firms fall upon good times and bad times. A well established company can suddenly merge with another, and until the two different management groups harmonize, product quality may suffer. Or a firm that has been in the doldrums for a time may decide to capture a larger slice of the market, and offer a range of bikes at exceptionally keen prices.

Your best guide to the current situations is the advice of a reputable cycle dealer. These people are in the business of selling bikes and do not long endure if they give poor counsel.

In fact, it is now a fairly common practice with many of the better shops to improve on manufacturers' specifications, and to offer a well-known model as a 'Special' with, for example, better quality hubs and alloy instead of steel rims. A number of shops also do their 'own' brand models and these are often a superior value if you are willing to compromise on colour, selection or some other detail.

So I repeat, use the technical information in this chapter, and take my recommendations as a starting point for the kind of bike you would like to have, and can afford. For an up to date listing of available bicycles, plus a star selection checklist of best buys in each price grade, pick up a copy of *The Bicycle Buyers Bible* (newsagents and bike shops).

Women

Gender division of bike frame types is misleading. A woman can ride a 'man's' bike as readily as anybody else. A 'woman's' pattern frame is structurally weaker and less responsive than a diamond pattern frame;

it is not available for all models, will come in fewer sizes, and often will have a different specification or a mattress saddle and flat handlebars in place of the racing saddle and dropped handlebars supplied with the diamond frame model. All the way around it is not much of a deal, and my advice is to go for the better value and performance of a diamond frame. Of course if you are on the short side you will find that only a very few production bikes are available in your correct size. If you can afford it, one way round this difficulty is to order out a custom built frame. In such an event, discuss with the builder the possibility of a slightly raked top tube, sloping from front to back. This allows adequate bottom bracket height, a comfortable straddle when stationary and, because a longer head tube can be used, increased frame flexibility (small frames tend to be stiff).

Conventional women's frame   Mixte frame   Triangulated frame

Everybody

In derailleur gear bikes, a basic model with a heavy frame and steel wheels can be a viable means of plain transport. But if this is the extent of your budget, then I strongly suggest that you consider buying a used bike (see next chapter) with a better quality frame and alloy wheels. This way you can have the essential elements of efficiency and responsiveness that make a bike really worth riding.

A basic bike from a reputable manufacturer is one kettle of fish, and what I call an El Cheapo is quite another. You see these around in unlikely places – petrol station forecourts, hi-fi equipment shops, and so on – and they are mostly absolute junk.

Here, some manufacturers and distributors have given in to unprincipled consumerism. Many people do not know much about bikes. They want, say, a 10-speed with chromed fork tips and quick-release wheels – a 'racing' bike – and look for a machine with these features at the lowest possible price. Flashy paint and glittery 'Tour de Galaxy' stickers hide a frame with all the vitality of a cast iron bathtub. Wheels are only marginally classifiable as round. Saddles are floppy bits of bare plastic. Bearings grind and bind. Derailleurs are low grade units that malfunction remorselessly. Brakes are criminally inadequate. You get on one of these machines and life is such a torment that in a short while you decide the whole idea is worthless. And if you seek recourse to a bike shop you are likely to find little joy. There is no way to put an El Cheapo right except to start from scratch, and such a course is decidedly uneconomic. You may think that the shop is being unkind, but in fact, tinkering with an El Cheapo is just heading further down a road with no possible good end.

In buying a bike the problem is not to save money, but to be sure you get what you pay for. Do not be duped by charisma and colourful brochures filled with pictures of happy types sporting about on garbage machinery. Use the fundamentals given in this chapter to work out a solid idea of the design, quality level and features you want, and buy a bicycle that really will bring you joy and pleasure.

Roadsters

In both heavy duty and sports roadsters – Raleigh set the standards. Their Popular (black with red lining), Royal Roadster (black with silver lining) and Superbe models (green with gold lining) are all well made and finished authentic heavy duty (45 to 50 pounds weight) roadsters with $1\frac{1}{2}$ inch wide tyres and roller lever brakes. Variations will be found in fitments such as single or three speed gears, part or full chainguards, propstands, fork locks, toolbags and lights. These are modern museum pieces, but they are elegant, rugged and reliable. Pashley are another firm producing this type of bike.

In sports roadsters with flat handlebars, mattress saddles, side-pull calliper brakes and $1\frac{3}{8}$ inch wide tyres, the Raleigh range again offers a choice in regard to single or three speed gears, chainguard size, lights and colours. All models are straightforward utility bikes suitable for town use, moderately pitched terrain and very light touring. You choose on features and looks – the women's Cameo, for example, has an attractive loop frame and is finished in a deep burgundy colour with gold lining. An interesting bike is the Classique from Peugeot, which includes lights, rear carrier, stainless steel mudguards and full chainguard, and also lightweight features such as an alloy chainset.

In the main, roadsters are of basic quality; there's little point to using expensive lightweight materials with this design. There are some fairly nasty El Cheapo imports about, of course, but if you look over the models discussed you will be able to separate the wheat from the chaff. NB: Raleigh manufacture their bikes under many different brand names for sale in other types of retail outlets, and it is worth checking around to see what is available before making a final purchase.

"IXL," Price £15.   "CLYDE," Price £18.

Town bike

Also called a 'commuter' or 'lightweight tourist', the   town bike combines the padded saddle and flat handlebars of the roadster with the lightweight frame, alloy components and derailleur gears of the 'racing' bike. They are perfect for around town use and light touring, and their extra cost of £15 to £30 over a sports roadster is amply repaid in easier and more enjoyable cycling.

The standard-setter in this category is the Falcon Super Tourist, with Reynolds 531 double butted main frame tubes, 5 speed gears and all alloy components, including Sugino cotterless chainset, Shimano Altus gears, Maillard small flange hubs laced to Rigida rims, and Weinmann side pull brakes. The £175 price tag at this writing is a bargain. The only bike to compare is the Coventry Eagle Elite, which is identical save for paint finish and pedals, and sells at this writing for an incredible £150. With the exception of the Raleigh Richmond, other town bikes at this price level have steel rather than alloy wheels, and no other town bike up to £250 offers equivalent frame materials.

If you want better in the way of quality or gear range, then go for a touring bike and substitute flat handlebars and the appropriate brake levels at the time of purchase.

Sports bicycles

Called 'look-alikes' in the cycle trade, sports bicycles cosmetically resemble racing machines, but typically have the soft frame geometry of general use and touring bikes. Their main sale is to youngsters as a first 'real' bike, and a sure clue of this intention is the presence of 'shortie' mudguards. These may look crisp, but are functionally useless. The same bike, however, with full length mudguards and a wider gear range, can be very viable transportation. A typical example is the Falcon Harrier range, which includes the 5 speed Tear Away and 10 speed Sprint models, both with shortie mudguards and fairly narrow gearing, and 5 speed Sapphire (woman's) and 10 speed (man's) models, both with full length stainless steel mudguards, chromed rear carriers and wider range gearing. The latter two models verge on the touring bike classification, and will certainly serve for commuting and general utility use. In quality grade and price, the Harrier range is 'Low Basic': frames of welded steel tubing, steel wheels and handlebars, and mostly alloy components thereafter. The bikes are well made and robust, however, and the components are of a generally higher quality than on most similarly priced bikes.

A similar situation prevails with several of Peugeot's budget models. These bikes have a keen price for the quality of frame tubing and construction, and in the full length stainless steel mudguard and steel rear carrier models, provide effective basic transport.

A good basic beginner bike with unexotic but good quality components is the Raleigh Ace, available in 5 and 10 speed models, and also as the upmarket Raleigh Winner, with a flashier paint finish and foam handlebar padding. Frame, rims and handlebars of steel, alloy components thereafter. Good range of frame sizes.

If a dramatic colour scheme appeals, a few quid more will obtain the Dawes Lightning with a good frame for the price range, and budget but quality components.

If it were up to me to choose a colourful 'first' bike in the sans mudguards sports category for a youngster, I would go for the Raleigh Europa, a look-alike to the Raleigh Team bike that is more than cosmetic – the frame geometry is a genuine racing configuration. Steel and alloy bits in the usual distribution, but 700C narrow profile tyres and more sensible gearing than most. The only difficulty is that the youngster would have to be big, as minimum frame size is 21 inches.

In which case, and still within 'Basic' quality grade and price, the Peugeot Criterium will do nicely. Good quality Peugeot 103 steel frame, and alloy components thereafter, including Simplex gears and 700C narrow profile tyres. This bike would almost quality as a fast road training bike, and this is the category to look under if you want to spend still more money.

Touring bicycles

For many people, the 'soft' frame geometry and heavy load carrying of the touring bike make it an excellent urban commuting machine that will cope with bumpy streets and pack home a load of groceries with ease. A true touring bike, however, will have a good spread of low gears to help iron out the hills; most production bikes are supplied with 52/40 front to 14-28 rear, which is general use rather than touring gearing. So long as you do not contemplate steep hills, heavy loads and/or long distances, 52/40 to 14-28 rear will get you by. If you do intend serious touring, then ensure that the gear range is appropriate, or can be modified *without major expense*.

In 'Low Basic' quality and price, the Raleigh Medale comes in a generous range of sizes, and steel frame and wheels with alloy components thereafter. Unexotic, but sound, and woman's model has a wider saddle. Slightly less expensive and with fewer frame sizes but good Shimano Altus gears is the Marlboro Pennine. Also in this category and a touch pricy but very attractively finished is the Dawes Fox/Fleur.

In 'Basic' quality and price, the yardstick for some years has been and is the Falcon Black Diamond. A decent frame for price, steel wheels, and a well balanced selection of alloy components thereafter, including Shimano Altus gears. This is a popular, good value bike which a number of shops do as a 'Special' with alloy wheels.

Moving up in quality from the Black Diamond goes in a decisive jump to the 'Low Medium' quality Falcon Majorca, which sports a well finished chrome molybdenum frame and all alloy components including Shimano 600 EX gears. Other machines up to the grade of the Majorca do not have anything like as good a frame or specification

THE 'BLACK SWAN:' GOING HOME—'PACEMAKER COMING ON.'

balance, and cannot compare on value. Of course this holds true only so long as the Majorca stays within £30 of the Black Diamond; otherwise, 'High Basic' bikes such as the Raleigh Record and Peugeot Explorer become contenders. Both of these have steel frames and alloy components of good quality, but no performance comparison to the £10 to £15 more expensive Majorca.

There's another noticeable price jump to the 'Medium' grade and price, and the Carlton Corsair with Reynolds 531 double butted main frame tubes and Sun Tour gears. This is a pleasing, comfortable bike with good detailing and wheels of fair quality considering the keen price. Under a tenner more brings in the Falcon Olympic, with Reynolds 531 double butted main frame tubes, Shimano EXGS gears and a better 36/52 Sugino chainset. The Olympic is a long-time favourite that has seen many miles. About the same money also produces the 12-speed Saracen Touring, with Ishiwata Magny V frame tubing, Shimano hubs, Sun Tour ARX gears and a sensible 36/48 SR chainset. This is one of the few bikes with larger women's frame sizes.

The Raleigh Royal is a good value starter in 'High' grade machines, with Reynolds 531 double butted frame tubes and forks, Sun Tour VGT gears and 42/52 SR Custom chainset. A nice touch is Grab On foam handlebar padding. This is a purposeful but quick machine that will manage commuting or touring with equal facility. A tenner more draws down the long time standby Dawes Galaxy, with Reynolds 531 double butted main frame tubes and a similar specification to the Raleigh Royal. The Galaxy is a classic touring bike and long-time strong value, although the rear carrier is a waste.

With the Claud Butler Majestic and only a wink more money one finds an authentic 'High' grade bike. Reynolds 531 double butted frame tubing and forks, Sun Tour VX gears, 36/50 SR chainset and Super Champion rims, rightly regarded as among the best. The Majestic comes with narrow section tyres, which are fine for swift passage but a bit delicate for heavily laden touring, and in which case wider tyres can be substituted on the same rims. The Majestic is a popular machine that a number of shops do as a 'Special' with better hubs, rear carrier and other bits. These are nice machines, of about the minimum quality that I feel is appropriate for regular riding.

A nipping £80 or so more touches the end of the scale, with the Claud Butler Dalesman/Holdsworth Mistral, which has Reynolds 531 double butted throughout, of course, Sun Tour Cyclone Mark II gears, 32/50 SR chainset, Super Champion rims and Campagnolo hubs. This is talking business. The Dalesman/Mistral handles beautifully loaded or unloaded, and the wheels are well made and strong. This is the kind of bike that I think gives the best value in pleasure and long-term service.

SANGER RACER.   AAP

Fast touring bikes

Many of the gaps in the range of worthwhile pure touring bikes are filled by fast road or fast touring bikes. These are characterized by slightly stiffer frame designs and a preference for narrow section tyres, both of which give increased vitality of performance. The type is popular for general riding, and perhaps ought simply to be considered a modern touring bike. Touring they certainly will go, even with heavy loads. The difference is to be found in ride and pace. The classic pure touring bike can manage fairly rough surfaces, and moves along at a steady lope; a modern tourer has more kick, both over bumps and in performance. This kind of distinction applies more readily to some bikes than to others. The Galaxy and Dalesman/Mistral are classic touring machines, but many people would rate the Raleigh Royal, CB Majestic and Falcon Majorca as fast road bikes.

In any event, a modern, performance-minded touring bike is by definition a quality machine, and starts in the 'Medium' grade with the good value Raleigh Clubman 12, with Reynolds 531 double butted main frame tubes, Campagnolo 980 gears, Sun Tour freewheel and SR Custom chainset – one of the few Japanese models where the chainrings readily interchange with other makes. A handsome claret finish and contrasting chromoplastic gold mudguards give a beautiful bike, and the only restriction is that the Campagnolo 980 mech will not take wide ratio gears.

Only slightly dearer and a best buy is the Revell Ritmo, with Ishiwata 0245 chrome molybdenum butted main frame tubes and Reynolds 531 forks, Sun Tour gears and Stronglight TS chainset. The 531 forks make for good handling and overall balance, the frame itself flourishes with neatly brazed on bits, and the chainset is particularly suitable for touring as replacement chainrings in a range of sizes are readily available. A significant touch are Rigida rims, which are close in quality to Super Champion, and give strong wheels. The Ritmo is a real bike, well balanced throughout, and difficult to better for the money.

Bearing in mind that the Raleigh Royal and CB Majestic could qualify in this progression of modern touring bikes, next rung up the ladder is a long swoop to the Raleigh Record Ace, a player that has won many hearts. Reynolds 531 double butted, of course, Campagnolo GS gears, Sun Tour freewheel and SR Custom chainset. A very handsome bike that goes well and has mudguards too.

In the same price range, the Peugeot Routier, with Reynolds 531 double butted main tubes, Simplex gears and Stronglight chainset, is an extremely well regarded bike often used by knowledgeable people who could afford better. The Routier is closer to a training bike than a modern tourer, but will accept mudguards.

From the Routier, a definite economic gulp to the 'High' quality Revell Elite, with Reynolds 531 double butted tubing throughout, Sun Tour gears and versatile Stronglight 99 chainset. Nutrak tyres and Madison anatomic saddle supplied as standard. There's an optional good package price on a Blackburn carrier rack and water bottle cage, Truflo pump and Grab On foam handlebar padding. The Elite is a sure-footed, fast handling bike with an excellent specification that, like the Ritmo, includes strong wheels. Significantly bettering the quality of the Elite takes real money.

" UNIVERSAL " No. I, Price £14.   "UNIVERSAL," Price £I8.
" UNIVERSAL " SAFETY No. 2, Price £10 10s.

Fast training bikes

The fast training bike is distinguished from the modern touring bike by a greater committment to performance. Frame geometry is tight, and often precludes the fitting of mudguards. Gearing is high and narrow for the most part, 'Medium' quality and price is required to produce a viable machine in this category. Two exceptions are the 'High Basic' Carlton Criterium, with a good steel frame, Sun Tour gears, SR chainset and 700C alloy wheels, and the good value 'Low Medium' Dawes Jaguar, with Reynolds 531 double butted main frame tubes, Sun Tour gears and Custom DX chainset. The Carlton Criterium is a stiff bike firmly in the training mode, while the Dawes Jaguar is domesticated enough to be suitable for general use and will accept mudguard. The Jaguar weighs a good 3 to 4 pounds less than the Criterium, represents exceptional value and is well worth the extra cost.

Slightly dearer but good value are the Raleigh Rapide and carbon copy Carlton Pro-Am, with Reynolds 531 double butted main tubes, Campagnolo 980 or Sun Tour VX gears, Sun Tour Freewheel and SR chainset. Both are handsome and swift, and choice is a matter of colour preference.

Next come two off-beat bikes: the Puch Mistral EL, with Puch 2500 steel frame tubing, Campagnolo 980 gears and SR chainset, a natty number that will turn heads on a sprint to the office, but that spares dangerous living through a generous fork rake and forgiving handling; and the aerodynamically styled Peugeot Centenary, with Peugeot 106 frame tubing and Simplex gears, which goes as well as it looks – fast.

Entering 'High' quality country saddles the Dawes Renown, with Reynolds 531 double butted throughout, Sun Tour VX gears and Super Custom CT-5RG chainset. This is a real lightweight at 23 pounds, and a particularly handsome machine that is decidedly quick, but usable as general transport. It will accept mudguards. Comparable, but a tad more expensive on account of Super Champion rims and Suzue hubs, is the Holdsworth Avanti in a sharp red pearl colour.

A useful bit of change up the scale finds another duplicate combo, the Carlton Super Course and Raleigh Competition 12, with Reynolds 531 double butted throughout, Campagnolo GS gears, Sun Tour freewheel and SR Custom chainset. These are fast machines that will not accept mudguards, and choice is on colour.

A bit more money produces the Puch Mistral SE which, like the less expensive EL model, comes with generously raked forks that preclude dangerous living. It certainly looks dangerous, however, and if you can arrange for narrow profile HPs in place of the tubulars supplied as standard, you can clip a good ten minutes off an ordinary commuting run to the office.

More like the real thing is the Holdsworth Elan, with Campagnolo 980 gears, Suzue hubs and Super Champion rims. Tubulars or HPs to choice. It will take mudguards while blasting through town or along country lanes, and 1st place in a race if you are a good enough rider. This is a particularly fine bike.

The end of the training bike category is marked by the Dawes Imperial, available in light blue or pearl red, with a distinctive (and comfortable) white Kashimax Aero saddle as topping, and running 14 speeds through Sun Tour Cyclone Mark II gears. Like other fast Dawes bikes, the Imperial can be fitted with mudguards, but this is very much a performance machine that requires regular maintenance if used for general riding and commuting. The Imperial scored highly in a *Bicycle Magazine* road test, and those who favour a very crisp, quick and sleek bike should make a point of looking this one over.

Racing bikes

An off-the-shelf racing bike cannot be had for peanuts, but a local race meeting is nothing like you see in the movies. Many of the bikes at such an event will consist of a fairly good, cosmetically tatty frame prised out of an understanding friend or relative with little cash and much talk, and a random selection of bits and pieces to help the thing go and stop. Most common racing machinery aims to be versatile, and adaptable to different circumstances with the minimum of trouble and expense. This is why most racers automatically think in terms of a good frame, and their own selection of components. An off-the-shelf bike can be just as good or even better, however, and put you on the road with a minimum of fuss.

Classifiable as a training bike when used with HPs, and as a racer when used with tubulars, is the Falcon Pro, with chrome molybdenum frame tubing, Campagnolo 980 gears and Apex chainset. Next up the list is the Holdsworth Elan, discussed in the training bike category above. A similar machine is the Peugeot Routier, discussed in the modern touring bike category. Indeed, it is not until you pass the £300 mark that you find a clutch of bikes built for racing and nothing else: the Peugeot Roubaix, Barry Hoban Bordeaux, Falcon Super Pro and Raleigh Gran Sport. These are all authentic racing machines and differences between them are slight; you need to compare for yourself. Nearly a third of the money again gives the Peugeot Professional, a sleek, lovely riding machine that has won many races. Top of the list and good value for quality of machines is the Raleigh Team Replica – the real thing, as seen in major races.

Mountain bikes

This breed of bike is new in Britain, and some models are more cosmetic than functional. It is worth checking out current issues of *The Bicycle Buyers' Bible* and *Bicycle Action Magazine* for the latest gen on new iron. The veritable model T Ford of mountain bikes is the Madison Ridgeback at about £300. The Muddy Fox range from S&G Distributors is comprehensive, highly rated for performance and value for money, and includes the unique Bigfoot, a lovely 18 inch frame, 24 inch wheel model for small size riders.

Cruiser bikes

Best value is the Raleigh Bomber, and flash award goes to the Murray Baja, an all chrome frame with gold components.

Custom and bespoke bikes

One grand bit of fun is to build up your own bike, starting either with an off-the-shelf frame, or a frame custom built to order. Strictly speaking, an off-the-shelf frame will serve perfectly well for 98 per cent of customers, but the satisfaction of having a unique made to measure frame, finished and decorated exactly as you wish, can be tremendous.

The old time master frame-builders are a dying breed and their work is in great demand, but there are also many young, new frame-builders who turn out excellent products at very competitive rates. Most of these are to be found in smaller communities and rural areas where overheads are low, and many will make you welcome and let you watch while the frame is built. Never ask a frame-builder to do something he or she does not want to do. The responsibility for ultimate success rests with the builder, and it is not fair to give a scheme that could turn out wrong.

Creating your own 'superbike' is one of life's great pleasures, but do not attempt this until you are an experienced cyclist and know exactly what you want – any mistakes will be expensive.

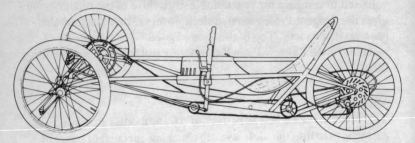

Recumbents!

Recumbent cycles are one of the most exciting development areas in pedal powered transport. Such machines are readily identifiable by the fact that the rider sits fairly close to the ground, with the legs extended forward, and the back elevated at least enough to allow forward vision. The reason for this configuration is improved aerodynamic efficiency. On a conventional bicycle at 20 mph, some 85 per cent of the rider's effort goes into overcoming wind resistance. A fully enclosed streamliner can reduce this drag by about 68 per cent, and a relatively upright recumbent such as the Avatar 2000 without a body shell has a 20 per cent reduction in drag. At 20 mph this translates as 25 per cent less effort than is required to move a conventional bicycle at the same speed.

Theory is one thing, practice is another. In physiological terms the recumbent position has advantages and disadvantages. Propulsion is by leg thrust alone, and it is not possible to stand on the pedals and use body weight as a help when climbing hills. The ability to pull and heave on the handlebars is also considerably reduced. There is a lot of lively debate on the subject, but the majority opinion is that recumbents are inferior to conventional bicycles for hill climbing and acceleration from a standstill. Acceleration from 15 mph is another affair, and hill climbing is only slower, not more difficult.

The recumbent riding position is extremely comfortable, with full support for back and buttocks, and there is none of the constriction in ability to breathe that goes with the crouched position used on a conventional drop handlebar bike. This makes possible a higher level of sustained effort, or pace. When combined with the inherent greater aerodynamic efficiency of the recumbent design, the net result is higher cruising speeds for less effort than with a conventional bicycle.

Recumbents come in three basic designs: tricycle, long wheelbase bicycle, and short wheelbase bicycle. To avoid overturning on corners, the tricycle configuration demands that the rider be placed very low to the ground. This makes for a visibility problem when riding in traffic. Its hard to see, and to be seen. A tricycle is stabler than a similarly low recumbent bicycle, however, and this is useful in stop-and-go riding. A nimble and quick tricycle recumbent is the Windcheetah SL from Burrows Engineering, 16 Thunder Lane, Thorpe, Norwich, Norfolk NR7 OPX, price at this writing about £550. This machine is immense fun, and also very practical. I've got one, and use it regularly for sport, commuting, shopping and last minute, high-speed deliveries of the kids to school. Winner of many races and practical vehicle contests, the Speedy (its common nickname) is perhaps the most versatile production recumbent available today. An additional option at £300 or so is a full body shell, windscreen and top. The extra weight inhibits acceleration, but once moving a fully faired Speedy will leave conventional racing bikes well behind. And you're warm and cozy if it rains!

Many people are diffident about very low-slung machines, particularly in traffic. Bicycle recumbents raise the rider for better visibility, and have other advantages.

There's nothing that will compare with a recumbent bicycle for cornering at speed. There is no problem with dragging pedals and the bike can be leaned over as far as nerve will permit. I've had few more exhilarating experiences than cannonballing down twisting country lanes with the Avatar 2000 while still pedalling through the corners.

Such antics bring up another important issue: braking capacity. A long wheelbase recumbent such as the Avatar has a resistance to cartwheeling that can only be overcome by running into a brick wall, and this allows uninhibited use of very strong brakes. With a short wheelbase recumbent bicycle, however, such as the American Hyper-Cycle, hard braking will result in a forward upset. This problem can be circumvented by lowering the rider, as with the Belgian Vélérique, but this reopens the can of worms marked handling, which becomes twitchier when the centre of gravity is lowered. So far as I can tell to date, in a recumbent bicycle the long wheelbase design is superior to the short wheelbase design for both braking and handling.

A further advantage of the Avatar type recumbent is that it deals well with potholes. The lightly loaded front wheel flies over the hole and, should the rear wheel break on impact, the rider settles down to the ground shoulder and stern first, in a short distance. There are many very good riders of conventional bicycles whose facial scars show the evidence of having come a cropper.

The only long wheelbase recumbent available in Britain at this writing is the Roulandt, made in Holland, a machine with a higher profile (and thus greater aerodynamic drag) than a regular bicycle. Race and road proven is the Easy Racer, from Easy Racers, Inc., 2981 Freedom Blvd., Watsonville CA 95076 USA.

So far as I am concerned, a recumbent bicycle is faster, safer and more comfortable than a conventional bicycle. It is exceptionally suitable for open roads and touring. In traffic it is an unusual machine that draws a lot of attention to the rider, but not at night on badly lit streets. Visibility to other road users can be a problem. Starting a recumbent bicycle from standstill is a definite technique and, although one does master it with experience, in thick stop-and-go traffic a recumbent bicycle is unwieldy. This problem does not obtain with a recumbent tricycle.

Other bicycles

Small-wheel bicycles

These are mini-bikes with 16 inch or 20 inch wheels, available with a variety of options, including hinged, folding frames. Their virtues are: (1) easy storage; (2) good luggage capacity; (3) manoeuvrability; and (4) easy adaptation to any size rider. Their drawbacks are (1) relatively high price, depending on number of gear speeds and accessories selected; (2) a weight of 40 to 50 pounds which makes them heavy to carry and hard to pedal; (3) an unstable ride due to the small wheels so that oil slicks, manhole covers, and gravel patches are likely to throw you; and (4) poor brakes, even in the calliper versions. This last is critical, since the net effect of the mini-bike's design is to restrict it to short local trips in urban areas where good brakes are premium.

Many people who take up cycling for the second time around get a mini. It's new. They like the crisp looks and easy way it goes. But if you are in this category I want to caution you specifically that these bikes are good for some things and not for others.

For getting the groceries it is hard to beat one of the shopper versions with baskets front and rear that come off quickly to carry around with you in the store. The manoeuvrability and small size of the bike make handling and parking easy. On the other hand, a conventional 10-speed with touring panniers will carry as much and more – *and* go touring. For shopping, the mini wins simply on grounds of convenience because with the 10-speed with touring panniers will carry as much and more – *and* go touring. For shopping, the mini wins simply on grounds of convenience because with the 10-speed there is always a certain amount of fumbling as purchases are packed away in the panniers and/or boxes are lashed on the rack. Some of the better panniers have been designed, however, to go on and off the bike in seconds, so you'd better check the section on touring and luggage before opting for the mini – which won't go touring very well.

Any of the small-wheel jobs have a darting manoeuvrability that is very handy for exploring urban locales. They will U-turn and turn right and left as fast as thought. You can get on and off hundreds of times effortlessly. They encourage spontaneity – nipping down a mews to look at an old house, pulling over to study a bookshop window, even hi-jinks cutting around obstacles. The price is paid in unsteadier handling at speed and sudden dumps on slippery surfaces like oil or leaves. Mini-bike brakes are just adequate so long as the sun shines and the rims and brake blocks are dry. In the wet the mini-bike's brakes go down to near zero. As a choice for steady, all-weather commuting, or habitual use by a rider weighing more than 12 stone, they are just not on.

Most mini-bikes come with quick-adjust seat and handlebars. This can be a very useful feature if several members of the family will be using the same bike.

In sum, the mini-bike is a local use machine with characteristics that give it the edge for multi-rider use, light shopping, urban exploring, and zesty handling. It is not so good for commuting or longer tours.

The best – and most expensive – 20 inch bikes are the Dawes Kingpin series. They are light, have slight edge in handling characteristics, and have quality features such as ball-bearing pedals and better grade saddles.

An interesting cross between a mini-bike and conventional size bike is the Pashley Patriot 24. This has a unisex frame 24 inch wheels for good handling and optional extras include a front bolt-on basket and rear child seat.

Folding bicycles
Conventional folding bicycles weigh 40 to 50 pounds and are bulky and difficult to manage. The Bickerton, constructed primarily from aluminium alloy, weighs only 20 pounds (22 pounds

for the 3-speed model) and folds down in 45 seconds to an astonishing 30 x 20 x 9 inches – about the size of a small suitcase. A stout canvas bag fitted on the front handlebars will hold up to 40 pounds of groceries or whatever, and also doubles as a carrier for the folded-bike.

The portability of the Bickerton has to be experienced to be believed. It is no trouble at all to take along in a taxi, train, or bus. Two Bickertons will fit into the boot of a mini. More importantly, the Bickerton obviates security problems. There is not need to bother locking it up, because you can take it wherever you go. A folded Bickerton will slide under a desk or workbench. It can hang from a cloakroom coat-hook. Storage in a flat or home with limited space is a snap.

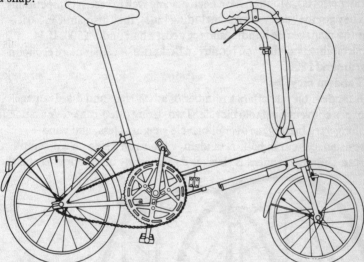

The portability of the Bickerton is a great asset for touring. Hopping by train, bus, airport, or car from one interesting touring area to another is easy. On country tracks the Bickerton can be carried in a backpack when the going becomes too rough for riding.

In performance a Bickerton will keep up with anything short of a flat-out racing or touring bicycle. The very light weight gives quick acceleration and easy uphill pedalling. Design and materials give the frame a surprising flexibility, so that despite the use of small wheels, the ride is very comfortable.

Of course the Bickerton is a mini-bike, and the handling is quick. Rapid downhill descents are unnerving. Very powerful pedalling from a standing start can 'bounce' the front wheel. The initial riding sensation on a Bickerton is distinctly odd. But once the distinctive characteristics are mastered the Bickerton becomes a very tractable and enjoyable bicycle to ride.

A bike in a class of its own is the Moulton AM-7. Where the Bickerton is designed first and foremost for portability, the Moulton is an altogether new engineering concept in bikes. It has the unique feature of independently suspended front and rear wheels, a frame geometry that gives a stable ride and excellent handling, and optional loading platforms that can manage up to 70 pounds of baggage. Riding a Moulton over rough cobblestones is a treat and while it is not strictly speaking a racing bike (the suspension tends to absorb sharp rider efforts), Moulton have been placing well in recent competitions. They go, they carry things (including kids), they dismantle in a trice into a manageable bundle, and they cost a hair under £500. If portability is all that you require, a Bickerton is rather more economic at around £200.

Tandem bicycles

A tandem bicycle offers a number of advantages and disadvantages over a conventional solo bicycle. Two strong riders can move a tandem along very briskly, as overall bicycle weight is less, and wind resistance is cut in half. A tandem will outrun a solo on a downhill run. Uphill, a tandem is slow. But over gently undulating terrain the

INVINCIBLE TANDEM.

greater mass of the tandem increases momentum, 'ironing out' small hills.

Two riders of unequal strength can have rest periods for the weak rider on the easy parts of a ride, and put in the muscle together when climbing hills. Togetherness is a very definite positive feature of tandem-cycling; it is easy to talk, and there is something very pleasant about the shared physical effort. The rear rider, or 'stoker', is free to enjoy the scenery to the maximum. Disadvantages include awkward handling in traffic, which riding should be done only be experienced cyclists, and the sheer size of a tandem, which necessitates a roof rack for transport by automobile, and generous storage space.

Only a lightweight (35 to 45 pounds) derailleur gear tandem is worth owning. The heavyweight (90 pound) models are just too much work to pedal. At double the weight of a solo bike, a tandem requires first rate brakes. At the minimum it should have cantilever rim brakes with oversize blocks. This would be for a lightweight racing tandem for use by experienced riders. Touring tandems should have drum brakes or disc brakes, or better still, cantilvers rim brakes and a drum or disc brake.

Tandem tyres take a beating. Tubular tyres and narrow section HP tyres are suitable only for racing or fast day riding. The technical editor of *Bicycling*, Fred DeLong, who has racked up many thousands of miles on tandems, recommends the sturdy 650-B tyres and rims for durability, comfort, and stable handling even on unpaved roads.

A good tandem is expensive but do not compromise on quality. A tandem must be soundly engineered and constructed in order to withstand the stress of two riders. My personal favourites are the tandems manufactured by Jack Taylor Cycles, Church Road, Stockton-on-Tees, Teesside TS18 2LY. Other quality builders are

Bob Jackson, 148 Harehills Lane, Leeds LS8 5BD, Mercian Cycles Ltd., 28 Stenson Road, Cavendish, Derby DE3 7JB and Tony Oliver, Maes Meredydd Uchaf, Rhosybol, Amlwch, Anglesey.

Two shops specialising in tandems are:
Beta Bikes
275 West End Lane   and   The Tandem Centre
London NW6 1QS   281 Old Kent Road
(catalogue available)   London SE1

and technical advice and help are available from
The Tandem Club
25 Henred Way Abingdon, Oxon OX14 2AN

Tricycles

These are popular items in retirement areas. They usually have 20 inch wheels to keep the weight down low and are quite stable as long as they are not driven briskly. A large rear basket-carrier, handy for carrying groceries, gold bricks, golf clubs, or whatever, is a popular accessory. People with poor balance or co-ordination, brittle bones, or other problems, should seriously consider a tricycle. But bear in mind also that many old folks do just fine with conventional two-wheelers, and in fact there are a number of bicycle clubs whose members are all over seventy.

One type of tricycle has a fixed gear on which there is no free-wheeling and the pedals turn when the wheels turn. People who have limited motion in their legs have sometimes found that the exercise provided by this type of machine helps recovery of leg mobility. For hilly terrain get a 3- to 10-speed model.

People with a taste for the unusual might want to consider a lightweight racing or touring tricycle with 26 inch or 27 inch wheels. In no way is this an old age toy. Many an experienced bicyclist has come a cropper first time out on a trike. It must be steered around a corner, a sensation completely at odds with the handling of a bicycle, and rider weight must be counter-balanced to the inside on even a moderate bend. It is quite easy to lift a wheel, and downhill bends in particular must be approached with caution. Changes in the camber of the road also easily upset balance.

At first I enjoyed trikes simply because I found them challenging. Now that I am more familiar and comfortable with their handling characteristics a number of advantages have emerged, and in fact the 'family' cycle is a tandem trike. It has very good load-carrying capacity, does not require a dismount when stopped, will park without having to be propped up, and will stay upright under slippery conditions. The baby's seat is located between the two rear wheels, giving some measure of protection should there be an accident. And it's easy to add an extra seat for another little 'un. All in all, the tandem trike works out as a very comfortable family bike for relaxed and social cycling. The handling does not inspired rapid downhill descents, but this is immaterial on a family bike.

Solo and tandem models are available from Ken G. Rogers, 71 Berkeley Avenue, Cranford, Hounslow, Middlesex TW4 6LF, and solo models from Jack Taylor Cycles, Stockton-on-Tees, Teesside TS18 2LY.

In Britain a trike is known also as a 'barrow', and there is a dedicated fraternity of adherents banded as

The Tricycle Association   Sec. J.H. Mills,
58 Townsend Avenue, West Kirby, Liverpool L11 8ND.

A good workhorse is the utility tricycle, weighing in at about 100 pounds. These feature a platform with a load capacity of 500 pounds, and have a great variety of industrial and commercial uses. A few examples would be: moving gardening equipment and lawnmowers around estates and parks; moving TV sets (or lawn furniture, or lace undies, or bags of cement – anything that a human being can pick up) around a warehouse; mounting a hot dog, ice cream, or vegetable stand; collecting rubbish from small litter bins. The great point in favour of the utility trike is that it is highly economical, and uses only the amount of power appropriate for the job at hand. It is also noise – and pollution – free. If you can think of and suggest an application for a utility trike where you live or work, you will be doing yourself and everbody else a big favour. A good range of carrier bicycles and tricycles is manufactured by W.R. Pashley Ltd., Masons Roads, Stratford-upon-Avon, Warwickshire CV37 9NL.

Sailing tricycle

The Rans Company, 408 Milner, Hays, Kansas 67601, USA, manufacturers sailing tricycles. These have a (30 square foot) sail just like on a boat, and will do up to 50 mph. Just be sure you have a lot of room!

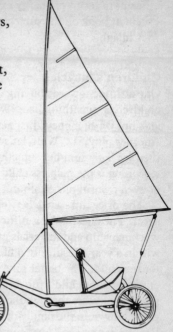

Unicycles

Pashley's is nice.

Flying machines

Human-powered airplanes have been designed, and in some instances built, virtually since the invention of the bicycle. Few got any appreciable distance off the ground until the epic *Gossamer Condor*, invented by Dr Paul MacCready, which captured the £50,000 Kremer Prize by flying a figure of eight course around two poles half a mile apart. In comparison to previous flying machines, *Gossamer Condor* requires relatively little power input; it has been flown by a grandmother!

Gossamer Condor was followed by *Gossamer Albatross* and an act that will be difficult to follow: winning the £100,000 Kremer Prize by flying on human power only over the English Channel.

Pedal machines

Machines using human pedal power include a garden tractor, lathes, food processing equipment, water pumps, lawnmowers, sewing machines, electric generators, hoists, cider presses, and many more. Particularly in developing countries where fuel and complex technology can be expensive, pedal power machines are often the most efficient in terms of energy expenditure and ease of application. An excellent book on the subject is *Pedal Power*, edited by J.C. McCullagh.

Children's bicycles

One attitude towards buying clothes, toys, and other materials for children is something like, 'Well, the kid'll grow out of it soon, so let's not waste money. Just get him/her something good enough.' Another ploy, is, "Well, let's first see if she/he is really interested – then we'll get him/her something better.' The victim of this faulty reasoning is the helpless child, who is saddles with some worthless or even painful pieces of junk and who is expected to be grateful for it. The price difference between a good bike and a cheap one is not great. The cheap bike is difficult and unpleasant to ride, and shoddy workmanship and materials guarantee that it will grace the junkpile within a year. Result: total financial loss and total lack of stimulation for the child. The better bike is not only a pleasure to ride, thus ensuring your child's fun and interest, but will also survive for a number of years through the hands of several children. It can be passed down in the family or sold for at least half the purchase price. Result: happier *children*, and less net expenditure. If you would like to save money or are on a tight budget, check the classified adverts in local papers and put up cards advertising for what you want at newsagents, laundromats, school meetings, etc., and buy a used bike.

A child can gain pleasure from a cycle as early as age two, but not necessarily as a means of transport. The initial use may be as the framework for a house or other construction. Let the child move at his or her own pace and they will eventually figure out what the thing can do. At this stage a tricycle is better than a bicycle with training wheels, and a particularly good children's trike is the Pashley Pickle.

A child is ready for a bicycle at about age four or five, depending on individual development and co-ordination. Training wheels will prove a mixed blessing. On the one hand they allow immediate use of the bike, but on the other hand are unsafe, as the bike can easily tip over, and only prolong the inevitable day when the child must learn how to ride properly.

The best way to teach anybody to ride a bike is to let them do it themselves. Lower the saddle so that they can touch the ground with

their feet when mounted. Remove the pedals if necessary. Set bike and rider on a very slight decline and let him or her progress by pushing along with the feet. Balance and steering ability will come quickly. The ideal first bike for a youngster should have:

• Pneumatic tyres for a comfortable ride, easier pedalling, and effective braking. Solid rubber tyres are three times harder to pedal, provide a jolting ride, and give bad braking.

• Steel steering head bearings. The plastic sleeve bearings used on cheap bikes result in bad handling and steering characteristics, and wear out quickly, compounding the problem.

• A large seat range adjustment so the bike can grow with the child.

If you can find one of the Viscount children's bicycles (the firm went out of business recently) still about, get it. These bikes have ball bearings throughout, and the high standard of quality gives exceptional value. Considerably more available, and of very good quality and value, are the Raleigh range of children's bicycles. In the models for children age seven or more these also have ball bearings throughout. Proper ball bearings give mechanical efficiency and a dramatic increase in pleasure that is well worth any slight extra cost.

Many children will want a BMX bike. These are machines for off-road riding and stunts and are more fun than a barrelful of monkeys. The tricks that kids can do with BMX bikes are mind-boggling. The machines are usually sturdily constructed and will stand a lot of wear and tear. I particularly like the fact that they are at their best when used off-road, away from the danger of motor vehicles. BMX machines litter the ground these days, and many are not of the first water. To avoid falling in the deep end invest in the excellent and comprehensive *Puffic BMX Handbook*, or a current issue of the periodical *BMX Action Bike*.

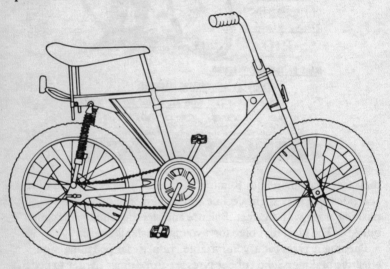

LUDGATE HILL.

3   The urban commuting bicycle

Road racing, cyclo-cross and track bicycles each have distinctive characteristics appropriate to their intended use. So does the urban commuting bicycle. Many city streets are obstacle courses filled with bumps, potholes, uneven surfaces, 'temporary' steel plates which are slippery when wet, broken glass, bits of sharp metal and other rubbish. In heavy traffic there is often not enough room for a cyclist to avoid an obstacle. A machine for these conditions must be tough. Theft is a constant problem in cities. An obviously expensive bicycle is more likely to be stolen, or stripped for parts. Finally, most regular commuters prefer a bike that requires a minimum of maintenance.

Several different types of bicycle are best capable of coping with urban conditions. Each has advantages and disadvantages according to your particular situation and needs.

The classic heavy-duty roadster offers a soft frame design which helps to iron out the worst of the bumps, enclosed hub gears which are well protected from wet and grit, robust $1\frac{1}{2}$-in tyres which have a fighting chance of surviving glass and other road litter, and an upright riding position which allows a good view of traffic conditions. However, at 50 pounds weight, the heavy-duty roadster is hard work to pedal, and is not suitable for long journeys or steep terrain. As far as security is concerned it is an odd-ball bike with a low black-market value and in theory would be less likely to be stolen.

The 3-speed sports roadster is much the same as the heavy-duty roadster except that it is lighter in weight, uses 26-in wheels with $1\frac{1}{2}$-in tyres, and is available in a wide range of frame sizes. It is still not much of a speed machine or hill-climber. One performance improvement is to fit alloy 26 in X $1\frac{1}{2}$ in rims and high pressure tyres. An inexpensive way of improving hill-climbing ability is to fit a larger rear sprocket of 20 or 22 teeth. This limits top speed to around 20 mph, but this is adequate for most traffic conditions. The bike is then more suitable for off-road riding. Sports roadsters are not the most valuable of bicycles, but are easy to re-sell. Security is a problem.

Derailleur gear bicycles are the obvious choice for long journeys and/or steep terrain. A longish wheelbase and fork trail, strong rims with thick spokes, and stout tyres, will maximize comfort and stability over rough surfaces.

There are a number of modifications to make a 10-speed more suitable for regular commuting. Fitting sealed bearing hubs, bottom bracket and pedals will increase maintenance intervals. Spokes should be 14 gauge plain, laced to strong alloy rims such as Super Champion. Stout tyres such as the Michelin Sports should be kept inflated *hard*, to help absorb bumps.

The present deplorable state of Kingston Bridge.

Ten-speed bike security is a problem. For locking up on the street, the only answer is a lock such as the Citadel or Kryptonite (see Chapter 4 for details). Many people disguise high quality frames with a coat of dull looking, sloppy paint, and substitute low grade components (saddle, derailleurs, chainset). The resulting bike looks like an old banger but still goes fairly well. Some people booby-trap their bikes by slacking off the brakes or wheels, or removing the saddle. These are last ditch measures.

The ultimate machine for urban cycling is the mountain bike. On an ordinary lightweight 10-speed, the sight of a jagged, yawning pothole will set your senses screaming with alarm. On a mountain bike you can laugh and attack the thing. Wide tyres and handlebars give a sure grip and utterly superior low speed handling. The only thing that will stop quicker than a mountain bike is a long wheelbase recumbent, and I wouldn't want to live on the difference. When it comes time to snap away from a traffic light, a good surge through the extra long cranks will leave even a pure road racing bike in the dust. You can go where you like – blazing down the fast lane, up and down kerbs, along canal towpaths, straight through parks – the mountain bike will do it all and more.

The problem here is attractiveness to those with sticky fingers. Mountain bikes are worth about £15 per pound weight, and look the part. Consider such a machine only if you have very secure parking facilities, or a guard swarm of crazed bees.

One way to bypass the security problem is to use a lightweight folding bike. These machines go where you go and can be tidily tucked away under a desk or in a restaurant cloakroom. If it suddenly starts to pour cats and dogs and you do not feel like getting wet, a folding bike is little trouble to take on a bus, train or taxi. This makes such a machine the favoured contender for mixed mode transport.

In performance, lightweight folding bikes need make little apology. They will go. But there is no way that small wheels will give the stability of large wheels over bumps and through potholes, and braking capacity is not of the first water. If you can, ride large wheels.

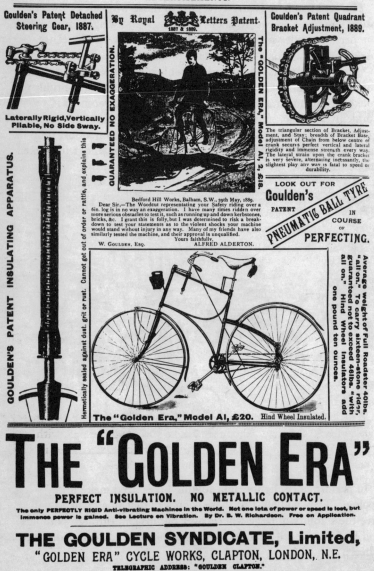

4 Buying and keeping a bike

New bikes

The best place to buy a new bicycle is a bike shop. You can
sometimes save money at a department or discount store, but you
are virtually guaranteed disproportionate headaches and problems.
In the first place, the quality of merchandise is almost always
inferior. Secondly, the sad fact is that not even the finest machines
are defect-free when they come from the manufacturer.
Department and discount stores do not employ trained bicycle
mechanics, and so the bikes they sell are often unassembled, or
have been put together by some cretin who has done more harm
than good. It takes a good bicycle mechanic to assemble a new bike
without damaging anything, check all the parts, and iron out the
inevitable defects. Even then, problems are not likely to be over. If
a department or discount store gives a guarantee – few do – they
have no mechanics to take care of after-sales problems. And if there
is some totally basic defect in a machine you buy, it takes weeks for
a refund or replacement.

A bike shop will assemble the machine. Although you must
check their work carefully, chances are they'll do the job right. If
some problem comes up later, they are available right away to fix
it, and so are replacement parts. You get a guarantee, which should
be for a minimum of a year, and is sometimes longer. And you will
want to deal with a bike shop anyway, for servicing, parts,
accessories and advice.

The kind of bike shop makes a difference. Try to find one that
deals only in bicycles. The more local a shop you can deal with, the
better. Any bike shop must meet certain basic requirements in
quality of bikes and service, but convenience means a lot. A
guarantee from a shop 50 miles away is useless for anything except
a major disaster. If there is a local shop and they don't have what
you want, talk it over with them. Perhaps they can order a bike for
you.

If their 'brand' of bike is not the one you had in mind, take a good
look at what they offer. All other things being equal, as they may

well be since many manufacturers use the same components, the convenience of a local shop is an excellent reason to switch 'brand'. Just make sure you get a fair value. Ask about servicing and parts. If their guarantee isn't good enough, explain the problem. Don't expect, however, that they will be able to offer as good a deal as a high-volume super-powered bike shop. What you pay a little extra for is the fact that they are around the corner. Also, perhaps, the general feeling is friendlier.

At any rate, stay away from discount and department stores. I have not regaled you with horror stories about machines purchased from such sources, but they are legion, and cover everything from kids' tricycles to ultra-fancy racers. The tiny bit extra you spend in a bike shop buys an awful lot.

Taking delivery

Anticipate that any new bike will have something wrong with it. Dealing with a good bike shop minimizes this possibility but by no means eliminates it. When I picked up a new dream machine from one of New York's finest shops I was too bedazzled to give it anything but the most cursory inspection. As I accelerated away from the shop, the rear hub and freewheel exploded in a blizzard of metal flakes and chips. Most problems you are likely to encounter are not apt to be so spectacular, but the point cannot be emphasized too strongly that a thorough inspection of any new bike is necessary. The best way to learn what to look for is to read the Maintenance and Repair sections of this book. Here are the main points to watch:

●Check the frame for straightness. Stand behind or in front of the bicycle and see that the wheels are in line. Next, hold the bicycle by the saddle only and wheel it around the shop. If the frame or forks are bent, it will tend to veer to one side. Finally, if you do a test ride, at some point when you are clear of traffic hold the handlebars as lightly as possible, even riding hands off if you have the skill. The bicycle should go straight, in control, without pulling to one side. Reject any bicycle which fails these tests. A bicycle which will not track accurately is tiring and unsafe to ride.
●Check quality of lug welds on frame. Sight down frame to check for bends.
●Wheels should spin easily. When held off ground weight of valve

stem should pull wheel around so valve is in six o'clock position. Wheel should be centred in fork arms or chain stays. If wheel can be moved from side to side and there is a clicking sound, hub cones are out of adjustment. Check that rim is true by holding a pencil next to it and spinning the wheel. Brace the pencil on a fork arm or chain stay to keep it steady.

● Pluck spokes. All should be evenly tight and give the same 'twang'.

● Brake blocks should hit rims squarely and not drag when released.

● Gears should work smoothly and with no slippage. Test first with wheels off ground and then on a ride.

● Pedals and chainwheel should spin easily but without side-to-side play.

● Ride the bike around the vicinity of the store for a few miles.

You may think that all this is a lot of trouble to go to. I have bought a fair number of bikes for myself, family, or friends. There was something wrong with every one of them, and a few I rejected outright. You will save yourself a lot of grief if you invest some time at the outset on a careful inspection.

A good bike shop will watch all this activity with tolerant amusement. A bad shop will register irritation and this is immediate grounds for considering making your purchase elsewhere. But be fair. You cannot expect a £100 bike to sing with quality, or for the shop to spend a great deal of time fiddling with it. What you have the right to expect of any bike is that it is roadworthy.

After you purchase a bike, check that all nuts, bolts, and screws are secure. Every last one. After riding 50 miles or so, repeat this operation. New bicycles 'bed in', and it is very common, for example, for the brake bolts to work loose. Cranks, particularly the cotterless type, are bound to need tightening. See the appropriate section under Maintenance for details.

For the name of a bike shop near you, consult the Shop Directory in a current edition of *The Bicycle Buyers' Bible*. You may be far from a suitable bike store. The following mail order firms sell bicycles, components and accessories by post:

Freewheel   Richmond Cycles
Unit 7   36 Hill Street
Oxgate Lane   Richmond, Surrey
London NW2 7HT

Both of the above are reputable, reliable firms. There are also other, newer mail order firms that advertise regularly in the cycling press and which offer bikes at up to 25 per cent off list price. This kind of trading has been going on in America for several years, and the rules are clear: be able to set up, remedy any defects and service the bike yourself. You will not have much change, if any, out of trying to induce a regular bike shop to do the work. Quite understandably, they take a dim view of mail order firms. Exceptions include Freewheel and Richmond Cycles, who offer quality merchandise at good value prices but do no discounting.

Used bikes

Good bikes can be elusive, especially when you actually want one. But they are a good way to save money. Expect to pay about 75 per cent of the list price for a machine in excellent as-new condition, and about 50 per cent of the list price for one in average condition.

Sources of used bikes depend on where you live. A few bike shops sell used machines but turnover is quick and you will need some luck to catch the machine you want. *Exchange & Mart* has classified ads for bikes. The weekly *Cycling* has lots of ads, mostly for racing machinery. *Cycletouring* (from the CTC, Cotterell House,

69 Meadrow, Godalming, Surrey GU7 3HS) has ads for touring bikes.

But if you are really trying to go on the cheap, then look around locally. Most cities and counties have classified publications listing all kinds of stuff – including bikes – for sale. Check also the classified ads in the local papers. Sometimes families and people moving house sell off furniture and household goods and there is often a bicycle in the pile. Keep an eye open for ads in your local newsagent's window, too. Auctions are sometimes useful. A good bet in the spring are local bulletin boards at universities and colleges. Put up some cards yourself or take an ad in the student newspaper. Naturally, the more prosaic a bike you seek, the faster you will be likely to find it. But if you just put the word out, something will turn up eventually.

Understand exactly what sort of bike you want. Converting a racing bike to a touring bike can be expensive – new freewheel, chain, chainrings, and possibly new derailleurs and wheels. Be particularly careful of winding up with a lemon. Try to find out the history of the machine. It's best if you can talk to the owner. Was she or he interested in the bike and in taking care of it? Or did they just leave it out in the rain? Where did they ride? I would rather pay a few pounds more for a well-loved bike than make a saving by risking on a machine with a dubious or unknown past. And I would give away a bike to a good home rather than sell it to possible bad times. Your own keenness can be an economic asset if, as is often the case, the vendor has a soft spot for the bike on offer.

In inspecting the bike, cover all the points listed for a new bike. Pay particular attention to the frame. Wrinkled paint on the forks or where the top and down tubes meet the head tube are an almost certain indication of a crash. A coat of nice new paint can hide a multitude of flaws. I know of instances where badly repaired crash-damaged bikes have fallen apart, killing their unfortunate new owners. What you want to see are a certain number of the inevitable nicks and scrapes, but no major dents, rust spots or welds.

Count into the cost of a used bike a complete overhaul and lubrication, including possible replacement of the cables, chain and sprockets. Read the sections on maintenance and repair in this book to learn how to assess components for wear and useful life.

A final word about used bikes relates to the problem of keeping your bike. There are plenty of stolen bikes for sale, particularly in street markets. Prices can be 25 per cent of list price, or even less. In case the proposition seems even remotely attractive, let me remind you that to get a bike this way is a crime. Legally and morally. Simply put, you are helping to steal. Additionally, it is not some money-greedy company's candy bar or rip-off piece of junk which you are stealing, but a possession somebody quite probably loves and cherishes.

THE ROVER SAFETY BICYCLE (PATENTED).

Safer than any Tricycle, faster and easier than any Bicycle ever made. Fitted with handles to turn for convenience in storing or shipping. Far and away the best hill-climber in the market.

Keeping your bike

This is a serious problem. Twenty-five per cent of the respondents to a *Bicycle Magazine* survey reported suffering the theft of a bike. If you do not take suitable precautions, then the loss of your bike is virtually certain.

Some of you may know that I used to have a commercial involvement with a lock called Citadel, an announcement that is mandatory for this flat statement: maximum bike security is only possible if you use a Citadel or Kryptonite lock. Ordinary cable and

THE NEW CLUB CRIPPER TANDEM QUADRICYCLE ROADSTER.

chain type locks can be cut in seconds with common tools.

For a *Bicycle Magazine* survey of locks, we locked a bike to a fence railing on a busy street, positioned a photographer on the first floor of a building directly opposite the bike, and sent in our very own professional 'thief'. The dirty deed was accomplished within seconds. A voluminous raincoat concealed the actual snipping of a cable lock, which the thief tidily tucked away in a pocket before absconding with the bike. People only yards away did not notice a thing. We could hardly believe how easy it was. We repeated the experiment six times, progressively making the theft more and more obvious. On the final go, the thief marched directly up to the bike, hauled out the snippers and cut the cable lock in full open view of nearby pedestrians, and still got away with the bike. One person took notice of what was happening, but did nothing about it.

The Citadel and Kryptonite locks are made of specially through-hardened steel and are very nearly bomb-proof. One unfortunate individual in Newcastle locked up his bike with a Citadel and lost the keys. It took the combined resources of the Police, Fire Brigade and engineering department of the local technical school a night and day to open the lock.

Both Citadel and Kryptonite back their locks with a one year performance warranty: if your bike is stolen as a result of the failure of the lock to prevent the theft, they will pay you the value of the bike up to £150 – a solid indication of the effectiveness of these products. A Citadel or Kryptonite will set you back around £20 but if you settle for less, then one day you are likely to find your bike – gone.

A good lock is your baseline for security, but is only a start. When locking up on the street you should:

● Lock the bike to seriously robust and immobile items such as lamp posts, parking signs, heavy iron railings and the like.

● Run the lock through the frame and back wheel. Remove the front wheel and either take it away with you, or run the lock through it as well.

● Be selective about location. Slum neighbourhoods are a bad bet at any time. Even if the bike is not stolen, bits and pieces may disappear. In any neighbourhood, look for a busy, well-travelled spot, not a dark alley.

● Try to enlist help. The cashier for a cinema will usually keep an eye on your bike. Newsagents and other merchants will often help, particularly if you are a regular customer. The local cafe may give you indigestion, but if the chef waves a meat cleaver at anybody who bothers your bike, the place is worth cultivating.

● Keep a written record of your bike's particulars, including the serial number stamped on the frame – most often found on the underside of the bottom bracket, but sometimes on a seat stay or tube.

●Have your bike post-coded. This involves the stamping of your house number and post code on the bottom bracket and enables the police to return your bike to you if they recover it after a theft. Various police departments, bike shops and cycle campaign groups will perform the service for a modest charge or even for free.

●Insure your bike. One gang of filth tried to steal a bike locked with a Citadel and vented the frustration of failure by wrapping the bike round a lamp post. Another evil crowd greeted a Citadel lock by cutting apart the frame of the bike, just to get the components. These kinds of things happen, and the only resource is insurance. The cheapest way to obtain this is as an extension of a household policy. Membership in organisations such as the British Cycling Federation and the Cyclists' Touring Club automatically includes various third party insurances and legal aid, but specific insurance cover for a bike costs extra. Together with the membership fee, insuring a bike can cost up to 25 per cent of the bike's value – not a very good deal. General Accident (General Buildings, Perth, Scotland PH1 5TP) offer competitively priced insurance schemes, and so do the National Association of Cycle Traders (you can arrange this through bike shops with an ACT sticker in the window) and some campaign groups, such as the London Cycling Campaign, Tress House, 3 Stamford Street, London SE1.

A COUNTRY POSTMAN.

Finally, on the subject of security, there's the problem of direct assault. Britain has its share of tough neighbourhoods where a good bike is an easy candidate for liberation. But mostly this kind of problem will arise only if you are dreadfully unaware of immediate circumstances. At any sign of social difficulty that does not require your personal intervention, just step on the pedals and get moving – at 20 to 30 mph you will leave most trouble behind before it happens.

5   Fitting and gears

Getting the most out of your bike requires careful fitting, e.g.
placement of handlebars, seat, and controls. The standard formulas
for this process are the result of considerable work and study by
genuine experts and will probably work the best. After you have
finished setting your bike up 'according to the book' the resulting
position may feel a bit odd. Give yourself at least 50 miles to get
used to the new arrangement before making alterations. You may
find the 'odd' position considerably more efficient and less
fatiguing than a 'comfortable' position. At the same time, no two
people are exactly alike, and some variation from the norm may be
in order. Just give the orthodox position a fair trial, and make
alterations gradually.

For how to make alterations in the position of seat, handlebars,
stem, and brake levers, look up Adjustment under the relevant
heading in the Maintenance and Repair sections.

Frame

Frame size is measured from the seat lug to the centre of the
bottom bracket axle. There is no single method for calculating
proper frame size that applies to everyone. Three rough rules of
thumb are:
1. Inside length of leg from crotch bone to floor, measured in
stocking feet, less 9 inches.
2. Height divided by 3.
3. Two-thirds inside length of leg.
Thus, a person 68 inches tall with a 32 inch inseam would have a
frame size of (1) 23 inches, (2) 22.6 inches, and (3) 21.3 inches! In
fact, correct frame size is a matter of trial and error, and experience
in what is 'right'. I'm 68.5 inches tall with a 32 inch inseam, and
ride happiest on 23 inches. Bron Lewis of *Bicycle Magazine* is 64.5
inches tall with a $31\frac{1}{4}$ inch inseam, and rides best on 20.5 inches.
The smaller frame size suits her (comparatively) shorter torso.

In any event, at least 2 to 3 inches of seat pillar should be
exposed when the saddle is at the correct height (see below), and
you should be able to straddle the frame comfortably with your feet
flat on the ground. If the top tube digs into your crotch, you can be

sure that sooner or later you will suffer a nasty slam where it hurts the most.

Novices are prone to select a frame which is too large. An oversize frame, particularly when touring, feels a bit more secure and steady. It may also have a slightly easier ride, as small frames tend to be stiffer than large frames. All this can create a definite prejudice towards a frame that is slightly larger than 'normal'.

British cycle manufacturers often exacerbate the situation by offering a poor selection of frame sizes. A typical range of diamond frame sizes might be 21, 22½, 23½ and 25¼ inches – bad luck to those who need a 19½, 21½, 22, 23, 24 or 24½ inch frame! In this respect the continental manufacturers usually offer a much more comprehensive range, as for example 19½, 20½, 21¼, 22, 22¾, 23½ and 24¾ inches.

In selecting a bike or frame, it will pay you to keep size in mind from the very start. There is little harm and possibly even merit in undersizing slightly – a longer seat pillar and stem will put matters right. But do not oversize by more than ½ inch. An excess of 1 inch or more will significantly compromise handling, speed and most importantly comfort.

Saddle

The position of the saddle determines the fitting of the rest of the bike. For most riders the correct fore-to-aft position is with the nose of the saddle 1¾ inches to 2½ inches behind a vertical line through the crank hanger:

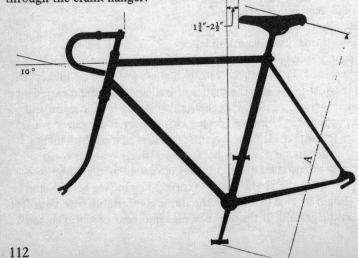

A more precise way of determining fore-to-aft position depends on rider height. A person 5ft 6 inches tall would normally have the nose of the saddle 1 inch back of the bottom bracket, while for a person 6ft 3 inches tall the distance would increase to 3 inches. Thus for someone 5ft 10 inches tall the usual position would be 2 inches back. However, there are many variations. Touring riders often use a slightly rearward saddle position together with handlebars set on the high side. They are interested in comfort and steady power over long distances. Sprint riders and traffic jammers who use brief bursts of sharp energy use a more forward saddle position. This is the reason sprint frames come with a steeper seat tube angle. For around-town use, if you are a vigorous rider, you may like a more forward saddle position. For extended going and best overall efficiency, however, stick to the normal position.

The horizontal tilt of the saddle, i.e. height of the front relative to the rear, is crucial. There is, in your crotch, a nerve. Pinching it even just slightly over a long ride can disable you with numb crotch for weeks. Start with the nose and rear of the saddle dead level, and if you experience any discomfort, immediately lower the nose a degree or two. It can make all the difference. This is where a good quality seat with micro-adjusting bolts is important.

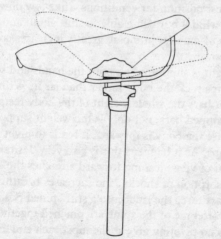

I have never seen a serious racing or touring bike with a back-tilted saddle.

Most saddles are set too low. A rough rule of thumb is that while sitting on the bike with your heel on the pedal at its lowest point, your leg should be straight. This means that when riding with the ball of your foot on the pedal, your leg is almost but not quite fully extended at the bottom of the stroke.

A precise formula for the best saddle height has been worked out in a series of scientific tests. Measure inside length of leg from crotch bone to floor without shoes. Multiply this length (in inches) by 1.09. Example: 32 inches × 1.09 equals 34.88, or $34^7/_8$ inches. Set saddle so distance A (opposite page) from top of saddle to centre of pedal spindle in down position with crank parallel to seat tube is $34^7/_8$ inches.

This formula has been put together by experts. They found that an alteration in saddle height of 4% of inside leg measurement from the 1.09 setting affected power output by approximately 5%. So once the saddle is set, give it a good long trial before making changes.

Handlebars

Let's settle one thing now: there are many reasons why dropped bars are more efficient and comfortable than flat bars. Here are a few:

(1) A much greater variety of positions is possible. Not only can you select the best position for conditions – like low down when headed into the wind – but being able to shift about and bring different groups of muscles into play greatly increases comfort, to say nothing of power.

(2) Because weight is supported by both the hands and seat, road shocks and bumps rock the body rather than jar it. With conventional flat bars the whole weight of the body rests on the saddle. With dropped bars, not only is the weight supported by the arms, but because the body is forward, it tends to pivot at the hips going over bumps. As it happens this is also very desirable from an anatomical point of view: leaning forward stretches the spine, allowing the absorption of shocks, and increases breathing capacity. Conventional bars force the rider into a stiff-spined position where the individual vertebrae of the spine are pinched together. Further, because there is no pivoting give at the hips, each and every jolt and bump is transmitted directly up the spine, greatly increasing fatigue.

(3) The better distribution of weight allowed by dropped bars provides improved stability and steering characteristics.

Positioning of the handlebars is crucial. For conventional use they should be set so that the top bar is just level with the nose of the saddle. Sprint bikes have the bars a whole lot lower, and if you do a lot of traffic riding you may want to set yours down a bit. Mine are about 1½ inches lower than the saddle. Just remember that if you opt for short-term speed it will be at some cost to overall efficiency.

The stem should position the bars so that the distance between the nose of the saddle and the rear edge of the centre of the handlebars equals the distance from your elbow to your outstretched fingertips. Another way to determine this distance is to sit on the bike in your normal riding position while a friend holds it steady. Without changing position, remove one hand from handlebars and let arm dangle fully relaxed. Now rotate your arm in a large arc without stretching. If, as your hand comes back to the bar, it is ahead of or behind the other hand, the bars need to be moved. Stems come in increments of length, or you can buy an adjustable stem. This costs and weighs more.

The standard rake for the ends of drop bars is 10° from the horizontal:

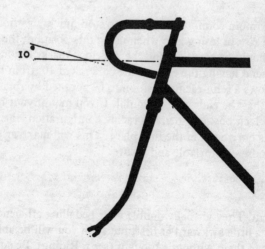

Start with this setting, which makes the tops of the bars level and thus affords the greatest variety of riding positions, and make changes as you desire.

Brakes

Do not tape new bars until you have ridden the bike enough to fully fiddle with and set the position of the brake levers. On racing bikes, for example, the hands are often primarily on the 'hooks', inside the curved section of the bars, and the brake levers are accordingly set at approximately 3 o'clock so as to be within ready reach of the fingers. Tourists and urban riders, however, tend to favour a more upright position and place their hands mostly on the tops of the bars or, particularly in traffic, on the brake lever hoods:

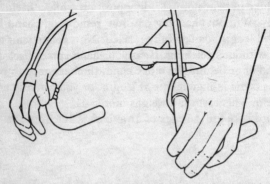

For maximum comfort and ability to stop quickly without undue effort or risk of losing grip when using this position, the brake levers should be set at around the 2 o'clock mark. If you use this, I recommend having the ends of the bars raked 10° from horizontal. This allows a semi-racing position to be adopted by rotating the bars so that the ends are horizontal. If you mount your brakes in the 3 o'clock position to give a racing configuration, then set the bar ends horizontal in the first place. This will make grip on the hooks more comfortable and secure.

Toe clips

Use them! They virtually double your pedalling efficiency. They may be a little awkward at first, but soon you will be able to slip in and out of them without a thought (see 6 Riding). Be sure to get the size which corresponds to your shoe size: small for women with small feet, medium up to size 8, and large size 9 and up. To avoid scratching up fancy shoes, tape the fronts of the clips with a little cloth tape.

116

Cleats

Cleats are metal or plastic strips fastened to the soles of bicycling shoes. Used in conjunction with toe clips they hold your foot to the pedal with a vengeance, and are quite unsafe for traffic riding unless you use very loosely set straps. But they are essential for racing and great for touring. To fit cleats properly, ride your bike for a few miles without toe clips so that the soles of your shoes take an impression from the pedals. Then simply position cleats so cleat tunnel is aligned exactly with the pedal marks. Then fit toe clips.

Gearing

Fitting also includes the selection of gearing. Understanding this subject requires some knowledge of basic riding technique. Some of the information I am going to give you now is rather technical. Just use it as you need it.

When I bought my first 10-speed I was surprised to find that the gears, instead of each having a separate range like on a car, overlapped considerably. One gear really wasn't much different from the other. The reason for this is that there is a rate of cadence – the speed with which the cranks are spun around – which is the most efficient. For most people this rate is from 65 to 85 strokes per minute. Racers run 120–130 and up. The idea behind a multitude of gears it to allow the rider to maintain the same cadence regardless of terrain.

In consequence, a racing bike will have close-ratio gears, each one much the same as the next, while a touring bike will have wide-ratio gears, with much greater differences between each gear. The reason for this is that touring bikes frequently pack heavy loads up steep grades. They are also – rightly – usually the choice of the novice rider. Only expert riders in good condition can comfortably use close-ratio gears.

What determines ratio? The number of teeth on the front chainring divided by the number of teeth on the back sprocket (or cog). Thus a 60 front and a 15 rear give a 4 to 1 ratio. For competition a typical set-up might be a rear cluster of 23, 21, 19, 17, 15 matched to front chainrings of 49 and 52. For touring it might be 28, 24, 20, 17, 14 rear and 40 to 50 front.

To make everything a little simpler, gear ratios are expressed as a single number. The formula is:

$$\frac{\text{Number of teeth on front sprocket}}{\text{Number of teeth on back sprocket}} \times \text{wheel diameter} = \text{gear ratio}$$

In general, 100 is the top range and is hard to push, 90 is more common, and 80 the usual speed gear. 60 and 70 are the most often used, 40 and 50 are for hills. Below 40 is for extremely steep terrain and heavy loads. Most people gear too high and pedal too slowly. This increases fatigue. It is much better to pedal briskly against relatively little resistance.

There are other factors besides range to consider in setting up gears. Ease of transition from one gear to another is important. If you have to shift both front and back sprockets every time, it is laborious. For example:

		Rear				
		14	17	21	26	31
Front	52	100.2	82.3	66.9	54	45
	47	90.4	74.5	60.2	48.6	40.8

means that to run up through the gears consecutively requires continuous double shifts. On the other hand, a set up like:

		Rear				
		14	15	17	19	21
Front	54	104	97.2	85.6	76.7	69.4
	38	73.2	68	60	54	49

means that you can run up through the gears using only one shift of the front derailleur. (Never use the small front to small rear or big front to big rear. I will explain why later.)

If you use wide gaps front and rear there is almost bound to be some duplication of gears:

		Rear				
		14	17	21	26	31
Front	52	100.2	82.3	66.9	54	45
	42	81	66.7	54	43.5	36.4

and yet curiously enough, many good
bikes are set up this way. It really depends on what you want the bike for, because in balancing the various factors of range, ease of shifting, and number of different gears, you are just going to have to make compromises.

Teeth on Sprocket	26	28	30	32	34	36	38	40	42	44	45	46	47	48	49	50	51	52	54
12	58.5	63.0	67.5	71.9	76.5	81.0	85.5	90.0	94.5	99.0	101.2	103.5	105.8	108.0	110.3	112.5	114.7	117.0	121.5
13	54.0	58.1	62.3	66.4	70.6	74.7	78.9	83.1	87.2	91.4	93.4	95.5	97.6	99.7	101.8	103.8	105.9	108.0	112.1
14	50.1	54.0	57.7	61.7	65.5	69.4	73.3	77.1	81.0	84.8	86.7	88.7	90.6	92.6	94.5	96.4	98.3	100.3	104.1
15	46.8	50.4	54.0	57.6	61.2	64.8	68.4	72.0	75.6	79.2	80.9	82.8	84.6	86.4	88.2	90.0	91.8	93.6	97.2
16	43.9	47.2	50.6	54.0	57.3	60.8	64.1	67.5	70.9	74.2	76.0	77.6	79.3	81.0	82.7	84.4	86.1	87.7	91.1
17	41.3	44.4	47.6	50.8	54.0	57.2	60.3	63.5	66.7	69.9	71.5	73.0	74.6	76.2	77.8	79.4	81.0	82.6	85.7
18	39.0	42.0	45.0	48.0	51.0	54.0	57.0	60.0	63.0	66.0	67.5	69.0	70.5	72.0	73.5	75.0	76.5	78.0	81.0
19	36.9	39.7	42.6	45.4	48.3	51.2	54.0	56.8	59.7	62.5	64.0	65.4	66.8	68.2	69.6	71.0	72.5	73.9	76.7
20	35.1	37.8	40.5	43.2	45.9	48.6	51.3	54.0	56.7	59.4	60.8	62.1	63.4	64.8	66.1	67.5	68.8	70.2	72.9
21	33.4	36.0	38.5	41.1	43.7	46.3	48.9	51.4	54.0	56.6	57.9	59.1	60.4	61.7	63.0	64.3	65.5	66.8	69.4
22	31.9	34.3	36.8	39.2	41.7	44.2	46.6	49.1	51.5	54.0	55.2	56.4	57.7	58.9	60.1	61.4	62.6	63.8	66.2
23	30.5	32.8	35.2	37.5	39.9	42.3	44.6	47.0	49.3	51.6	52.8	54.0	55.2	56.3	57.5	58.7	59.9	61.0	63.4
24	29.3	31.5	33.7	36.0	38.2	40.5	42.7	45.0	47.2	49.5	50.7	51.7	52.9	54.0	55.1	56.2	57.3	58.5	60.7
25	28.0	30.2	32.4	34.5	36.7	38.9	41.1	43.2	45.4	47.5	48.6	49.7	50.8	51.8	52.9	54.0	55.1	56.2	58.3
26	27.0	29.0	31.1	33.2	35.3	37.4	39.5	41.5	43.6	45.7	46.7	47.8	48.8	49.8	50.9	51.9	53.0	54.0	56.1
27	26.0	28.0	30.0	32.0	34.0	36.0	38.0	40.0	42.0	44.0	45.0	46.0	47.0	48.0	49.0	50.0	51.0	52.0	54.0
28	25.1	27.0	28.9	30.8	32.7	34.7	36.6	38.6	40.5	42.4	43.4	44.4	45.3	46.3	47.2	48.2	49.2	50.1	52.0
29	24.2	26.0	27.9	29.7	31.6	33.5	35.3	37.2	39.1	40.9	41.8	42.8	43.7	44.6	45.6	46.5	47.4	48.4	50.2
30	23.4	25.2	27.0	28.8	30.6	32.4	34.2	36.0	37.8	39.6	40.5	41.4	42.3	43.2	44.1	45.0	45.9	46.8	48.6
31	22.6	24.4	26.1	27.8	29.6	31.4	33.1	34.8	36.6	38.3	39.2	40.1	40.9	41.8	42.7	43.5	44.4	45.3	47.0
32	21.9	23.6	25.3	27.0	28.7	30.4	32.1	33.8	35.4	37.1	38.0	38.8	39.7	40.5	41.3	42.2	43.0	43.9	45.6
33	21.3	22.9	24.5	26.2	27.8	29.45	31.1	32.7	34.4	36.0	36.8	37.6	38.5	39.3	40.1	40.9	41.7	42.5	44.2
34	20.6	22.0	23.8	25.4	27.0	28.6	30.2	31.8	33.4	34.9	35.7	36.5	37.3	38.1	38.9	39.7	40.5	41.3	42.9

Number of Teeth on Sprocket

Gear Chart for 27-inch Wheel (subtract .037% for 26-inch wheel)

Stock gearing on many production bikes is definitely a compromise:

Rear		14	17	20	24	28
Front	52	100	83	70	58.5	50
Front	42	81	67	57	47	40.5

This selection of ratios is adequate for town riding, but the bottom 40.5 inch gear is not low enough for touring in hilly terrain or carrying heavy loads.

Tourists want lower gears spaced closely together, and the classic method for doing this is to use smaller front chainrings and a modest spread of cogs:

Rear		15	17	19	21	23
Front	46	83	73	65	59	54
Front	28	50	44	40	36	33

This arrangement has a lot going for it: four close ratios at the low end of the range for climbing hills, a simple shifting sequence, and four good ratios for level ground. The drawbacks are a fierce jump between the small and large chainrings (44 to 59), and a limit on top speed. Also, it is a type of arrangement that made sense in the days when derailleurs were pushed to handle a cog with 28 teeth (T). Modern wide range derailleurs can manage a 34T cog, or even a 38T in the case of the Sun Tour AG. In consequence, some bikes are set up with a large rear cog and widely spaced ratios as:

Rear		14	18	23	30	34
Front	52	100	78	61	47	41
Front	42	81	63	49	38	33

This gives a wide range, but the large jumps between ratios make it difficult to maintain an even pedalling cadence, and many of the ratios are duplicates. Another method is to reduce the size of the small chainring as:

Rear		14	17	20	24	28
Front	52	100	83	70	58.5	50
Front	36	69	57	48.5	40.5	34.7

The advent of 6-speed blocks and narrow chains makes it possible to have both fairly close spaced gears, and a 'stump-puller' for hills:

Rear		13	15	18	21	26	32
Front	52	108	93.6	78	67	54	44
Front	42	87	75.6	63	54	43	35

This arrangement gives a reasonable hill-climbing gear, a good spread of middle and high gears, and an 'overdrive' for zooming down hills.

Racing and fast road bikes want narrow jumps between gears, as in this 14-speed arrangement:

Rear		12	13	14	15	17	19	21
Front	52	117	108	100	93	82	73	66
Front	42	94	87	81	75	66	59	54

The main points to bear in mind when working out a selection of gear ratios are:

1. Emphasis – for touring, a good range of low gears; for competition, a good range of high gears; and for town riding, a good range of middle gears.

2. Bottom low – for touring in hilly terrain this should be around the 20 inch mark. A gear this low is thought by some to be for weaklings and called a 'granny' gear. With it, however, you will be able to pedal when others have to walk. Some of the strongest riders I know use a bottom gear of 19 inches for touring. Town bikes want a bottom gear in the low 30s, and competition bikes can start with a 45 or 50 inch gear.

3. Top high – there are many world champion riders who like to use big gears. In general, however, most racers gain speed by

pedalling faster, not harder. The great Eddy Merckx, for example, used a 77 inch gear when he broke the one hour time trial record. For practical purposes anything over 100 inches is an overdrive giving more speed on downhills. Fine if you like excitement or are racing, but otherwise, consider that the hard work – and main need for gears – is going *up* the hill. Let the gravity do the work down the other side, while you relax and enjoy the view.

4. Shift sequence – make it as simple as possible.

5. Derailleur sequence – this is a function of the difference in size between high and low sprockets, and large and small chainrings. A 14-28T block has a 14T difference, and 52/42 chain rings have a 10T difference. Together, the difference is 24T. If you opt for a wide-range 14-34T block, for example, you may need a new derailleur with greater capacity.

6. Derailleur type – 'although this is expressed as the largest size of rear cog that a derailleur can handle, it is really a matter of type. Competition derailleurs work best on close-ratio freewheels kept well within capacity. Touring derailleurs work well on wide-ratio freewheels and indifferently on close-ratio freewheels.

 7. Number of gear ratios – six-and seven-speed freewheels (which give 12 and 14 speeds with double chainrings) are not uncommon on production bikes. Set up with close-ratio cogs they are great for competition, but are more trouble than gain when set up with a wide range of cogs for a town or touring bike. For one thing, gear ratios have a greater tendency to duplicate, negating the point of the exercise. For another, a narrow chain is required, which makes shifting more fiddly. To make room for the 7-speed model, and certain of the 6-speed models, the wheel must have more dish (off-set of the hub) and is therefore weaker – not the thing for bumpy urban streets or heavyweight touring. Finally, a 7-speed block matched to double chainrings in actual practice gives 10 speeds at most and not fourteen.

Why? Because even with a 5-speed block and double chainrings you should never run the big front chainring to the big rear cog, or small front chainring to small rear cog. It causes the chain to cut
.across at too severe an angle, creating excessive wear, a tendency to

rub the derailleur cages, and reduced efficiency. With a 7-speed block the problems are even worse. At most you can use only 5 of the 7 rear cogs on each front chainring, and it is better to limit the number to 4 – a rather anaemic total of 8 speeds out of a possible 14. Throw in a couple of duplicated gears and you are down to 6 usable ratios – the minimum that even a poorly designed 5-speed block/double chainring combination will produce!

For really effective wide range gearing, the route to take is triple front chainrings. You will not gain all that many more ratios, but they will be exactly where required and certain types of difficult gear shifts will be easier. With a triple the inner chainring should be the smallest available, say 28T or 26T. This allows the use of a moderately sized largest rear cog, saving weight and improving shifting. It is always much easier to drop the chain from a large to small front chainring than to lift the chain up on to a large rear cog. With a triple, shifting into low range is a simple matter of banging home the shift lever for the front derailleur.

The next advantage of a triple is that the middle chainring can be ideally sized for level cruising, and be used on all five rear cogs without chain deflection problems. Most of the time you just run

on the middle ring, and have only one shift lever to worry about.

When there is a tail wind or a downgrade it's up on to the big chainring and go. With the middle range nicely taken care of by the centre chainring, you can afford a couple of final drive ratios plus an overdrive ratio off the big chainring.

The disadvantage of a triple chainring are expense, a possibly tricky shift to the middle chainring (at first, you will have to look at and centre the front derailleur with evey shift to the middle ring), and a greater need for attention to detail when setting up the arrangement if it is to work properly in the first place.

If you are seriously interested in using triple chainrings, sort matters out at the time of bike purchase. You will almost certainly have to make substitutions. At this writing there is only one creditable production bike fitted with a triple chainset, and it is a make with very poor availability of spare parts. Although some of the prestige racing chainsets such as Campagnolo and Ofmega will accept an inner chainring, the smallest size is usually limited to 42T. The largest selection of chainring sizes and best availability of spares is offered by T.A. Cyclotouriste (26 to 68T), and is interchangeable with Stronglight 49D (that is, you can use Stronglight rings on T.A. arms and vice versa, but you cannot mix up the two makes of rings on the same arm). Stronglight 99 gives a selection from 28 to 54T, and is interchangeable with Sakae Ringyo (SR) 5-TG. Preferably you should start with one of these systems from the outset, and none of them are particularly common on production bikes.

Furthermore, a triple chainset often requires a longer bottom bracket axle to adjust the chainline and keep the inner chainring clear of the bike frame. Sometimes it is possible to use an ordinary double axle by inserting a spacer washer between the fixed cup and the frame. All these matters want sorting out when you buy the bike, and only by a shop experienced in dealing with triple chainsets. If you are a complete novice, or are spending less than £200, then my advice is to leave the whole affair to another day.

Gearing is a quite complicated subject about which I can only give some general guidelines. For a comprehensive guide to gearing obtain the October, 1982 issue of *Cyclist Monthly* (Oakfield House, Perrymount Road, Haywards Heath, Sussex). This has an excellent article on gearing by Frank Berto, who probably knows more about the subject than anyone else alive.

6 Riding

Anybody can ride a bicycle. You just get aboard and pedal. Heh!
Try following an experienced tourist on a 100-mile run or a
competition rider around the track. Physical condition of course
plays a part, but here technique counts more than anything else.
Fifty-year-old grandmothers can and do run rings around fit young
adults. Attention to the basics of technique will make riding easier
and more enjoyable, and give you greater freedom than if you had
not bothered with the subject at all.

Of course even basic technique varies somewhat with conditions.
And there is a lot more to riding than technique. The following
chapters on traffic jamming, and touring and racing, amplify
considerably the information you need in order to cycle safely and
comfortably.

Shifting

Take it easy when first learning to shift. Once you get the knack
you can make smooth split-second gear changes, but let your skill
develop gradually and avoid damaging 'clunk' sounding shifts.

3-Speeds: To shift up to a higher gear, ease pressure on pedals,
move selector to next gear, resume pressure. Extra-fast shifts may
be made by maintaining pedal pressure, moving the selector, and
then pausing momentarily when the shift is desired. If done too
hard, this may damage gears. Going down to 1st from 2nd or 3rd
and coming to a stop, back-pedal slightly. If not stopping use same
procedure as for upshifts.

10-Speeds: Never, ever shift a 10-speed unless pedalling. To see
why, hang your bike up so that the rear wheel is off the ground,
rotate the cranks, and manipulate the gear shift levers so you can
see how they work. Shifting a 10-speed without pedalling may
result in a bent or broken chain or gear teeth. If you park your bike
in the street, always give the gears a visual check to make sure
passers-by have not fiddled with them. It happens often.

When going up or down through the gears, ease pedalling
pressure during shift. The shift levers do not have stops for the
different gears, and you have to learn where they are by feel. Do
not let the derailleur cages rub the chain. Sometimes it is necessary

to make a small adjustment in the front derailleur when using a wide range of rear sprockets in order to prevent this. Do not run the big front sprocket to the big rear sprocket, or the small front to the small rear. It causes the chain to cut across at too severe an angle, greatly increasing wear and reducing efficiency. Proper shifting should also take into account the demands of cadence (see below).

Pedalling

Ride with the ball of your foot on the pedal, not the heel or arch. The fundamental technique for easy cycling is called ankling. This is where the foot pivots at the ankle with each revolution of the crank. Start at the top of the stroke (12 o'clock) with the heel slightly lower than the toes. Push with the ball of the foot and simultaneously pivot at the ankle on the downstroke so that the foot levels out between 2 and 3 o'clock, and continue this motion so that at the bottom of the stroke the toes are lower than the heel:

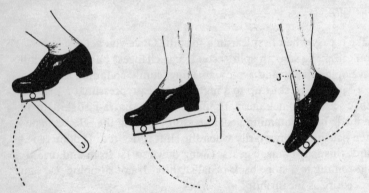

With toe clips pull up on the upstroke as well. The main thing to strive for is smoothness and steady, even pressure. Practise this slowly, in a high gear, and away from traffic so you can concentrate on watching your feet.

Toe clips are a great boon. By allowing you to pull up on the pedals as well as push down, they virtually double pedalling efficiency. They are completely safe. Smooth-soled conventional shoes can always be slipped out even when tightly strapped down. If using bicycling shoes and cleats, keep the straps loose in traffic. The technique for getting under way is simple: start with loose

straps. Straddle the bike, slip a foot into a pedal at the 1 o'clock position, and tighten the strap. Push off, using the downstroke of this crank to get you under way, and simultaneously reach down with the free foot, give the pedal a light tap to spin the toe clip around to the proper position, slip foot in, bring crank around to 12 o'clock position, and tighten strap. It sounds more complicated than it is. The key is the deft, light tap to the pedal to bring the toe clip around so you can slip your foot in. Practice will soon make it second nature. When coming to a stop, reach down and loosen one strap so you can get your foot back in easily when under way again. Do not worry about being trapped by toe clips. I have made zillions of emergency stops and have always been able to get my feet free. On the other hand, do not tempt fate by riding in heavy traffic with ultra-tight straps. And if you use sneakers or other soft-soled shoes (bad – not enough support), or cleated bicycling shoes, keep the straps loose when conditions warrant.

Cadence

This subject was mentioned in connection with gearing. Briefly, human beings pedal most efficiently at a certain number of strokes per minute. The optimum cadence varies with the physical condition and technique of the individual rider. Generally, novices run from 60 to 85 strokes per minute, experienced tourists approach 100, and racers run 120-30 and up.

Most people gear too high and pedal too slowly. They don't think they are going anywhere or getting any exercise unless they are pushing against resistance. It is precisely this pushing which creates fatigue. It is much better to pedal rapidly against relatively little resistance. Especially when first starting with a bike, always try to pedal as rapidly as you can without going into orbit. Soon you will find your natural cadence, and should always try to maintain this as a uniform rate of pedalling. Allow this to be one of the primary functions of the gears, and always shift up or down as necessary to maintain an even cadence. Learn to shift just before you need the new gear. Do not let a hill slow down your cadence, for example, but shift just before you hit it, and as needed going up. The way you will be able to churn along will be absolutely amazing.

RUSHING A RISE.

Bumps

When you come to bumps, pot-holes, cables, etc, put most of your weight on the pedals and handlebars. This allows the bike to pivot underneath you, reducing shock for both you and the bike. You know how motorcycle scramble riders stand up on the pegs? Like that.

Braking

Try to use your brakes as little as possible. This will help you to 'look ahead' and anticipate traffic conditions in advance. Be careful of braking too hard and skidding or pitching yourself over the handlebars. It is the front brake which does most of the work, and the more rapidly you decelerate, the more work it can do. This is because weight is transferred forward, increasing the coefficient of friction between the front tyre and the road surface. Simultaneously, weight on the back tyre is lessened slightly, decreasing the coefficient of friction and making it more liable to skid. The technique for a rapid or panic stop is thus one of keeping the body weight as far back as possible, progressively increasing pressure on the front brake, and holding pressure on the back brake to just below the point where the wheel will lock and skid. It is a question of feel and can only be learned by practice. Start with quick stops from low speeds and gradually increase velocity. After you feel reasonably adept, have a friend give you emergency stop signals at unexpected moments.

In slippery conditions or when banked hard over in a turn, favour the rear brake. The rear wheel does have a greater tendency to skid, but if it goes you may still be able to keep yourself upright, and at worst will land on your hip. A front-wheel skid will pile you on your face.

The police have strict orders to arrest any Bicyclist riding without a bell or whistle

4.—Friends and Foes.

In wet conditions frequently apply the brakes lightly to wipe water off the rims. Otherwise you may need four or five times the distance for stopping with dry brakes.

Going down long hills avoid overheating the brake shoes or wheel rims by pumping (on-off-on-off-on etc.) the brakes. Always be able to stop.

Turning

If you ride a bicycle then by definition you can turn it. But there are different methods and styles of turning.

Under way, a bicycle is in a constant state of imbalance. A tendency to lean one way will be corrected by the rider, the bike will move through centre of balance to a lean the opposite way, and the rider will correct again. Most turning consists simply of taking advantage of a lean in the desired direction. Instead of correcting, the rider allows the lean to continue and thus effects a turn. The *feeling* is that the rider has changed balance and the bike has followed to suit, and in that bicycle geometry is designed for a certain amount of self-steering, the feeling is accurate enough. The rider does in fact change balance. This type of turn has two faults: it is slow, and it puts rider and bicycle weight in one single line down to the point of tyre contact with the road.

In racing, and in traffic riding, it is often necessary to turn FAST! This can be done by hauling back on the handlebar end opposite to the direction in which you wish to go. The bike will move out from under you, you will start to fall, and then you will TURN. Can you see it? In the 'normal' turn you topple to one side gradually; in the 'haul handlebar' turn you snatch the bike out from underneath you, and immediately fall into a turn. It is very handy for avoiding unexpected obstacles such as broken glass. In effect, you go one way, the bike goes the other, and afterwards you catch up with each other. Like panic braking, this type of turn must be learned slowly, and with lots of room for manoeuvring.

Another type of turn consists of laying down the bike, while you remain relatively upright i.e., the bike 'leans' more than you do. This is useful when the road surface is rough, because then a percentage of the rider weight pivots as the bike moves up and down, lessening the load on the wheels. Better for the bike, better for you. It is also a quick turn, although not as fast as hauling handlebar.

Another type of turn consists of leaning the body more than the bike. I think – but cannot assure you – that this helps lessen the chances of a skid. At any rate, when I unexpectedly encounter a wet manhole cover or oil slick while turning I throw the bike *up* while keeping my own weight down. This, and the lay down turn, can be done by moving the whole bike underneath you while you pivot sideways at the hips, and can be accelerated by hauling on the handlebars as well.

Haul, lay down, and set up turns are esoteric in description but relatively simple in practice. For your own safety you should be able to execute a haul turn instantly and automatically whenever circumstances require.

S.T.D.

DOWN HILL.

7   Fast is safe

For most people the greatest single deterrent to cycling is fear of an accident involving a motor vehicle. The statistics on this subject are incomplete and misleading, but I am not going to add to the confusion by debunking them. In plain fact, cycling in traffic is dangerous. The people frightened away from riding a bike have ample justification for their fears.

Taking a bath is also a risky affair. You can learn to cycle, or bathe, with a level of knowledge and skill that greatly reduces the risk of accident. At first prospect cycling in traffic makes anyone in their right mind very nervous. It is extremely important to understand from the outset that there is something you can do about the danger. Your precise gift as an entity is an ability to manage environment or circumstances, and the outcome of cycling in traffic depends less on the situation than on what you do.

Your commitment in this respect determines the extent to which you should ride in traffic. Although the basic principles are the same, there is a considerable difference between mixing it up with heavy weekday commuter traffic and cycling a few blocks to the park on Sunday. Efficient, safe cycling requires attentiveness. Especially in traffic, you must know everything that is going on, from the size of the pebbles on the road to the debris which might fall on you from a construction project to the number and type of vehicles before and behind you – absolutely everything. Traffic riding requires total concentration. There is no place for wool-gathering here, or idyllic pastoral pleasures. Some people are just born inattentive. If you are one of these and a survivor, you've probably already learnt to steer clear of risky places and situations. You prefer walking to cycling or driving a car, because it does not require much attention and leaves your mind free. Great, but if you are keen on cycling, then I recommend off-road riding. Because if you do not pay constant attention when cycling in traffic, you may only survive as a statistic.

It's not all downhill. Attentiveness has benefits. First of all, total engagement is refreshing. For example, I like physical challenges but spend most of my time pushing a pencil. For me the change of pace represented by traffic jamming is at times exhilarating. It does, as they say, take your mind off your troubles. Secondly, once you gain a little experience you will hopefully still be alert, but relaxed. Is crossing the street a C.B. DeMille production for you? In a more relaxed state you will appreciate the benefits of attentiveness, and see more, notice more, feel more. Getting from one place to another will be a distinctly real experience, and something *you* do.

I would like to deal with two other drawbacks to traffic jamming which unfortunately have no redeeming features.

Air pollution

The inhalation of motor vehicle exhaust fumes and other air pollutants is a serious health hazard for the cyclist. Motor vehicles contribute up to 85 per cent of all air pollution in urban areas. As a cyclist you are at nose level with the maximum concentration of pollutants, and you are breathing harder and faster.

In correspondence with me, the National Society for Clean Air suggested that I say: 'The hazard of air pollution should not be disregarded; but the benefits you will gain from the exercise of riding will certainly offset any damage you may think can be caused by inhaling the various pollutants in the air.' To some extent this is true. The body has natural defense mechanisms against airborne pollutants, and when the body is more active so are the defense mechanisms. But it is pure horse-feathers to suggest that cycling through polluted air is good for you.

Motor vehicles – which are pretty well the beginning and end of the problem – emit lead, unburnt gas, nitrogen oxides, sulphur oxides, carbon monoxide and small quantities of grit. The worst for the cyclist are lead and carbon monoxide.

Ninety per cent of the lead in the air comes from petrol, and amounts to between 7,500 to 10,000 tons annually. In London alone, five tons of lead pollute the air each day. For the urbanite, it means breathing air containing up to 10,000 times as much lead as would occur naturally, and carrying a body weight of lead 500 times greater than when his or her ancestors relied on biomechanical and renewable energy sources.

How dangerous is lead? Very. The list of possible damages is amazing, and ranges from headache through a string of severe disabilities including arthritis, gout and heart disease, through to

Thanks to Francis Arnold and Judith Thomas for much of the information here.

simply shortening your lifespan. But probably the worst is that lead makes you stupid. Eminent researchers in the United States, Germany, Australia and Britain have all shown that children exposed to high lead levels are associated with low intelligence, low verbal skill, bad hearing and slow reaction times. Quite a package.

The Russians eliminated lead from petrol in all their major cities as early as 1959. In the United States the 1970 Clean Air Act established stringent requirements for motor vehicle exhaust emissions, and now half the cars there run on unleaded petrol. Just about all the cars in Japan run on unleaded petrol, and from 1985 all new cars in Australia will do the same. West Germany, Sweden and Switzerland have all reduced their levels of lead in petrol to 0.15gm per litre, and signs are that the Germans will eliminate it altogether in the near future.

In Britain, the current level of lead in petrol is 0.40gm per litre. The Government has not been quick off the mark in calling for a reduction. The oil companies have been told to realise a standard of 0.15gm per litre by 1986. Why do we lag so far behind so much of the world?

Nobody needs lead additives in petrol, least of all motorists. The stuff promotes wear and tear, and to get it back out of the motor, scavenging agents are also added to the petrol, along with carcinogenic anti-wear agents. It's a real witch's brew and completely unnecessary. Lead is added to petrol to improve the octane rating. There is now a cheap octane improver of very low toxicity, MTBE (methyl tertiary butyl ether), which burns better and does less damage to the engine.

MTBE is not used because the major oil companies have a good thing going in lead additives. The firm Associated Octel controls the majority of the markets for lead additives outside North America, and is owned jointly by BP, Chevron, Mobil, Shell and Texaco.* In 1979 net profit before tax was £6.8 million. They got government subsidies as well. And two Queen's Awards for exports. All by poisoning you. By making you stupid. Remember that, the next time some oil company says you can be sure of them, or that your future is safe in their loving hands.

Carbon monoxide is a classic poison which interferes with the oxygen-carrying capacity of the blood. Long before it kills, this action results in decreased alertness, headaches, vague dizziness, and nausea. Just the ticket for cycling in traffic. For a bonus, heart problems, memory loss, emphysema and cancer. Whee.

Well, one note of cheer is that your chances are a lot better if you take in an adequate amount of vitamin C. It reduces the toxicity of all sorts of things, including lead, carbon monoxide and nitrogen dioxide. In an ideal world one should not need extra vitamins; this is not an ideal world. There are also those who contend that the alleged benefits of vitamin C are a lot of hogwash. There are plenty of other smart people who feel that the stuff is useful.

A well-balanced wholemeal diet, with as much real, fresh food as possible, will go a long way toward equipping you to deal with pollutants. One nice thing about cycling is that your fuel – food – is important, and this helps create a predisposition toward things that are actually nutritious. So in a way, matters take care of themselves. Air pollution is not a reason for abandoning cycling; cycling just makes you much more aware of the problem. If you're interested in increasing the public pressure for lead-free petrol try contacting CLEAR, 2 Northdown Street, London N1 9BG.

Harassment

Motorists routinely harass cyclists. In the majority of instances this is through sheer incompetence; the motorist does not take sufficient notice of the cyclist, and unthinkingly drives inconsiderately or even dangerously. There are also a number of motorists who deliberately endanger or attempt to harm cyclists.

*Thomas, Judith, 'Breathing Heavy Metal', *Bicycle Magazine*, Vol. 1, Issue 11, November 1982, p. 43.

Driving a motor vehicle in traffic requires controlled aggression, a firm indication of what you propose to do in relation to other road users and then, ideally, a subsequent execution which precludes a different course of events. In light traffic this give and take methodology functions more or less smoothly; in heavy traffic it can easily get out of hand. Just as when laboratory mice population densities are intensified and the mice demonstrate an activity increase that can become frenetic, motorists in heavy traffic tend to generate greater amounts of aggressive effort. The more retarded the journey, the angrier they become.

A PRACTICAL DEMONSTRATION—I.
County Councillor (to distinguished foreign guest): "You will get an admirable idea of how we sand the roads on an extensive scale. With this huge van we can cover the ground in one-third the time, and distribute ten times the quantity of —

A PRACTICAL DEMONSTRATION—II.

This natural course to ruin is exacerbated by the fact that very few people treat motor vehicles strictly as a means of transport. The emotional qualities of ego, status and territoriality intertwine closely with the possession and operation of a motor vehicle. It is these psychological factors, rather than mechanical elements such

137

as braking capacity, which are the main cause of 'accidents'.

Marketing people know perfectly well that driving a car is a sexually based expression of power and potency. That this kind of thing leads to risk-taking and accidents can easily be seen in the differential rates for motor vehicle insurance; it costs more if you are young, male and /or operate a powerful vehicle, and less if you are experienced, female and/or operate a vehicle of modest power. The common factor to each of these contingencies is a greater or lesser tendency towards aggressiveness, or lack of good judgement.

In sum, traffic is an environment of regularised confrontation that also involves fundamental and strong human emotions. In such circumstances, the immediate physical frailty of the cyclist is a serious disadvantage. The motorist is enshrouded in a strong metal cocoon and in any confrontation the cyclist risks bodily harm. The motorist does not. Unlike the gentle giants of myth, who knew their strength and size and trod accordingly, motorists routinely abuse their immense physical advantage over cyclists.

However, much depends on the cyclist's level of riding skill. For novice cyclists who are unfamiliar with operating any kind of vehicle at all, the confrontative and competitive aspects of riding in traffic will at first appear incredibly stupid, and probably very daunting. One frequent outcome is a timid riding style where the cyclist often fails to take existing right of way, and therefore continually runs afoul of the faster, more aggressive motor vehicles.

Intermediate cyclists are capable enough riders, but still find that motorists are frequently alarmingly aggressive. At this level frustration with the unfairness of it all can be acute, and the reaction to abuse from a motorist one of extreme and unsettling anger. I once had a cabbie try to push me off the road going into an intersection, but held ground and foxed him to a stop in the middle of the junction. I leapt off the bike, ground my fist against his nose and threatened to put it between his ears if he did not behave. He said 'hang on' and removed his glasses. In my blind rage I hadn't even noticed. I stayed off my bike for a week afterwards while I sorted that one out.

The first instinctive reaction to physical danger is to cower, and the second is to strike back. Often this is an excellent idea. For many motorists who endanger cyclists, the fact that they can be yanked out of their protective shells and made to suffer physical tit for tat is a shocking revelation of the real life terms of the encounter.

But this modus operandi has problems.

The precisely infuriating characteristic of most cyclist-motorist confrontations is that the cyclist is helpless to do anything but preserve life and limb, and the motorist escapes. Once you do catch up a motorist, the accumulated frustration can erupt in violent anger. Rough justice perhaps, but a steady diet of this sort of thing is debilitating for you and at odds with having a good time. Additionally, venting your spleen can be counter-productive, and cause the motorist to become more wrong in an effort to be right. Finally, a terminal altercation is generally an unpleasant business. From the standpoint of your own peace of mind, it is much better if you can calmly point out the facts of the situation, and then watch with interest to see if the other party is alert enough to connect with the idea that you qualify for human rights.

Once you become a skilled urban cyclist, you will find that you can fairly well stay out of trouble in the first place. You'll ride careful but comfortable. Most of the potential bad incidents can be spotted in advance and avoided, including the unconscious or deliberate evils of motorists, and these only generate a wry grin of amusement. One day at a T-junction a fellow in a van cut sharply in front of me and slammed on the brakes, nearly piling me into a parked car. I pulled alongside and with genuine curiosity asked why, and he replied 'you should have been further left'. I asked if he thought killing me was an appropriate measure for this supposed misdeed and he again replied 'you should have been further left', indicating clear insanity. I contemplated the ruinous effect of a blood-boiling fight on an otherwise wonderful day, and went on my way.

Interestingly, had the man succeeded in killing me he would have suffered little penalty. Homicidal intent with a motor vehicle is difficult to establish. Typically, when a cyclist dies at the hands of a motorist, the worst charge is negligence, and the penalty a fine and perhaps a period of time for which the motorist's licence is revoked. Often there is no penalty at all.

Alfred Hubbard, a farmworker, was cycling home from Cambridge one Saturday night in August 1965 when he was struck by a hit and run motorist. Unaided, Alfred Hubbard slowly bled to death. Four months later the motorist, an American serviceman, was put on trial for manslaughter on account of failing to stop and render assistance. The prosecution showed that the motorist was aware of having struck the victim, and further testimony established that Alfred Hubbard would have probably lived had prompt aid been given. The defense contended that there might be a moral duty to help, but that no duty existed in law. The judge agreed and the driver went scot-free.

In cyclist-motorist confrontations the law is definitely not on the side of the cyclist. If you take matters into your own hands and attempt to fight back on a direct physical level, you will probably qualify for a charge of criminal activity. There are times when you should retaliate, and later on I will explain some of the methods for bringing a motorist to grief. But in general, responding to the threat of danger with anger is non-productive, serving only to destroy your peace of mind and, possibly, get you into trouble.

Why, you must now be asking, am I telling you these cheerful things about air pollution and harassment by motorists? Well, how would you feel if I recommended swimming in a stretch of ocean, and neglected to mention that the waters were infested with sharks? The analogy is interesting, because for most people the fear of sharks is disproportionately great in light of the actual danger. Similarly, if you do not have an idea of what to expect, cycling in traffic can be fearsome or enraging, depending on your turn of mind. If you do have some rational notion of what is happening, then your chances of understanding and usefully channelling your own powerful feelings improve considerably. You might even enjoy cycling (or swimming with sharks).

Riding

There are innumerable physical hazards to look out for while riding in traffic, but it is motor vehicles which are your main concern. Theory says that bicycles have the same rights and privileges as other types of vehicles. The facts are otherwise.

A motor vehicle is an inherently rapid piece of equipment. For most motorists, anything which obstructs forward progress – such as a slow-moving bicycle – just should not be there. The motorist may be wrong, but it is essential for your survival to understand how he or she thinks. As a cyclist, you are a relative nonentity. As often as not, motorists will cut you off, make turns in front of you or sit right on your tail when there is no room to pass. It never occurs to them to put on the brakes and give you room to manoeuvre, as they would for another motor vehicle. Not that many car drivers are game to cut up a large lorry.

Matters are made worse by the fact that many motorists are not fit enough, or competent enough, to drive. Licensing qualifications are so basic as to be laughable in the face of real road conditions. Many motorists are under the influence of alcohol or drugs or both. Any cross-section of drivers will find elderly, obese and otherwise infirm people with the motion capacity of a frozen sloth.

Many motorists have never ridden a bicycle, and are unfamiliar with the problems of the cyclist. The Department of the Environment gives financial support to the National Cycling Proficiency Scheme, which trains cyclists in riding skills and the Highway Code, but does nothing for motorists. The Ministry of Transport's manual, *Driving,* has only a few sparse words on cycles. For most motorists (even if unconsciously), cyclists are not road users of equal status but a peripheral, obstructive nuisance.

Accordingly, riding successfully and comfortably in traffic requires a blend of determination and knowing when to give in. For example, try never to block overtaking cars. But if it is unsafe for you to let them pass, then do not hesitate to take full possession of your lane so that they *can't* pass. Both you and the other human have exactly the same right to use the street or highway. Possession of a motor vehicle confers no automatic additional rights or privileges. If anything, it is the other way round. The wasteful consumption of energy and vicious pollution of the environment by motor vehicles is a serious infringement of your rights.

So far as society in general is concerned, cyclists are a great improvement over motorists. In addition to holding the main responsibility for indirect damages through pollution, worldwide motorists annually directly kill 219,000 people and 144,000,000 birds and animals, and hospitalize a further 1,825,000 people.

A terrible thing about this carnage is that it is largely needless. Cycling *per se* not only causes little damage, it is usually more efficient. The majority of journeys are short, and would be quicker and less expensive if accomplished by cycling rather than motoring. Like a call for nuclear disarmament, riding a bike is both a personal affair and a general political statement.

In your relations with motorists, it is of paramount personal importance that you understand and believe in your own significance as an organic entity. The business of living is more important than immediate expediency. The early American Indians

MOORE DEL.

never just cut down a tree. First they sat down and talked things over with the tree, pointing out how it could continue to live in a vital capacity as a boat, a part of a dwelling, or whatever. Similarly, motorists have no inherent right to shunt you to one side as a matter of convenience. Like the tree, you are a living entity entitled to a fair minimum of respect and care.

This kind of thinking can be useful for your own self-esteem but do not carry it too far. In the name of peace, national governments threaten the world with bombs. Similarly, the scheme for motorised transport has put a lot of people behind the wheel who are authentic maniacs. I've heard individuals say that they intend to run down a cyclist and, believe, it happens. No matter how right or important you are, any final confrontation with a motor vehicle will wind up with you the loser.

As a cyclist, you may not always be accorded a rightful place in the scheme of things, but you should nevertheless be capable of riding according to the Highway Code. If you are not familiar with the basic rules of the road, the meaning of various signs and lights (a selection is shown on the next page) and the proper techniques for turns and roundabouts, then get a copy of the Code from a post office or bookshop and study it. You can also enrol in the National Cycling Proficiency Scheme which trains and tests in the fundamentals of cycling and the Code. It takes only a few hours and is free. I recommend it as compulsory for children. Enquire at your police station or school.

This may all seem like a bit much to you. In my view, any user of the road whether by bicycle, lorry, roller skates, or pogo stick should pass a test. Getting about on roads is a serious business which, if it is to be done safely and with consideration for the rights of others, requires that you know what is going on. I've done a lot of bad-mouthing of motorists, but they do have rights that deserve consideration. Further, claiming your own equal status and rights is possible only if you know the rules in the first place.

In general, the Highway Code requires that you ride as well to the left as is consistent with safety; obey traffic signs and signals; give way to pedestrians at zebra crossings; and signal turns and stops. Left turn is left arm held straight out to the side, right turn ditto with the right arm, and stop a downward patting motion of the extended right arm.

In law, cyclists are dangerous characters subject to prosecution for endangerment of self or others, recklessness, dangerous riding, speeding and riding under the influence of drugs or alcohol.

A knowledge of the rules is essential, but is only a bare beginning. As a relatively defenseless cyclist, you cannot rely on your 'rights' for protection, but must assume that if there is some way for somebody to get you, they will. So . . .

●Hands near or on brake levers at all times. With modern synthetic brake blocks you should be able to exert the maximum possible braking force. If you need to stop quickly on a bike with poor braking capacity, try twisting the front wheel as you apply the brakes. So long as you're not going too fast, the bike will melt into the ground in a controlled crash as the wheel and forks buckle.

●Keep your eyes constantly moving both fore and aft. When looking behind do not twist your head; duck it down. Easier to do, quicker, and smoother. Do this constantly. At any moment you might have to swerve to avoid an obstacle, and must know if you have the room to do so. Any bike used regularly in urban traffic should be equipped with a rear view mirror (see 11 Accessories). The contribution this makes to safety, comfort and speed is immense.

●Be definite. Save meandering for country lanes where you can see for a long way in both directions. Ride in a straight line. Signal all turns clearly. Make right turns from the right lane and left turns from the left lane, if on a wide street. If you are going to do something, do it. Being definite takes the form of a certain amount of aggressiveness. Don't get bulldozed into immobility – nobody is going to give you a break. Make and take your own breaks. As far as most motorists are concerned, you either don't exist or are some alien foreign object which they want behind them. Draw attention to yourself and be super-clear about your intentions. Colourful clothing is a good idea.

●Always assume the worst. You can't see around the stopped bus? *Assume* a pregnant woman who is the sole support of 21 children is going to come prancing out. There is a car waiting to cross your lane? *Assume* it will, because *it will*. In 4 out of 5 accidents involving bicycles and motor vehicles, the motor vehicle committed a traffic violation. Always ride within a margin of control which allows you to stop or escape should absolutely everything go wrong.

Those with Red Circles — Mostly Prohibitive

Stop and Give Way

No Entry

Stop

No Right Turn

No Left Turn

No U Turns

No Cycling

GIVE WAY

Give Way to Traffic on Major Road

Blue Circles with no Red Border - mostly Compulsory

Route for cyclists only.

Turn left past the sign

Route shared with pedestrians.

Route shared with pedestrians, but with dividing line.

Route for cyclists — but other vehicles may be on it.

Warning Signs mostly Triangular

1:10

Steep Hill Downwards

Level Crossing without Gate or Barrier Ahead

•Look for openings in traffic, driveways, streets, garages, etc, that you can duck into should the need arise. Try to plan where you would go should you and the bike part company. The natural tendency in a collision situation is to try desperately to stop. Many times your interest will be better served by launching yourself over an obstacle. Far better to hit the road at an angle than a car head-on.

•While not exceeding a speed which gives you control, try to keep moving. Within reason, avoid using brakes. This will have the effect of making you figure out well in advance what traffic situations are going to occur. There is a car double-parked in the next block. Are you going to be able to swing out? Also, a lot of the danger from other vehicles in traffic comes from differences in velocity. If you are going slow, cars bunch up behind, crowd, become impatient, etc. A racing bike can easily keep up with and pass a lot of traffic. You may find it a bit unnerving to run neck and neck with cabs and lorries at first, but it is safer than offering a stationary target. Try to *integrate* yourself with the traffic.

•To this end, always be in a gear low enough to give you power and acceleration. In heavy traffic an even cadence is difficult to maintain, but try to keep your feet churning away and avoid getting stuck in a 'dead' high gear. As a cyclist, you have only a fraction of the power available to the motorist. To stay integrated with traffic requires that you be prepared to accelerate hard and quickly.

•On the other hand, do not follow the car in front too closely. Car brakes are better than bike brakes. Most bike accidents consist of the bicycle running into something. Leave plenty of room up front. This is where motorists accustomed to running bumper-to-bumper will try to pressure you from behind, even though you are moving at the same speed as the car you are following. Maintain position and if they give you the horn give them the finger.

•Be extra-cautious at intersections where you already have right of way. Cars coming from the opposite direction and turning right will frequently cut straight across your path. Even if the vehicle is seemingly waiting for you to pass, don't trust it, for at the last moment it will leap forward. Letting a motor vehicle precede you to clear the way is often a good tactic.

Another danger at intersections is cars coming up alongside from behind and then making a sudden left turn. One way to stop it is for you to be in the centre of the lane. However, if the intersection you are entering has a light which is going to change soon, then traffic from behind may be storming up at a breakneck pace. You'd better be out of the way.

•In any city anywhere in the world, taxi drivers are a hazard. All things are relative and in London, for example, most cabbies are decent. In the US of A cabbies have the highest ulcer rate of any occupational group, as well they might considering their working conditions and how they drive. Abilities vary, but most are just no good. New York City cabbies are the bottom of the barrel.

The reason cab drivers are often a problem is that they are professionals. Driving in traffic every day, they soon know exactly what is going on and become accustomed to moving ahead at every opportunity. It is second nature, and does not even require hostile intent on their part. It is just something that they do. Every day. As long as you ride clearly and decisively cabbies will present you with few difficulties; but if you start to fumble and wonder what to do, then they will quickly become impatient, and shut you in behind a bus, or cut you off, or submit you to some other unpleasantry about which you can do nothing.

•Very often you will be riding next to parked cars. Be especially careful of motorists opening doors in your path. Exhaust smoke and faces in rear-view mirrors are tips. Even if a motorist looks right at you and is seemingly waiting for you to pass, give her/him a wide berth. Believe it or not, you may not register on her/his consciousness, and she/he may open the door in your face.

THE CITY CYCLIST.

•The law requires you to ride to the left of the left lane as far as is consistent with safety. This is a very elastic and sometimes abused definition. Cyclists have been ticketed for causing an obstruction by riding too far to the right, and there have also been instances of opening car door/cyclist accidents where the cyclist was held to be at fault. Always allow enough manoeuvring room to avoid road litter and potholes. Pass parked cars with room to spare should a door open. If somebody objects to your 'obstructing', ignore them. If you get a ticket, it is a far better deal than a trip to the hospital.

When the road or street is too narrow for overtaking vehicles to pass you with enough room, then ride bang out in the centre of the lane. Do not let them pass, or if it is a two-way road or street, make them pass in the opposite lane. Vehicle drivers may hoot or shout, but this is far safer for you than letting them pass with only inches to spare. You are equally entitled to road space and safe passage.

•On multi-lane roads or streets where there is a left-turn-only lane at an intersection, and you intend to go straight through, get into the right through-lane well before the intersection. Ditto if there is a bike lane. In fact, even if there is no left-turn-only lane, it is better to move out of the bike lane into the next lane right for going straight through an intersection. This helps minimize the chance of a left-turning vehicle cutting you off.

Lane changing in fast, thick traffic can take muscle. John Forester does it by eyeball to eyeball contact with a particular motorist while positioning himself with the clear intention of moving right.* If the motorist makes room, Forester then changes lane. The method has a distinct advantage in that both hands stay on the brakes, where they belong in heavy traffic. However, if you have enough room in front to take one hand of the bars and stick it out in a jabbing, emphatic signal, the situation is then much clearer to other road users.

•Keep an eye on the road surface. Watch out for broken glass, stones, potholes, etc. Plenty of bumps and potholes are big enough to destroy a bike – and you. Going over bumps, cables, etc, get off the saddle and keep your weight on the pedals and handlebars.

*Forester, John, *Effective Cycling*, Custom Cycle Fitments, 782 Allen Court, Palo Alto, CA 94303 USA. The best and most comprehensive book on cycling that I know of.

•Quite a few things can dump a bike:

Oil slicks in the centre of traffic lanes at busy intersections and on sharp curves. When cars stop or turn hard, a little oil drops off. The resulting slick can send you off the road or sliding out into the middle of a busy intersection.

Newly wet streets. There is a light film of oil which until it is washed away mixes with the water to make a very slippery surface.

Wet manhole covers and steel plates can dump you in a hurry. So can wet cobblestones, wet autumn leaves, gravel and sand. Many storm sewers are just the right size to swallow up a bicycle wheel.

•Ride with the traffic. Sometimes when there is no traffic coming the other way, it is better to ride in the opposite lane.

•The velocity of traffic on free-way style streets which have no parking is usually too high to permit safe cycling. If you run in the centre of the lane, you block traffic. If you go to the side, cars whizz by you at high speeds with only inches to spare. Stick to streets with parked cars and look out for opening doors.

•Cars and lorries have a habit of pulling out unexpectedly and without signalling. Look out for driveways, building entrances, construction projects, cab ranks, and any other possible source of a vehicle. Remember, you don't exist for many drivers. They look right at you, the image is flashed on their brain, but they don't comprehend. They don't *see* you.

And perhaps some do. One time in New York City I had the lights in my favour at an intersection with a police car waiting on the cross street. The eyes of the driver fixed steadily on me and he waited until I was just going through the intersection before pulling through a red light and right in front of me. Expect the unexpected.

•Pedestrians are another unreliable bunch. They don't think 200 pounds of bike and rider coming towards them at 30 mph means anything, and will frequently jaywalk right in your path. Your odds are much better here than when mixing it up with a car, but even so any collision is going to hurt you, the pedestrian, and your bike. Use a horn, yell – and give them the right of way if you have to.

•Kids. As much of a hazard to the cyclist as to the motorist. Any child has the potential to race out suddenly into the street.

•Other cyclists. I don't know why, but many cyclists and especially children are erratic. Give them a wide berth.

•Footpaths. It is illegal to ride on a footpath. However, a cyclist is closer to a pedestrian than a car is to a cyclist. Mixing cyclists and pedestrians together on footpaths is not only much safer than mixing cycles and cars on roads, it is not even dangerous. The accident statistics from Stevenage, where pedestrians and cyclists have mixed for over twenty years, bear this out. A number of factors make this so, but the most fundamental is that the cyclist, like the pedestrian, is vulnerable and exposed and has every interest in avoiding conflicts.

Riding on footpaths must be done with discretion – dashes through Sunday parks filled with strollers are inconsiderate – and you must give clear priority to pedestrians, dismounting if necessary. But many footpaths are little used and offer a more sensible transit than running with the road traffic. Just remember – however rational your case, to ride on a footpath makes you liable to infringement of the law, an alternative you may prefer to risking your life.

Fast is Safe

Cycling in traffic seemingly involves girding yourself for battle and inducing a constant state of morbid apprehension for your life. At one level this is true. The idea of mixing cars and bicycles together is crazy. Cars are an atavistic idiocy responsible for millions of deaths and injuries. It is entirely logical to want nothing whatsoever to do with them.

However, once you have a working appreciation of the hazards to be encountered in traffic, you will find that the situation can be made to work to your advantage. Riding fast promotes your own safety. This is because moving quickly demands that you anticipate and avoid the troublesome situations that would otherwise retard your journey. The best way to do this is to ride what I call the high side.

So long as you shift along quickly enough to keep pace with the other road users, riding in the mainstream of traffic is safer than trying to stay out of the way by keeping to the low side. Riding the high side largely eliminates hazards such as kerbside road litter, opening car doors, cars overtaking and turning left across your path

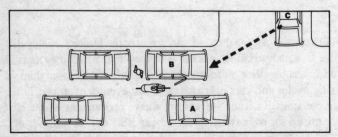

Low Side: hemmed in by vehicle A, the cyclist has no way of avoiding the opening door of vehicle B. He is also invisible to the driver of vehicle C waiting at the cross junction.

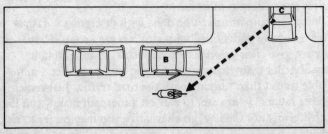

High Side: the cyclist is out of the way of the opening door, and visible to the driver of vehicle C.

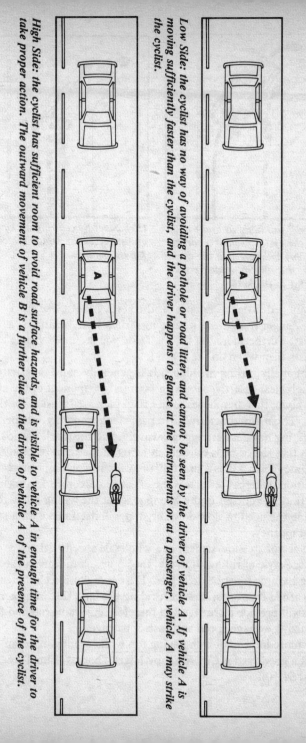

Low Side: the cyclist has no way of avoiding a pothole or road litter, and cannot be seen by the driver of vehicle A. If vehicle A is moving sufficiently faster than the cyclist, and the driver happens to glance at the instruments or at a passenger, vehicle A may strike the cyclist.

High Side: the cyclist has sufficient room to avoid road surface hazards, and is visible to vehicle A in enough time for the driver to take proper action. The outward movement of vehicle B is a further clue to the driver of vehicle A of the presence of the cyclist.

153

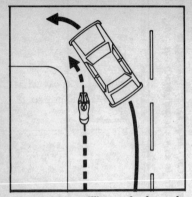 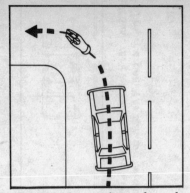

Low Side: unwilling to brake and follow the cyclist around a corner, or possibly unaware that the cyclist is there, the turning vehicle crowds the cyclist to the kerb.

High Side: by centring on lane, the cyclist forces the motor vehicle to follow behind.

and stray pedestrians stepping off the kerb. All of these are a greater danger than the risk of being struck from behind by a motorist. Furthermore, on the high side you are more visible to motorists than when on the low side.

Emotionally, riding the high side is generally more satisfactory. Although clear assertiveness is an essential component of the high rider's style, this diminishes rather than increases tension for the cyclist. The main imperative is to pass along smoothly, neither accelerating nor decelerating excessively, and the mark of the high rider is that she or he is efficient at being in the right place at the right time. This skill is a function of awareness and a positive orientation, whereas tension is the negative outcome of worrying about finding yourself in the wrong place at the wrong time. Just reducing the need to slow down or stop will itself make for a more relaxed journey.

This is not an endorsement of a wholesale speed trial or kamikaze style of riding. Initially, the approach to learning about cycling hazards must be defensive. First save your neck. Once you have learned the ropes, however, riding the high side in urban traffic will provide a creative and therefore enjoyable method for maximizing average speed and ease of passage.

For more information on having fun while cycling in urban traffic, a good read is *City Rider* by Nigel Thomas (Elm Tree Books, £4.50).

8 Bang!

It is all very well to dispense information on how to stay out of trouble when riding a bike, but the cyclist should also know what to do should an accident actually occur. The problem is not so much knowing what to do, as being able to do it.

Most people react to an imminent crash with panic. They may freeze into immobility and do nothing, or blindly clamp down on

"AN AGED WOMAN ON HER BACK,
TWO BABES IN GUTTER PRONE."

the brakes and lose directional stability. This can make a bad situation fatal. For example, if a car is about to hit you from the side and you death grip the brakes, locking up the rear wheel and sending the bike down in a slide, then when the car hits you, you are likely to be rolled up underneath it. If, on the other hand, at the moment of impact you try to get clear of the bike and make a dive for the hood of the car, you may slide along to the windscreen and perhaps even over the roof. Not fun, but the survival chances are much better than if you are underneath the car.

Panic-induced muscular tension increases physical damage in a crash. The person who falls or is thrown and is able to stay loose and relaxed will suffer less injury than the person who tenses and tries to save him or herself.

The ability to exercise the best of a series of bad options, and stay physically relaxed in a situation offering damage, can only be learned through experience and practice. I have been an avid skier since I was four, a high diver since I was seven, and when I suddenly find myself flying through the air upside down I am automatically loose, looking to tuck and roll when I hit.

If you do not know how to fall, try to have someone with training – fighting experts, skydivers, skiers – give you some pointers. I find that fast woods riding with an old trasho bike is useful. A few spills are inevitable, and as long as they are in loose dirt, usually little damage results.

Practise the braking and turning techniques discussed in the Riding chapter. Think of how to use them in various circumstances. If a car pulls up alongside you and then unexpectedly turns left, cutting you off, a sudden application of the brakes will simply pile you into the car. A rapid haul turn however, just might avoid an accident, and if you do hit, you will both be going more or less in the same direction. Suppose a car pulls out in front of you from a side road or driveway. There may be enough room for a haul turn so that you hit the car a glancing blow. If there is not enough room to turn, then brake as hard as possible without skidding, and just before hitting the car launch yourself clear of the bike. You may be able to sail right over the car. Stay loose and roll when you hit the pavement.

If you are hit from behind DO NOT BRAKE. Try to get away by steering to the side.

Having it back

When a motorist does you dirt, one acceptable response is an explosive yell. It's the cycling equivalent of blowing a horn to signify potential or immediate danger.

A good yell can help you to release some of the adrenalin energy that danger generates. It can make a motorist just a touch uncomfortable, and is more effective if there are passengers in the vehicle. A lot of ruckus and commotion means that the motorist is doing something wrong, and the more passengers as audience, the greater the awareness of discord.

One of the most frequent sins of the motorist is to overtake a cyclist and then suddenly brake and turn left. The motorist knowingly creates trouble for the cyclist, and hopes to get away with it through sheer greater size. This is a moment of opportunity. The cyclist is usually in the blind rear quarter of the vehicle and invisible to the motorist, who will be under some tension about the outcome of his or her misdeed. In such circumstances, a well-timed yell can startle a motorist a clear six inches off the seat up into the air, and cause a momentary loss of vehicle control. If there is a traffic bollard or other nearby obstruction, the motorist may hit it.

Another unsettling tactic in a situation where a motor vehicle is actively risking an accident is to hit it hard with the flat of your hand. This makes a tremendous bang inside the vehicle (especially if done on the roof) and again strongly suggests that something is out of order. The best moment for a direct attack is when a vehicle entering the roadway from the left and intending to turn right cuts across your path. By swerving behind the vehicle, you create the welcome safety of diverging trajectories and with good timing you can give the vehicle's stern a noisy bash. Do not use this ploy without a clear escape route. If you bang on the roof of a vehicle which is running alongside and crowding, you are just asking for the motorist to panic and do something wrong, or for a hot-head to give that little twitch of the wheel that will smear you forever.

It is sometimes tempting to deliberately have an accident. This is illegal. The most appealing moment for such a gross infraction of the rules is when a motorist noses out in front of you from a side road, forcing you to slam on the brakes to avoid a collision. Sooner or later it will cross your mind to deliberately slack the brakes just a little and hit the side of the vehicle, rolling on your shoulder and back over the bonnet to a safe landing, but thereafter continuously complaining of an unspecified pain in your back. You must never do such a terrible thing.

Do bear in mind that in discussing this having it back business, I am walking on the dark side and speaking of evil things. Well, that is how people feel sometimes. Evil.

9 Touring

Touring is the real joy in biking. The only better way to see the country is to walk or roller skate. A bike has advantages in mobility and luggage-carrying, however, and the aesthetic sacrifice is not too great. Touring can be done in a tremendous variety of ways. You can go for an afternoon's jaunt or spend a summer or more travelling thousands of miles. You can go as a self-contained unit with your own camping gear, or ultra-light and stay in inns, guest houses, hostels and hotels. You can count the miles travelled, or concentrate on the scenery (yeah!). Your journey can include transit by auto, bus, train, boat, and plane, so that you can hop from one interesting place to another. You can have a plan, or absolutely none at all. Touring is a call to adventure, beauty, new sights and experiences.

There's a lot to touring, and plenty for you to think about. At the same time it can be quite simple. Any bike headed for the sticks should have a tool kit, unless you don't mind pushing your

'A merry heart goes all the way,
   Your sad tires in a mile, a.'—*Shakespeare*.

bike a few miles to a garage and/or the possibility of an overnight stay until it opens. Equipment makes a difference, but the main thing is to get out there. My greatest, happiest tour was on a battered 1935 BSA whose vital parts shed like water.

Part of the fun of touring is figuring it out and planning or not planning for yourself. Some people insist that the only way to tour is with a meticulous and detailed plan; others heave map and compass into the bushes and go wherever fancy takes them. For some the fun and relaxation comes as a result of planned and concentrated effort; for others it is through not thinking about anything. There is no 'right' way to tour. Each to his or her own. Accordingly, this chapter tries simply to give basic information about touring. It is not a step-by-step guide. It's up to you to decide where and when you want to go, and what sort of equipment you expect to need.

An Essex Farm near Epping

Where

One source of information is books. *Adventure Cycling in Britain*, by T. Hughes (£6.95) covers basic touring techniques and equipment, and lists specific tours varying from easy day rides to strenuous mountain 'rough-stuff'. *Adventure Cycling in Europe*, by J. Rakowski (£6.95) covers 27 countries and is a gold-mine of practical information. Another contender is *Cycle Touring in Britain and the Rest of Europe*, by P. Knottley (£4.95). Specific routes are listed in *The CTC Route Guide to Cycling in England and Ireland*, by C. Gausden and N. Crane (£2.95), and in *Weekend Cycling*, by C. Gausden (£6.95). Some of the above books are in book and cycle shops, and all are obtainable from Selpress Books, Dept RB, 35 High Street, Wendover, Bucks HP22 6DU.

General information on touring, brochures, accommodation lists and so on can be obtained from tourist authorities:

British Tourist Authority
Tourist Information Centre, 64 St James's St, London SW1.

England
English Tourist Board and London Tourist Board, 4 Grosvenor Gdns, London SW1.

East Anglian Tourist Board, 14 Museum St, Ipswich, Suffolk.

East Midlands Tourist Board, Bailgate, Lincoln.

English Lakes Counties Tourist Board, Ellerthwaite, Windermere, Westmorland.

Isle of Man Tourist Board, 13 Victoria St, Douglas.

Isle of Wight Tourist Board, 21 High St, Newport.

Northumbria Tourist Board, 8 Eldon Sq, Newcastle/Tyne.

North-West Tourist Board, 119 The Piazza, Piccadilly Plaza, Manchester.

South-East England Tourist Board, 4-6 Monsoon Rd, Tunbridge Wells, Kent.

West Country Tourist Board, Trinity Ct, Southernhay East, Exeter, Devon.

West Midlands Tourist Board, 1 Shaw St, Worcester.

Yorkshire Tourist Board, 312 Tadcaster Rd, York.

Wales

Wales Tourist Board, Welcome Hse, High St, Llandaff, Cardiff.

Mid-Wales Tourism Council, 3 China St, Llanidloes, Mont.

North Wales Tourism Council, Civic Centre, Colwyn Bay, Denbighs.

South Wales Tourism Council, Darkgate, Carmarthen.

Scotland

Scottish Tourist Board, 23 Ravelston Terrace, Edinburgh 4.

The Borders Tourist Association, 66 Woodmarket, Kelso, Rox.

Clyde Tourist Association, c/o Information Centre, George Sq, Glasgow.

Grampian Tourist Association, 17 High St, Elgin, Moray.

Highlands and Islands Development Board, Bridge Hse, Bank St, Inverness.

South-West Scotland Tourist Association, Douglas Hse, Newton Stewart, Wigtowns.

Northern Ireland

Northern Ireland Tourist Board, 48 High St, Belfast.

Touring clubs and groups

One way of getting into touring is to join a club. You get a variety of planning and insurance services, and riding with fellow members you receive a planned tour, the benefit of a group leader who will set a pace within your capacity, and lots of free friendly help and advice. First and foremost is The Cyclists' Touring Club, Cotterell House, 69 Meadrow, Godalming, Surrey GU7 3HS. I recommend this organisation to every cyclist, tourist or not. The largest and oldest (1878) national cycling association, it not only provides an extraordinary range of services, but also safeguards and champions the rights of cyclists at every level of government and municipal authority.

The CTC is divided into 55 District Associations and each has a programme of rides throughout the year, mainly on Sundays but also during the week. There are also local, national and foreign organised tours led by experienced members, numerous national competitions and rides, and an annual grand fête and get-together, the York Rally. Club services include the Touring Department,

A CTC HOTEL

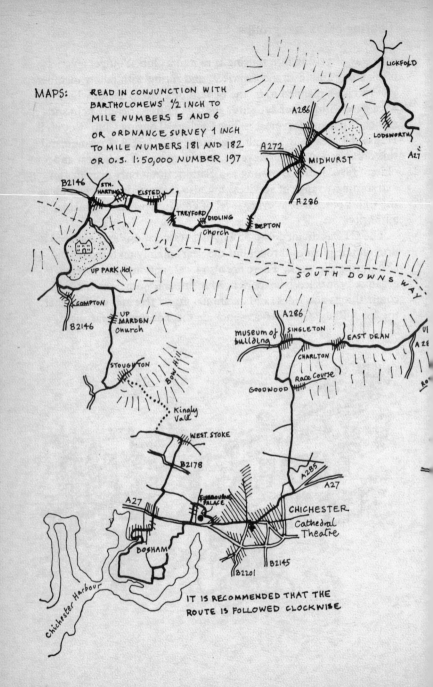

MAPS: READ IN CONJUNCTION WITH
BARTHOLOMEWS' 1/2 INCH TO
MILE NUMBERS 5 AND 6
OR ORDNANCE SURVEY 1 INCH
TO MILE NUMBERS 181 AND 182
OR O.S. 1:50,000 NUMBER 197

LICKFOLD

A286

LODSWORTH

A272

MIDHURST

A27

A286

B2146

STH.
HARTING

ELSTED

TREYFORD

DIDLING
Church

BEPTON

UP PARK Ho.

SOUTH DOWNS WAY

COMPTON

UP
MARDEN
Church

B2146

A286

museum of
building

SINGLETON

EAST DEAN

U

A2

STOUGHTON

Bow Hill

CHARLTON

Race Course

GOODWOOD

Ro

Kingly Vale

WEST STOKE

B2178

FISHBOURNE
PALACE

A285

A27

A27

CHICHESTER
Cathedral
Theatre

BOSHAM

B2201

B2145

Chichester Harbour

IT IS RECOMMENDED THAT THE
ROUTE IS FOLLOWED CLOCKWISE

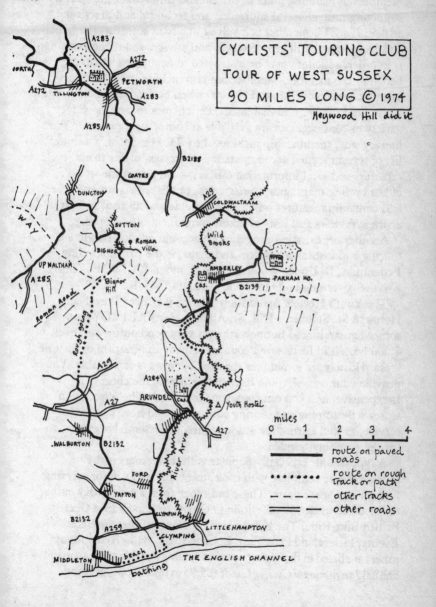

ICKFOLD

A283
A272
ORTH
A272
PETWORTH
TILLINGTON
A283
A285

CYCLISTS' TOURING CLUB
TOUR OF WEST SUSSEX
90 MILES LONG © 1974
Heywood Hill did it

B2188
COATES
DUNCTON
A29
COLDWALTHAM
WAY
SUTTON
Roman Villa
Wild Brooks
BIGNOR
UP WALTHAM
AMBERLEY
A285
Bignor Hill
Cas.
B2139
PARHAM HO.
Roman Road
Rough going
A29
A284
A27
ARUNDEL
Cas.
△ Youth Hostel
A27
WALBURTON
B2132
River Arun
FORD
YAPTON
CLYMPIN
B2132
A259
CLYMPING
LITTLEHAMPTON
MIDDLETON
beach
THE ENGLISH CHANNEL
bathing

miles
0   1   2   3   4

——————— route on paved roads
········· route on rough track or path
— — — — other tracks
———————— other roads

165

which has a large library of comprehensive, personally researched tours complete with maps (see overleaf), and which will assist members in planning tours in Britain and throughout the world, supplying routes, useful addresses, and technical and practical advice. If a CTC member is involved in a road accident, the Legal Aid Department will give free help and advice, and if compensation is in order, solicitors may be instructed to negotiate a claim on behalf of the member. Membership also includes free third party insurance with cover up to £500,000 when cycling anywhere in the world, and further optional insurance schemes to cover a wide variety of contingencies are available at competitive rates. On the literary side, membership includes the CTC Handbook – a thick list of recommended accommodation addresses, places to eat, cycle repairers and local information officers – and one of the world's oldest cycling magazines, *Cycletouring*, published six times a year and containing features on touring at home and abroad, technical articles, reviews and tests of bikes, components and clothing.

Another organisation providing an accommodation handbook, touring and insurance services and maps, is the British Cycling Federation, 16 Upper Woburn Place, London WC1 0QE. This is also the governing body for cycle racing in the UK.

The Youth Hostels Association (National Office: Trevelyan House, 8 St. Stephen's Hill, St. Albans, Herts AL1 2DY) is a somewhat straitlaced but nevertheless very good outfit with over 4,000 hostels in forty-seven countries, many in beautiful or historic areas. Hostels are sometimes spartan, but always serviceable. You provide your own sleeping bag, and help with the chores. Inexpensive, and you can cook your own food. The Association stores sell camping and touring equipment and have a tourist service, as well as running guided tours. An essential organization for the economy-minded.

A type of tour especially popular with newcomers is the organised ride complete with cook, mechanic and van for carrying luggage and spare parts. These can range from a simple day outing to the three-week 900 mile John O'Groats to Land's End Great British Bike Ride. The best known organizer of these is Bike Events, 1 Cleveland Place East, London Road, Bath, Avon. Many others are listed in the spring issues of cycling periodicals, and in the annual *International Cycling Guide* (£5.95 in bike shops, or from

Selpress Books, Dept RB, 35 High Street, Wendover, Bucks HP22 6DU).

So. Where you go depends on your own temperament, equipment interests and physical condition. If you favour back roads off the beaten track and camping, you are going to have to deal with equipment for both you and the bike; touring on better roads and sleeping in inns means less and lighter equipment. I would suggest that you make your initial rides about 20 miles or so, and work up to longer tours and overnight stays as you get used to it. Until you are quite experienced, do not target over 50 to 60 miles a day, and try to balance hard runs with days of relaxation and shorter jaunts. Excess zeal will turn you into a basket case. Start easy and finish strong.

Riding

I recommend taking the smallest, least travelled roads practically possible. These are B-class roads and smaller. Not only are they almost always more interesting, but the fewer cars there are around the more comfortable you will be. Motor vehicles in the country are a serious hazard for the cyclist. The speed differences between cycles and cars are much greater. On the dual-lane carriageways,

A CLUB RIDE IN THE COUNTRY

for example, the vehicles run at 70 mph plus, often bunched so tightly together that the drivers' vision is limited by the vehicle they are following, and hence they do not see the cyclist until the moment of overtaking, when they no longer have the time to swing out and give room. This danger is acute at night-time. Often there are footpaths adjoining such roads, little-used and a sensible alternative, but keep a keen eye out for broken glass and other litter. On the two-way A and B class roads many vehicles move smartly, particularly if the driver 'knows the road', and hare around tight corners at 40 to 60 mph. With an up to 50 mph difference in speed between the motor vehicle and the cyclist, and limited space for manoeuvring, a bad situation can develop faster than the many drivers who over-rate themselves think is possible. There are fewer accidents in the country, but a far greater percentage are fatal.

The best bet for the cyclist are small roads which keep vehicle speeds down to about 30 mph, at which rate there is almost always enough room and time to prevent serious accidents. These roads meander and take longer, but are usually more interesting. The point of cycling in the first place is to savour and enjoy, and so for reaching somewhere in a hurry use other transport, or take you and your cycle by rail or air.

An alternative to roads are bridlepaths (which cyclists are legally entitled to use) and footpaths (which they are not). These honeycomb Britain and I have taken many long tours touching road for only a mile or so. The scenery is usually fantastic, and the riding often demanding. Most bikes will stand up to this sort of use well enough, and can be shod with extra tough expedition tyres. Or you can use a purpose built machine such as a mountain bike. As far as the legality of footpaths is concerned, I again suggest using your head. A popular walking area filled with Sunday strollers is a poor choice and you should dismount and walk. But most times there is nobody around and you will have the outdoors to yourself.

Safe country road riding is largely a matter of common sense. Most of the rules for traffic riding apply here also.

●The cardinal rule is 'what if?' Look and think ahead. Don't for example, time your riding so that you and an overtaking car reach a curve at the same time. If a car – or worse yet a lorry – comes the other way there just isn't going to be enough room.

•Bear in mind the tremendous relative velocity of cars. In traffic you can pretty much keep up, but in the country cars will have up to 70 mph over your 5 to 15. If you crest a hill, for example, and there is no oncoming traffic, move over into the opposite lane for a while. This avoids the hazard of overtaking cars who cannot see you over the crest.

•Try to have a hole to duck into should everything go wrong. Where will you go if that tractor pulls out? If a car comes around the corner on your side of the road, are you going to try for the ditch or a tree? You may wreck a bike going off into a field, but this is a lot better than colliding with a car. Think about this as much as you can and try to make it an automatic process. This way, when an emergency arises, instead of freezing in panic you may be able to save your life.

•Be particularly wary, when you have to speed up, of people doing odd things. Cannonballing down a hill, you may be doing 30-50 mph, a fact that many motorists and pedestrians do not comprehend. They see a bicycle, and automatically class it as slow and unimportant, dismissing it from mind (as you can be sure they would not do for a large lorry), and step out or pull out on to the road, or pass, or whatever. This capacity for visual recognition with no subsequent cognitive comprehension may seem bizarre, but I assure you it is so. Never trust other road users – you cannot afford to do so.

•Mind your brakes. After running through puddles or wet grass, dry off by applying them lightly as you ride. When running down steep hills, do not hold the brakes steady, which causes heat build-up and fade, but pump on and off. This also tells you if you have something in reserve – which you always should.

On long downgrades where there is ample room, do not be afraid to let your bike stretch right out and breathe. Past 20 mph air resistance provides a significant retarding effect, and you can save a lot of wear on the brakes by raising or lowering your body to control speed. Just remember that when it comes to actually stopping, air resistance will not be any help.

●Run well to the left (or right, on the Continent) but leave yourself a little bit of room to manoeuvre. There are all sorts of broken pavement, sewers, and odd bits of litter which crop up unexpectedly at the road's edge.

●On two-lane roads watch out for overtaking motorists coming towards you. They often do not see or just plain ignore a bicycle coming towards them. If you move out to the centre of your lane most motorists will return to their lane. Some will not and you must be prepared to stop on the shoulder of the road. You might care to have a few rotten tomatoes handy for such moments.

●Beware the Hun in the Sun. At sunrise and sunset motorists with the sun in their eyes may not see you.

●Rural farm traffic is a law unto itself. Many farmers operate machinery on local public roads as if they were in the middle of a field.

●Watch for loose gravel, dirt, or sand, and especially at driveway and side road entrances.

●Bridge gratings, cattle guards, railroad tracks, etc. can all swallow up a bicycle wheel and send you flying.

●Dogs. Dogs and other creatures of the field and air are a menace to the cyclist. I was once attacked by a large and very determined goose. Dogs are the main problem, though, and you need to keep a constant lookout for old Towser. Most experienced cyclists have at least one dog attack story to tell and in America, for example, 8 per cent of all bicycle accidents are caused by dogs.

There are many theories about why dogs attack two-wheeled vehicles, but it seems reasonably clear that the spokes make a noise which drives them nuts; they snap at the wheels and not the rider. There are also a distressing number of dog owners who take a not-too-secret pleasure in having vicious, attack-prone animals, and others who should not try to take responsibility even for a cockroach. One couple expressed puzzlement to me after their dog bit my riding companion: every time the dog was disobedient, they said, they beat it till their arms hurt. Why wouldn't it obey? With

treatment like that, any dog will become vicious and irrational.

Understanding that old Poochie may not be directly at fault does not make a dog attack more fun. Dogs are fully the responsibility of their owner, and excepting dogs crazed by disease, can be trained to leave cyclists bloody well alone. I like dogs very much and accept that some adjustment to their particular natures and quirks is necessary if they are to be around. I do not accept being knocked off my bike by some giant hound.

The vital thing to understand is that the problem is not so much being bitten, as being startled out of your wits, losing control of the bike and crashing. If you are confident that you can, if necessary, deal with a dog attack, the risk of a panic-induced accident is reduced. So also is the risk of being bitten. Like sharks, wolves and other predators, dogs are even more stimulated to attack if the victim is afraid and out of control.

Most dogs attack according to a pattern. They circle to the rear of the cyclist and come up from behind. If you are on a downhill incline and/or the dog is diminutive, you may be able to outrun it. Most times this is either not possible or unwise (the dog is too large and too fast), but 99 times out of 100 there is still no serious problem. All you have to do is stop, dismount and face the dog directly. Often he will come up wagging his tail. If the dog is still aggressive, point your arm at him and say firmly, 'go home', 'depart ye henceforth' or whatever articulation you can muster. It is only the rarest of dogs that will attack a human being who appears confident and obviously prepared to deal with matters. When you leave, walk away like all 'normal' (to the dog) people do, and the matter will be forgotten.

What about an actual attack in which you are being bitten and savaged? Unfortunately, my publishers will not allow me to explain in detail some of the methods for defending yourself. Dog lovers have threatened legal action on the grounds of prevention of cruelty to animals. These are not people who have had to spend a month picking bits of gravel out of their legs and face because a dog knocked them off a bike. They have not had to undergo the long and extremely painful series of rabies shots which are mandatory if you are bitten outside Britain and the dog gets away. They do not have anything useful to say about the little girl who lived down the road from my parents' place and who was pulled down by three dogs and torn to bits.

So be it. For the time being at least, rabies is not a problem in

Britain. You are far more likely to die or come to serious injury as a result of losing control of the bike than from a bite. But if you are attacked, make every effort to find and identify the dog and owner. Ask in local homes. shops, petrol stations and so on. If bitten, however lightly, obtain immediate medical treatment.

Report any attack to the police. Any dog is allowed one bite, and a charge is then issued to the owner to keep the animal under control. Two bites are very serious and three are terminal: the dog is put down. I love dogs very much and find this possibility extremely distressing, but appreciate even less the prospect of serious personal injury or death. Owners who do not control their dogs cannot have them. By law.

If you sustain damages as a result of a dog attack, hitting a dog or seeking to avoid hitting a dog, while cycling in accord with legal requirements, the owner bears full responsibility. If the dog owner is uncooperative, just find a solicitor. Unless you have done something completely hare-brained (no lights at night, whizzing through a public park, etc.) the law is completely and absolutely on your side.

—EN ROUTE TO THE LAKE—

Technique

Cadence (see Riding for basics) plays an extremely significant part in the technique of long-distance touring. In a short sprint you can drain your body's resources and strength, but on a long tour output must not exceed ability to continuously replenish fuel and oxygen. Which makes it sound simple: just take it easy and have something in reserve. Not quite.

If you are interested in covering a lot of ground (not everybody is) and in feeling comfortable, then you must strive for an exact balance between energy output and the body's ability to synthesize and store energy. There is a *pace* which works best. Go too fast and the result will be fatigue and possibly strained muscles that will dog you throughout the tour. But go too slow, and you will become sluggish and lethargic, and mistake this for genuine tiredness.

A rough indicator of pace is respiration and heart-beat. You simply cannot sustain for long periods effort which noticeably increases either. Thus, the exact pace you can maintain depends on your physical condition, not on your strength.

I particularly recommend that you take it easy at first, sticking to the lower gears and not pushing hard against the pedals. This will help you to find your own cadence and pace, and perhaps avoid excessive initial effort. Most people tend to lean into it hard the first day. The result is strained and sore muscles, and the next day they can hardly move. You'll go farther and faster if you take it easy at the start.

Riding position can make a tremendous difference. Going into the wind try to get low down. With a strong tail wind, straighten up and get a free push. In Europe many riders use home-made 'sails' resembling kites strapped to their backs. These are effective even with a quartering wind. Position determines the muscle groups in use: hands high on the bars eases the back, stomach, arms, and hands; down positions do exactly the opposite and are best for hill climbing.

Equipment

Bike

Choice of bike depends on the kind of touring you do. A 3-speed roadster is good for durability, but heavy weight and an inefficient gear train make it a poor choice for distance work. For all-round use, a derailleur gear bike is best by far. It can be set up to favour durability and carrying heavy loads or to favour performance and fast road riding. Tourists who mix transportation modes frequently, going by bus, train, plane or car from one place to the next, may find a portable folding bike the most convenient.

Most general use sport bikes can easily be altered for touring, and the discussions of luggage, lights, etc. below will suggest what bits and pieces are necessary for your needs. The most important thing is for your bike to be geared correctly for the terrain you will encounter (see Chapter 5). If you do not already own a bike, then pick up a copy of the current *Bicycle Buyers Bible* for the latest scoop on touring machinery.

One excellent form of sport/touring is along tracks and bridlepaths and cross-country. The going can get muddy and rough, and even on smooth sections there are concealed rocks, limbs and other debris. A derailleur gear touring bike can manage this sort of thing on a sometime basis, but a steady diet of off-road work will noticeably increase wear and tear. The economic and simple route to an off-road bike is to equip a beat-up 3-speed roadster with an extra large rear sprocket, cut down alloy mudguards, cage pedals and knobbly speedway tyres. It cannot be jumped and bashed like a BMX racer, but is inexpensive and also still perfectly useable as a road bike.

The definitive but expensive route to an off-road machine is the mountain bike (see 2 Choosing Mounts for details). This is just made for punishment and you will not believe what these machines can do until you try one for yourself. Tyres can be selected for optimum traction in sand and mud, or in fast road versions that work almost as well in the dirt.

An association devoted to off-road riding is The Rough-Stuff Fellowship, 4 Achray Avenue, Callander, Perthshire FK17 8JZ.

Tyres

The development of narrow profile, high-pressure clincher tyres precludes the use of tubulars by all but a handful of affluent fanatics. For poor roads and/or very heavy loads use a $1\frac{1}{4}$ inch heavyweight tyre, or at the ultimate, a 650-B $1\frac{1}{2}$ inch tyre. For more performance, use a lighter, $1\frac{1}{4}$ inch high-pressure gumwall, and if you really want to blast along, then use a $1^1/\mathrm{s}$ inch high-pressure 100 p.s.i. tyre. Remember: the narrower and harder, the faster and the more punctures.

Tool kit

What you need depends on how far you go and how you maintain your bike. I keep basic tool kits for each type of bike (3-speed or 10-speed, wire-on or tubular tyres), and expand the tool kit with extra tools and parts when necessary. At the minimum, have:

Tyre repair kit including levers and spare valve
Tyre inner tube
Dog bone or 4 inch adjustable spanner
Screwdriver
Chain tool and spare links
Any special Allen keys required for your bike.

For longer journeys add:
A few assorted nuts, bolts, and screws
Brake and shift cables
Spokes and nipples, spoke key and small file
Brake pads
Do-all spanner to fit hub cones, brake locknuts, etc., *or* hub cone spanners and assorted small spanners as necessary
Spare tyre (use the compact folding type)
Wire cutters
Freewheel remover

Cotterless crank extractor
Lubricants, including grease
Any special gizmo you might need. A small container of waterless hand cleaner can be a real pleasure.

A WELL-KNOWN SPOT ON
THE GODSTONE ROAD.

The ROSE & CROWN
Riddlesdown

Sounds like a lot, but it can all be packed into a compact bundle. On group rides cut down on the number of spare parts per rider, and share one set of tools. Your lighting system as a matter of course should carry spare bulbs. Include a bit of wire and tape for longer runs.

For mending yourself, a basic first-aid kit. I generally also carry: a multi-purpose pocketknife, compass, waterproofed matches, button thread for clothing repairs, game snares, or fishing line, and when appropriate, a snake-bite kit. If you are fond of following sudden fanciful notions and exploring odd by-ways when riding a bike, then a lightweight reflectorized survival blanket is a good investment. After all, you could crash and be disabled, etc., and if you are alone in such circumstances a survival blanket could make a life or death difference.

Lights

A requirement at night. Most tourists prefer generator lights as they are consistently bright and less expensive than battery lights. However, some people do not care to pedal against the resistance of a wheel or hub generator, and wiring tends to snag and break at inconvenient moments. Unless fitted with a storage battery (see 11 Accessories), generator lights go out when the bike stops.

Battery lights are simple, can be used off the bike for map reading or roadside repairs, and left off the bike altogether on a fast daytime run. They are best for off-road riding, as they do not dim if you go slowly, and there are no wires to snag.

What is best for you depends on how you ride. Generator lights are about the only sensible answer for strong lights and extended night runs. However, if you are riding when the days are long, and need lights only for an hour or so at a time, then lightweight battery lights will do. In either case, have a spare light in case the main system fails.

I strongly suggest using a warning flasher unit (see 11 Accessories). Another good item is the Matex flashlight, which straps on the arm or leg and shows a white light to the front, red light to the rear. It will also do as a camp light or for roadside repairs.

Mudguards

Unless you do not mind a wet stern and gritty muck all over the tender mechanical bits of your bike, mudguards are a requirement for British and Continental touring. Plain plastic models are inexpensive and light, but eventually warp and allow water to spray. Far superior are the ESGE chromoplastic models, which are lightweight and will stand extraordinary abuse for many years. Alloy and stainless steel mudguards are heavy, but are sturdy and offer mounting points for lights and other nick-nacks. They have an annoying characteristic of transmitting sound, but this can be cured by using an undercoating paint, available at motor accessory shops.

Bicycle shoes and cleats

There are two basic choices: shoes made to be used without cleats and suitable for walking when off the bike, and shoes made for use with cleats and suitable only for cycling. In theory, if you are really rolling on the miles and want the strongest possible shoe, then steel shanked leather soles and cleats give the maximum get up and go. In fact, there are many ultra-long distance tourists who are perfectly happy with dual purpose cycling/walking shoes such as the Madison, Adidas, Rivat, Sidi, or Bata, and they have the advantage of not having to carry an additional pair of shoes for use when off the bike.

My suggestion is to start off with a pair of dual purpose shoes. They'll be useful anyhow for general riding. If you find them suitable for touring, fine. If not, buy a pair of proper cycling shoes and fit them with cleats. In my experience nothing beats these for comfort and efficiency.

Baggage

Loading a touring bike is an art. There are two cardinal principles: load low and load evenly. Piling gear up in a high stack or all in one place creates tremendous instability for the bike. Bicycle carriers are designed to distribute loads properly. There are three basic kinds: handlebar bags, saddlebags, and panniers. People travelling light can get by with a saddlebag. These fasten to the seat and seat post and can hold a lot of gear.

An alternative is the handlebar bag. This has the advantage of ready access for maps, food, cameras and other things you need often. The disadvantage is an adverse effect on steering.

A revolution in cycle baggage occurred with the introduction of the Jim Blackburn Low Rider front pannier rack. Instead of holding the panniers up high, these centre the panniers on the front hub. The improvement to bike handling has to be experienced to be believed. Front panniers will carry more than a handlebar bag and are not that difficult for access. Maps can be held to the handlebars with a spring clip. The only need for a handlebar bag that comes to mind is when carrying sophisticated cameras. In such a case the handlebar bag should be of a type which is held by a wire frame slung from the handlebars, and secured by elastic tension cords to the front forks. This will help minimise the tiny sharp vibrations which are particularly harmful to cameras. Given a choice, however, I'd rather use Low Rider front panniers, and trust the camera to a foam lined Camera Care Systems pouch.

Campers will want rear panniers, and for the best load distribution, front panniers as well. Panniers come in one of two basic designs: single bag, which allows maximum cramming in of gear, and multi-compartment bag, which separates gear for easy access. Most panniers made today are quick on or off the bike, and some can be converted into backpacks.

Good brand names are Karrimor, Carradice, Pakit, Andrew Hague and Eclipse. Recommending one over the other would not be fair as different models suit different uses. You really need to go to a bike shop and inspect the merchandise personally. One product worthy of special mention, however, are the Trelock ABS plastic panniers. These are a fixed shape and do not have great carrying capacity but have the advantage of a swinging lid with a single catch that can be locked, thereby also locking the pannier to the bike. This can be a remarkably handy feature when touring; in order to preclude theft, ordinary fabric panniers must either be stashed away or carried about the person. My recommendation is to use fabric panniers only if maximum load capacity is paramount.

Panniers want the support of a stout rack. Those supplied on production bikes are often flimsy. There are two types: aluminium alloy and steel. Aluminium alloy racks are light and strong. Generally ranked the best and expensive are the Jim Blackburn models. Also stout but much less costly is the Andrew Hague line, which includes a model where the parts screw together. This allows custom fitting to the bike, and should be easier to repair if something goes wrong while off in the sticks. The Blackburn racks are heli-arc welded and while breaks are very rare, they have been known to happen. In such an instance special equipment is needed for a repair. Blackburn racks have many copies, and with these you get what you pay for. So far as I am concerned, there is no substitute for the real McCoy.

Steel racks are less expensive and of course heavier than aluminium alloy. but have the advantage of being easy to repair with ordinary welding equipment. This can be significant if you are off in Africa or Asia, but is not a vital concern in Britain or on the Continent. The Karrimor rack has been around for many years and is a proven performer.

When you load your bike, put heavy gear at the bottom of the bags, light bulky stuff like sleeping bags at the top. Give yourself a few shakedown trial runs. The extra weight takes getting used to, and nothing is quite so irritating as rebuilding a luggage rack in the middle of a tour. After the rack bolts and screws have bedded in, use a locking material such as Loctite to hold them firmly in place.

Maps

A compass is not only useful in conjunction with a map, but can itself guide you in the general direction you want to go without strict routing. Sometimes it is fun to dispose of maps altogether. Just go where fancy takes you, and ask directions on the way. You get to meet people, and often they can suggest really interesting routes, scenic attractions, swimming places, and the like. But have a map in reserve.

As well as keeping you on a desired route, maps have the vital function of keeping you off main arterial roads, and out of industrial areas. Petrol station maps are inadequate. Excellent are the Ordnance Survey maps, a catalogue of which is available from the Director-General, Ordance Survey, Romsey Road, Maybush, Southampton SO9 4DH. The maps are obtainable in many bookshops, and from Ordnance Survey agents, a list of which is obtainable from:
(for England and Wales)
Cook, Hammond & Kell Ltd
22-24 Caxton Street, London SW1

(for Scotland)
Thomas Nelson & Sons
18 Dalkeith Road,
Edinburgh EH16 5BS.

Working out a selection of maps that will be useful without being planning, the OS (Ordnance Survey) 1:250,000 (about 4 miles to 1 inch) maps are suitable. For local navigation nothing can beat the OS 1:50,000 maps, which show individual buildings, private roads, churches, ancient ruins, telephone call boxes, and the like. The difficulty is that some 200 of these maps are required to cover Britain, and a selection for a tour can be extraordinarily bulky. The OS do produce a number of tourist maps at 1 mile to 1 inch (about the same as 1:50,000) for popular holiday areas, and these are extremely useful. If you are riding bridlepaths and cross-country, then you will find the OS maps essential. If you are loping along on roads, a practical compromise are the $\frac{1}{2}$ inch scale Bartholomew's maps, also obtainable in bookstores or direct from John Bartholomew, 12 Duncan Street, Edinburgh EH9 1TA.

ON THE WRONG ROAD.

Clothing

Shorts are pretty much universal garb. For touring I like the Madison shorts, which have a terry cloth lining and lots of handy, closeable pockets. Been Bag also do a nice model with a removable, washable liner. Traditional cycling shorts use a chamois liner which is very comfortable, but requires rubbing with a softening cream to prevent hardening after washing.

For shirts and so on, wash-and-wear is probably the most convenient, but I prefer plain cotton next to the skin. The only exception is the remarkable Helly Hansen Lifa thermal underwear. This is made of a polypropylene fabric which wicks moisture away from the skin, and to be fully effective needs to be worn underneath a cotton or wool garment that will absorb and then evaporate wetness. Lifa underwear is very thin and comfortable to wear, and for negligeable weight, probably the warmest thing going in cold weather. When the sun is shining, take off your outer shirt and the underwear goes into reverse gear, as its wicking properties then serve as a kind of air conditioner.

A proper cycling jersey or jacket with big pockets at the rear is a very useful all-around garment. For keeping dry there is nothing to beat a jacket and pants made of Gore-tex (see Accessories). There is a case to be made for carrying along a glad rags outfit for special occasions so that you can mix with the general populace without discord, but I suggest minimising your load wherever possible.

Camping

Membership of The Camping Club of Great Britain and Ireland Ltd 11 Lower Grosvenor Place, London SW1 includes an International Camping Carnet, insurance services, a handbook on camping, and a guide to 1,500 sites in Great Britain and Ireland. Site lists are also available from the British Tourist Authority, 239 Old Marylebone Road, London NW1.

Camping gear
Personal experience and preference are the main basis for scope and choice of camping equipment. Some people need a prepared campsite with loos, showers and even a TV set. Others get by with a bivvy sack and a candle. If you are unfamiliar with living

183

outdoors, do some research before investing heavily in a lot of paraphernalia. One excellent and definitive tome is *Backcountry Bikepacking*, by W. Sanders (try Selpress Books, Dept RB, 35 High Street, Wendover, Bucks HP22 6DU). There are camping equipment stores in most cities and towns, but be selective. A lot of the gear is designed to be carted around in an automobile. Cyclists require light weight and quintessential function. The YHA stores always offer a good range of equipment at keen prices.

1. Sleeping bag. A tent for protection and a fire for cooking can always be improvised with a fair degree of success, but only most skilled can keep warm in a bad bag. If you are freezing and cannot sleep, you will have many long hours to brood on the economic and practical merits of having got something that would do the job in the first place. Get the best bag you can afford. Consider also that good equipment will make late autumn and winter touring a viable possibility.

The best bags, pound for pound, are filled with down. Down has the greatest range (temperatures at which the bag will work), resilience (bag packs small), recovery (gets loft back when unpacked), wicking properties (carries moisture away from body) and more character. Down bags cost from £50 to £100 and the less expensive, lighter (filled with $1\frac{1}{2}$-$2\frac{1}{2}$ pounds of down) models are adequate for warm weather. Down bags have two disadvantages: they can be too warm, and will turn into a useless soggy mess if wet.

One way around these problems is to use a multi-layer pile fabric bag such as the Buffalo (from shops or direct from G & B Trailers, Unit 7, Roman Ridge Road, Sheffield S9 1GB). These are actually a series of different size outer, inner, and liner bags that can be used individually or in combinations to suit a wide range of conditions. Pile fabric is a good deal easier to care for than down, and Buffalo bag outers will withstand all but a continuous heavy rainfall. A down bag cannot perform this trick without a Gore-Tex bivvy shell or plastic sheet. The penalty for pile fabric is weight, about 6 pounds as against about 3 pounds for down, and more bulk.

The least expensive bags contain synthetic fillers such as Dacron 88 and Astrofill. These run about £20, weigh around 6 pounds, and are adequate for warm weather at low altitudes.

Whatever sort of bag you favour, use a sleeping mattress or pad. Fabric air mattresses (avoid the plastic type) are comfortable but bulky. Ensolite pads are thin, but warm and comfortable. Karrimor's Karrimat is a proven performer.

2. Tents come in all shapes, sizes and grades, and are good for protection against bugs, rain, and to ensure privacy. Personally, I see little point in hieing to the Great Outdoors and then clamming up in a dark hole. A sheet of plain plastic can be rigged into a decent shelter with just a little ingenuity and is extremely cheap and light. But Britain tends to be wet at times, and nothing beats a proper tent for comfort.

A good shelter is the Pakit, weighing in at $3\frac{1}{4}$ pounds with minimal bulk, but roomy enough for two people. This is a proper double skin tent with a cotton inner to prevent condensation, and a ripstop nylon outer to keep off the rain. It even has mosquito netting. The Pakit tent is extremely good; other tents with comparable features usually weigh between 6 and 7 pounds (from bike shops and direct from Freewheel, Unit 7, Oxgate Lane, London NW2 7HT). If you have money to burn and would like a read of an interesting, colourful catalogue, check out the 2 pound Pocket Hotel from Early Winters Ltd., 110 Prefontaine Place South, Seattle, Washington 98104 USA.

3. Cooking stove and utensils. The days of scrounging up bits of wood for a cheery campfire are fairly well gone. Open fires are not allowed in many areas because of the risk of a general fire. Also, if enough campers pick over an area there can be ecological damage.

To be sure of a means for cooking, you'll need a stove.

Cheapest are the solid fuel jobs such as the Esbit, which will fold and actually fit into a pocket. The flame on these cannot be controlled, which means no cooking inside a tent, and in windy conditions matters can get impossibly out of hand.

More tractable are gas stoves with throw-away cartridges. These burn clean and pack tidily, but the cartridges have an annoying habit of running out when least expected; for regular use you will need to carry a spare refill.

Liquid fuel stoves variously use paraffin, meths or petrol. Operating a paraffin stove is something of an art. First the burner must be pre-heated with meths. Then you prick the jet with a wire to clear any possible obstruction, open a tap and, if all is well, the emerging paraffin vapourises and ignites. If, as is frequently the case, something is amiss, then the stove goes out and you are enshrouded in a cloud of oily black smoke. Paraffin stoves are one of the few mechanical devices known to possess intelligence. They always wait for the key moment when your back is turned before malfunctioning and erupting in a ball of flame (although there is no particular danger, so long as you are within quick striking distance of the controls).

Meths stoves are simple and reliable. An excellent make is the Swedish Trangia, which comes complete with its own frying pan, two saucepans, handle and kettle. The Trangia is clean and will cope with high winds. The snag is the cost and availability of meths. In fact, with both paraffin and meths you will have to

always plan ahead, and ensure that you have an adequate supply. This can make your life miserable with, for example, a compulsory Saturday morning ride in a torrential downpour to make town before the shops close.

Petrol is more easily available and is relatively cheap, but can blow you to kingdom come. So long as you are careful there should not be a problem, and many experienced tourists swear by the excellent performance and economy of stoves such as the Optimus 99. I think a petrol stove is fine if you are using it all the time and well in the habit of following the necessary precautions. For sometime use, meths or paraffin stoves are better, as their quirks are merely inconvenient and amusing rather than fatal. I abhor a world filled with empty gas cylinders.

For utensils I prefer a steel pot, a steel fry pan that will serve as a lid for the pot (and simultaneously keep its own contents warm) and a steel cup that can also go on the fire. Avoid aluminium utensils, as they are toxic. Skewers can be used on their own, or to form a grill, and are very compact.

4. Food. Dried lightweight foods are extremely convenient and quite palatable. I suggest carrying enough for emergencies only, however, and trying for fresh food along the route. Stock up on supper and breakfast at about 4 o'clock. Mixtures of dried fruit, grains, dried milk, protein powders, yeast, etc., are nourishing, tasty and easy to carry. Many health food shops have a dried fruit and nut mixture called trail food. Always have something more advanced than a candy bar in reserve, just in case you get stuck.

Please

If you camp or otherwise hang out in the countryside, please be tidy. Litter is not only aesthetically vastly unpleasing to other people, but is also very dangerous for animals. Livestock and wild creatures can cut themselves on tin cans and glass, and choke to death on plastic bags. Take away all your rubbish and if you find extra, do yourself a favour and take away as much as you can of that as well. In a very real sense the countryside belongs to everybody. But the people who live and work there are getting increasingly fed up with the sloppy ways of tourists and 'outsiders'. In popular holiday areas like Dartmoor there are farmers and other locals who really hate tourists, and with good cause. As a result, more and more real estate is being closed off. Do your bit to reverse this trend.

Getting there

Other forms of locomotion complement bicycles very well.

Cars

A 10-speed with the wheels off will fit into the boot of many economy cars and certainly on the back seat. For carrying several bikes there are two types of car carrier: rear end and top. Rear end versions hold two bikes and are easy to load. It is hard to get at the boot, however, and the bikes collect a lot of road grit and scratch each other. Top mounted carriers can hold up to six bikes and keep the machines clean, separate and out of harm's way. I particularly like the LP range of car carriers. This includes a Universal Rack which will mount on an already existing car rack.

Airlines

Most of these handle bikes well and some provide special bike boxes. If not using a box it is a good idea to remove the rear derailleur. Loosen the stem and twist the handlebars parallel with the front wheel. You may be asked to remove or reverse the pedals. The airlines are primarily concerned that there should be no sharp projections to cut up other luggage. Bikes sometimes travel for free, and sometimes for a charge.

Railways

Trains are perfect for speeding you to a particular area, or for skipping over uninteresting sections on a long tour. Load the bike into the luggage van yourself, and use elastic straps to hold it firmly in place. British Rail has an impossibly complex method for allowing or disallowing the carriage of bikes on its various trains. You'll just have to ask and be guided accordingly. Final say, whatever the rules, rests with the van guard. Being nice to these people will pay dividends. You can always fox everybody by popping your bike into a bike bag (from some bike shops or by post from Freewheel, Unit 7, Oxgate Lane, London NW2 2HT) or a large box (bike shops again); the bike then goes on as personal luggage, for free.

Special note: do not ever ship a bike unaccompanied by British Rail unles it is over-insured to the point of windfall. One bike shipped to me via British Rail was mangled into a worthless pile of junk – frame, forks and even the cranks bent beyond repair – and the question of compensation did not even arise. Insure, and be prepared for the worst.

The Continent

Cycle touring is a particularly satisfying way of travelling around the Continent, allowing you to explore and savour to a degree not otherwise possible. People are exceptionally friendly and helpful to cyclists. You really 'get into' the country. And for uninteresting or arduous sections of the journey, you simply take a train, boat, or plane. It is often easier and more convenient to pop over to France

AWHEEL IN FRANCE.

or the Benelux countries than to journey to a tour departure point in Britain.

Sources of information on continental touring are abundant. *Adventure Cycling in Europe,* by J. Rakowski (£6.95) tells everything you need to know for 27 countries. *Cycle Touring in Britain and the Rest of Europe,* by P. Knottley (£4.95) is another useful book with many practical tips from a veteran. A wonderful read and an indispensable font of practical information is *Cycling in Europe* by Nicholas Crane, covering the best touring areas in 16 European countries. The above books are obtainable from some cycle shops, or from Selpress Books, Dept RB, 35 High Street, Wendover, Bucks HP22 6DU. Articles on organised bike holidays and specific tours usually appear in the spring issues of the cycling periodicals.

The best single source of current information is the Cyclists' Touring Club. They have information sheets, pre-planned tours, maps, and insurance and travel services which make them unbeatable value for the tourist. They also conduct tours. So do the Youth Hostels Association, and membership includes a number of useful guides and handbooks. The British Cycling Federation does not conduct tours, but does offer insurance services and some 50-odd pre-planned tours.

And then there are always the traditional aids to travel – the Michelin Guides and various sight-seeing tomes. One of the nicest things about cycle touring is that you are not obliged to make a plan and stick to a schedule. Even in crowded holiday areas you should not have much difficulty in finding accommodation if you just veer off the beaten track – which a bike makes easy.

You can write to various national tourist offices and cycling organisations for information:

Albania – Federata Sportive Shgiptare-Bruga, Abdi Toptani 3, Tirana

Austria – Österreichischer Radsport-Verband, Prinz Eugenstrasse 12, 1040 Vienna.

Belgium – Ligue Vélocipédique Belge, 49 avenue du Globe, 1190 Brussels.

Bulgaria – Fédération Bulgare de Cyclisme, Boulevard Tolboukhine 18, Sofia.

Czechoslovakia – Ceskoslovenska Sekce Cyklistiky, Na Porici 12, Prague 1

Denmark – Dansk Cyklist Forbund, Kjield Langes Gade 14, DK-1367 Köbenhavn.

Eire – Irish Cycling Federation, 9 Casement Park, Finlas West, Dublin 11.

France – FUBICY, 7 avenue de la forêt noire, 67000 Strasbourg; Fédération Française de Cyclotourisme, 8 rue Jean-Marie Jégo, 75013 Paris.

Holland – ANWB, Wassenaarseweg 220, 2596 EC Den Haag; Netherlands Cycletouring Union, PO Box 240, 2700AE, Zoetermeer.

ENFB, Postbus 2150, 3440 DD Woerden.

Hungary – Hungarian Cyclists' Federation, Budapest 1146.

Northern Ireland – Northern Ireland Cycling Federation, 9a Great Northern Street, Belfast.

Norway – Norges Cykleforbund, Hauger Skolevei 1, 1351-Rud, Oslo; Syklistenes Landsforening, Majorstuveien 20, Oslo 3.

Poland – Polska Zwiazek Kolarska, 1 Plac Xelaznej, 00136 Warsaw.

Portugal – Federacao Portuguesa de Ciclismo, Rua Barros Queiroz 39-10, Lisbon.

Spain – Federación Espıanola de Ciclismo, Calle Ferraz 16-50, Madrid 8.

Sweden – Cykelfrämjandet, PO Box 2085, 103 12 Stockholm; Svenska Cykelsällskapet, PO Box 6006, 163-03 Spånga

Switzerland – Comité National du Cyclisme, PO Box 930, 1211 Geneva 3.

W. Germany – ADFC, Postfach 101123, D-2800 Bremen.

Africa

Bicycles are a common form of transport for Africans, but their machines are of course extremely stout and sturdy, as often there is simply no road at all. In Morocco, for example, south of the Atlas Mountains and into the Sarah Desert, the roads are dirt tracks resembling streambeds. Most of the locals simply cycle over the desert itself. However, in Northern Morocco the roads are quite

Der Weltradfahrer Willy Schwiegershausen. 1903

negotiable, and there are not many cars. I should imagine that similar varied conditions prevail throughout Africa.

Unless you run a local bike, parts are a problem, and in many areas so is thievery. Cyclists in Africa have been trapped in disease quarantine areas. There is always an ongoing selection of wars, revolutions, famines and other excitements to interest the tourist. In many places life is less than cheap. Still, I would say the prospects for cycle touring are good. I know a fair number of people who have toured in Africa. They all seem to share the characteristics of being self-reliant, energetic and able to get on well with people. *The International Cycling Guide* lists a few African cycling organisations, and the Cyclists' Touring Club has correspondents there. Guided tours are run by Bicycle Africa, 4247 135th Place Southeast Bellevue, Washington 98006 USA.

Asia and the Pacific
Much the same story as for Africa. There are a fair number of people who have cycled out that way, and most of them have a hair-raising story or two to tell. Try the Cyclists' Touring Club for up to date information.

United States
Bicycle touring is a fine way to see the United States. Unless you are extraordinarily perverse you will not find ghetto areas such as New York's Lower East Side or Harlem attractive, and so do not need to worry overmuch about personal safety. Most of your riding will probably be in the countryside where you are relatively safe. But be warned: the level of violence in many urban areas is considerably greater – shockingly so – than most people from civilised countries are prepared for. Americans no longer say in parting, 'Have a nice day', but 'Have a safe day'.

Another problem is that American drivers have not fully caught on to the bicycle boom. The idea that motor vehicles take precedence over any other road-users is much more prevalent than in Britain, and the problem of motorists not really noticing or thinking about cyclists is much worse. Most American cars are large, softly sprung, and do not handle well. Roads are wider and straighter. Accordingly, American drivers have not developed the same level of skill and expertise as their British counterparts, who have to cope with narrow, twisting roads. In terms of road safety, cycling in America is, overall, more dangerous than here.

These nasty things said, I am sure that if you go touring the States, you will have an excellent time. Although it is more dangerous than Great Britain, it is not so unsafe as to be inadvisable. And Americans are warm, open, friendly people.

The most useful organisation for the prospective cycle tourist is Bikecentennial (PO Box 8308, Missoula, Montana 59807). Membership includes discounts on equipment, maps and accommodation, and a raft of literature including the reference book, *The Cyclists' Yellow Pages*. Another organisation providing information and conducting tours in American Youth Hostels, National Campus, Delaplane VA 22025.

Commercial holiday tours abound in America and, as anywhere, can vary enormously in quality. A colourful brochure does not necessarily indicate that you will have a good time. A standard to measure by is: Vermont Bicycle Touring, RD 3, Bristol VT 05443. They have been in business for over ten years and are known to be good. If you write to a firm for holiday information, ask for the names of some people in your area who have been there.

Of petrol station maps, I have found Esso's to be the most detailed, but even these do not meet the needs of the cyclist. The best source is the US Geological Service, who publish contour maps for each state. If you know the exact area you'll be in, they also have local maps down to 1:24,000, a scale which shows walls, footpaths, tiny streams, etc. These are too detailed for anything but the most local use, but are extremely interesting. Many map stores carry the USGS maps, or you can order them direct (for local maps ask first for free state index map):

East of Mississippi	West of Mississippi
US Geologic Survey	US Geologic Survey
Washington District Section	District Section
1200 South Eads Street	Federal Center
Arlington, VA 22202	Denver CO 80225

If you plan a tour which includes travel by rail, be chary of baggage handlers. The make-work contingent has rigged it so that a baggage handler must load the bike aboard the train – badly. Stories of bikes mangled into oblivion by these clods are legion. Insist on personally supervising loading or don't travel by rail at all. Hang the bike from the ceiling or side of the luggage van if possible, and in any case see that it is lashed down securely and that no heavy objects can fall on it.

Take your own bike over with you. British bikes are expensive in America. Japanese bikes in America are good value, but frames tend to be less flexible. And incidentally, if you buy a bike there and remove it from the country within three months you get a refund on purchase tax. Between the price difference and the tax refund, if you sell your bike in the States at the finish of your tour you should at least break even. But a more important reason for taking your own bike is that it allows you to sort it out before going, and not waste vacation time hanging about a bike shop making adjustments and screwing on bits and pieces.

You may wish to purchase Stateside regardless, or need repairs. Bicycle shops litter the landscape and a current list of the better ones can always be found in the magazine *Bicycling*. One item to have for sure is a Citadel or Kryptonite lock. Bike theft in America is very common.

Canada
The Canadian Bicycle Book (D.C. Heath Ltd, Toronto; $3.95) is mostly an introduction to cycling but has some touring information. Organisations are: Canadian Cycling Association, 333 River Road, Vanier, Ottawa K1L 8B9, Ontario, and Ontario Cycling Association, 160 Vanderhoof Avenue, Toronto M4C 4B8.

South America
Check with the Cyclists' Touring Club.

Book Two

1. Maintenance and Repair

Maintenance Program

The subject of maintenance and repair of bicycles is usually clouded with negative feelings. It is regarded as something in the "must be done" category and approached as a chore. Bicycle repair books are fond of saying that any cretin can understand how to fix his machine, or that the book itself has the answer to any problem that might conceivably come up. Both approaches underestimate the reader's intelligence and compartmentalize maintenance and repair, keeping it separate from "riding". This is a basic mistake. The extent to which you get involved in working on your bike should be a direct function of how you ride. One follows the other like night and day. The awareness that riding a bike precipitates usually includes an awareness and interest in the bike itself. How the bike responds is very much a function of maintenance. Ideally, you are going to work on your own bike because you want a together, tight machine under you, i.e., you will do it because *you want to*.

As with all things, you get back in proportion to what you put in. It is essentially a question of fineness. It is the nature of bikes that they are at their best when well-lubricated and carefully adjusted. A sensitivity to this sort of refinement does not happen the instant you mount a bike. Give it time. As you ride you will become increasingly aware of your bike's characteristics. A well set-up bike fits you like a suit of clothes, and you will soon develop an "ear" for the sound of bearings and a "feel" for other parts, such as the brakes. The development of this sensitivity – the result of personal and direct participation – is part of the reason for owning a bike in the first place. Eventually, you will find that increased riding pleasure is not just a reward for doing your own maintenance, the mechanical sensitivity itself becomes part of the riding pleasure.

As I say, this is all something that you should grow into. The idea of having a bike is to have fun. A fair amount of latitude is possible in servicing bikes and you have hopefully chosen a machine suited to your level of interest. So you can minimize or maximize maintenance as per your own inclinations. But bear in mind that most machines, and certainly bicycles, need a certain amount of lubrication and adjustment if they are to function at all. Without it, they rust away, and because the parts are unlubricated and out of kilter, they slowly chew themselves to bits when ridden. I have seen "old dependables" that have been left out in the rain for years and have never seen an oil can or a mechanic. They make it for years – and then snap a chain in the middle of a tour or a brake cable at the start of a long hill. Or eventually the rust destroys them. There is no need for this. A properly maintained bike will easily last a lifetime (one of mine was made in 1920 and has seen plenty of hard service to boot). For reasons of simple economy and safety, if you can't be bothered to do routine maintenance then take your machine to a bike shop for servicing at least twice a year.

An excellent reason for doing your own work is that you are apt to do a quicker and better job than the shop. By and large, bicycle mechanics are not well paid, and are thin on the ground. A familiar sign to be found on bike shop doors is: 'Sorry, no more repairs this month.' For want of what is only a ten-minute repair job, your bike can be out of commission for days or even weeks. And no matter if the shop is good or bad, you cannot expect the mechanic to have a total interest in getting the job done exactly right. Once you learn the drill you will almost always do a better job. Further, if you suffer a breakdown late at night or far out in the sticks, you will be able to deal with it.

Another important reason for doing your own work is that it makes preventative maintenance almost automatic. Preventive maintenance is replacing parts before they wear out and break, usually at an inopportune time and miles from any bike store. If you are paying attention to the various parts of your bike and keeping it in tune this is pretty much going to happen as a matter of course. In turn, breakdowns and repairs will also be fairly well obviated.

I think this approach is the easiest and the most efficient. I have studied every repair manual I could find. Most stress fixing something *after* it has broken. Even though I know how to fix bicycles most of them lose me right away. Either they are filled with long passages of incomprehensible jargon, or they have computer-programming style directions ("If A, go to page 28C; if not A, go to B, page 34, then to page 28 D.") designed to reduce you to a mindless automation.

Here is my approach: each major component system of the bicycle such as brakes, wheels, gears etc. is broken down into four areas:-

How It Works   Routine Adjustments
Replacing Parts   Troubleshooting

The idea is to give you a basic understanding of what is happening – and make you a mechanic! How It Works for each section is required reading. It does no good for you to diddle with this or adjust that if you have no idea of how it works. And if something is broken it is impossible for you to fix unless you know how it works in the first place.

It will help a lot if as you read, you look at and feel the corresponding parts of your bike.

I don't cover everything. One wheel is pretty much the same as another. I have tried to include representative types of equipment currently in use but there are bound to be exceptions. If this happens to you try to find the item in this book which most closely resembles the part you are servicing or fixing. Pay particular attention to *function* and then analyze your own part the same way. This should get you through almost anything.

There are also some tasks which are just not worth doing. Getting into the innards of a coaster brake multi-speed hub is one of these. It takes a long, long time and isn't fun at all. Some people may resent these omissions. They want to do everything for themselves. Well, the point of diminishing returns is reached with attempts to service coaster brake 3-speed hubs. Even most bike shops refuse to overhaul these units and simply replace them – it's actually cheaper this way. If you insist on doing this sort of work detailed instructions are available from the bicycle manufacturer or from the hub manufacturer.

Tools

You can get by with amazingly little in the way of tools. However, for some kinds of work there are a few you will just have to get. Also, what you need depends on what kind of bike you have.

Before going into particulars a word on tool quality: do yourself a favour and buy good ones. Cheap shops, supermarkets, and even hardware stores carry cheap bargains like 10p screwdrivers and 40p spanners. These are a false economy, for they are made of inferior metals that will break or bend under stress, or they are made badly enough so that they don't even work. You do not need many tools, and the investment is well worth it in the long run.

For both 3- and 10-speed bikes:
Hardware shop
8-in or 6-in adjustable end spanner. Pliers. Hammer.

¼-in. tip, 4 – 5-in shank screwdriver.
⅛-in. tip, 2 – 3-in shank screwdriver.
Wire clippers. 6-in file, mill bastard.
Bike shop
Mafac tool kit – contains tyre irons, spanners, other gear, including tyre patching kit.
All-purpose tool like Raleigh give-away.
Thin hub spanners, 13 x 14 and 15 x 16. Spoke key.
Pedal wingnut spanner (for pedals with outside dustcap only).
Tyre gauge.
Tyre patch kit.
10-speed bikes:
Bike shop
chain rivet remover; freewheel remover, there are two basic types:

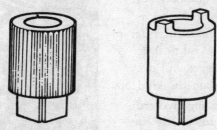

Look at your freewheel and see if it is splined or not on the interior to see what kind you need.
Set of metric Allen keys.
If you have a Campagnolo derailleur, a special Campagnolo combination Allen and socket spanner.
If you have cotterless cranks you will need a special crank-removing tool as per your brand of crank.
Other useful tools:
set of spanners, vice-grip pliers, channel lock pliers, small portable vice.

As you can see from studying the list, many of the tools are for specialized jobs so you do not have to acquire them all at once. Absolutely essential, and especially for trips, is the Mafac toolkit, a screwdriver, and an all-purpose combination tool like the Raleigh give-away.

If you have difficulty obtaining tools from local shops, or would just like to read over an amusing tool catalogue, write to The Third

Hand, 3945 High St, Eugene, ORE 97405, USA.

You will need some means of holding the bike steady. One method is to simply turn the bike upside down. With downswept handlebars use a narrow cardboard or wood box with slots cut in the side to support the handlebars and keep the brake cables from being bent against the ground. A nail driven into a doorjamb with a rope to hang the bike by will also suffice. Best of all is a proper work stand. These are rather expensive (£30 and up) but perhaps you could share one with friends.

Lubrication

This is a general discussion of lubrication. For details look under the part in question, e.g. brakes, hubs, gears, etc.

There are a number of different types and forms of lubricants. Each has advantages and draw backs depending on the kind of machinery and riding involved. Oil is the old standby. Be sure to use a good grade such as motorist's SAE 30, or Sturmey-Archer cycle oil. Do not use ordinary household oils.

Grease is used for bearings. Ordinary grease from a motorist's shop will work well enough. Lithium greases such as Filtrate and Cycle Pro are less likely to be washed away by water. Also good in this respect is Bardahl Multi-purpose grease. Best of all is waterproof grease, such as Phil Wood, Andrew Hague or LPS 100.

For the ultimate in slipperiness add a small quantity of Moly-Slip to your grease and oil. This contains molybedenum disulfide, a sub-microscopic substance that fills in microscopic irregularities on metal surfaces, reducing friction and wear.

Generally, a white lithium grease such as Filtrate or Sta-Lube will run more freely than a water-resistant grease such as Phil

Wood or LPS-100. You'll find that many racing people favor the lighter greases, and often brew up exotic mixtures of their own design. Remember however that these people usually think little of stripping down and re-lubing a bike for nearly every race. The tourist, commuter and recreational rider will usually prefer the longer interval between services provided by the stiffer water-proof greases.

Your bicycle has upwards of 200 ball bearings held in place by cups and cones:

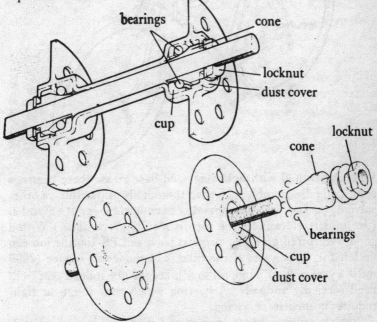

The cone remains stationary while the cup, and whatever part is attached to it – in this example it would be a wheel – rides on the ball bearings and spins around. The distance betwee the cone and the cup is adjustable and must not be too tight or too loose. Sometimes the ball bearings are held in a clip called a *race:*

Typically, this is positioned so that the balls are against the cup. You will find bearings at the headset, bottom bracket, wheels, and pedals:

When lubricated with lightweight oil-base grease these bearings are usually disassembled, cleaned thoroughly in paraffin or other solvent, packed with grease and reassembled, every six months. (See under relevant section for disassembly technique.) With a good waterproof grease or product such as LPS-100 the job can be left for three years if the bike is in moderate service (2000 miles a year or less). High mileage bikes (5000+ miles a year) will need servicing annually. A bearing which runs rough or tight requires immediate servicing.

Some bearings are both greased and oiled, and in particular, 2- and 3-speed hubs and hubs on ultra-fancy racing bikes. You can tell these by the fact that the hub has a small oil cap or clip:

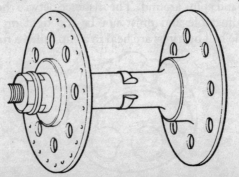

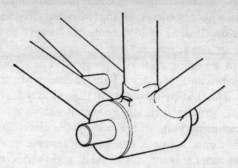

These need lubricating once a month: multi-speed internal gear hubs a tablespoonful, regular hubs about ½ teaspoonful, and coaster brake hubs 2 tablespoonfuls. Some bottom brackets are set up to use fluid as well as grease. A teaspoonful once a month. Use fluid wherever you find oil caps or clips. Too little is better than too much. If fluid leaks out of the sides of the bearings and dribbles all over your crankset or wheels, you are using too much.

I prefer the use of a dry lubricant for the chain, freewheel, derailleur, brake pivots, cables, and any other parts which do not use grease:

Dry lubricants usually come in spray form and contain an exotic and sometimes secret blend of ingredients. Often included is molybdenum disulfide. Dry lubricants can be used as a substitute for oil. They are not as long lasting, but ease of application makes more frequent servicing relatively painless. The important thing is that the lubricants are dry. The trouble with oil is that it attracts dirt which then mixes with the oil and forms a gooey abrasive mess, greatly increasing mechanical wear. Everything gets dirty, including you. In the case of the chain, for example, this means that once a month you have to remove it, soak it clean in paraffin or other solvent, dry it, oil it, and then reinstall it. It's time consuming and messy. If you use a dry lubricant you need do this job only once every two or three months. You must lubricate more often – bi-weekly in normal service, weekly in hard service – but with a spray this job takes only a few seconds. The same rationale applies for the freewheel and derailleur. The spray is particularly useful for the brake pivots and all cables. Oil has a tendency to leak out onto the brake levers and handlebars, and brake shoes. Once a month is sufficient.

The dry lubricant known to me through experience is LPS, which comes in three grades of thickness (LPS-1, -2, -3) and also as a paste which can be used as a grease for cables and bearings. Only LPS-1 is truly dry to the touch. LPS-100 grease is very long lasting and highly resistant to fling (that is, leaving the scene of the job) and water, but is quite stiff.

Note: Dry lubricants will usually dissolve ordinary greases and oils. Do not mix the two types!

Another dry lubricant is paraffin wax, available in grocery stores. It is extremely good for prolonging chain life. Clean your chain in the conventional manner with paraffin or other solvent. Melt the paraffin in a coffee can over the stove. Dump the chain in and then hang so that drippings fall back into can. Use oil or spray for the brake pivot points, freewheel and derailleur. The paraffin will not work well on these parts because it cools and hardens too quickly on contact with the metal to penetrate effectively. It is excellent for brake cables, however. Just run the cable through a block of paraffin a few times until it is well impregnated. Save and re-use the old paraffin. Paraffin, like spray, does not attract dirt.

Note: New bikes fresh from the dealer and bikes that have been standing around for a long time may be dry as a bone. *Oil evaporates!* Be sure to lubricate such machines before using.

General Words

There are a number of things to keep in mind when servicing bikes:

1. Do not use a great deal of force when assembling or disassembling parts. Bicycle components are frequently made of alloys for light weight. These are not as strong as steel and it is not hard to strip threads or otherwise damage parts. Always be sure that things fit. Be careful and delicate. Snug down bolts, nuts, and screws firmly, not with all your might.

2. Most parts tighten *clockwise* and come apart turning *counterclockwise*. This is called a right-hand thread. A left-hand thread tightens *counterclockwise* and loosens *clockwise*. Left-hand threads are not used often.

3. When fitting together threaded parts hold them as perfectly aligned as you can, and turn one backwards (loosen) until you hear and feel a slight click. Then reverse and tighten. If this is new to you, practice on a nut and bolt until you have the feel of it perfectly.

4. If you get stuck with a rust-frozen bolt or nut, soak it in penetrating oil, give it a few taps to help the oil work in, and then try to undo it again with a tool that fits exactly. If this fails try a cold chisel and hammer:

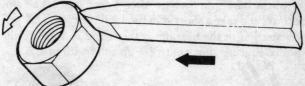

Go at this carefully since if you slip you may gouge a chunk out of your bicycle. If this fails, hacksaw or file the nut or bolt off. How did it get this rusty in the first place?

5. When assembling or disassembling try to be neat and organized. Lay parts out in the order which they came apart or go together. Put tiny parts in boxes or jars.

6. There are a number of little nuts and bolts on your bike for cable clamps, racks, brake lever mounts, gear shift lever mounts, and the like. These tend to get loose and need tightening about once a month.

7. The left side of the bike is as if you and the bike both point forward.

8. Solvents: paraffin and paint thinner are good. Gasoline is very dangerous. Another way of cleaning greasy parts is with a degreaser such as Spray Away or Gunk.

9. Finish: a good quality auto paste wax will preserve your paint job and make it easier to keep clean. Wipe the bike down once a week and after major journeys. Do not wax wheel rims where brake shoes contact.

10. Wire cable is used for brake and gear controls. If you need to trim a new cable to size, do so with wire snips for a clean cut. Pliers will fray the cable end so that it will not pass through the cable housing. After snipping, solder the cable end to prevent fraying, or alternatively, dip it in epoxy glue. File away excess solder or glue.

Ordinary cables and housings work very well but when replacement time comes consider using braided cables. These are extra strong cables running through a housing lined with teflon, perform excellently, and do not require lubrication.

11. Sealed bearing hubs, bottom brackets, and pedals are not covered in this manual. When servicing or repair is needed, usually special tools and techniques are required for each particular make of unit, and often the work is done by the factory.

Never put a bike into storage after a wet ride. Wait until the weather clears and take a short spin for a mile or two. This will force out any water left in the bearings, cables, and so forth. Otherwise even a 'sealed bearing' unit can freeze up solid with rust.

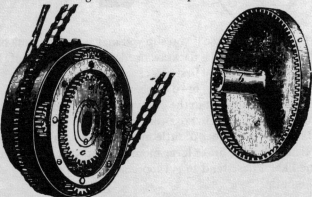

2. Brakes

Contents

General

Bicycle brakes come in three basic types: hub coaster pedal operated, disc hand operated, and caliper hand operated. The coaster is inferior on several counts. Under conditions requiring a quick stop it tends to lock the rear wheel, causing the bike to skid rather than slow down.* It has poor heat dissipating qualities and can burn out on a long downhill. It is difficult to service. It is for the rear wheel only, thus cutting braking efficiency below 50%, since it is at the front wheel that the greatest braking power can be attained. In fact, on dry pavement it is difficult if not impossible to lock up a front wheel. This is because braking throws the weight forward, increasing traction. If you have a bike which has only a coaster brake equip it with a caliper brake for the front wheel. Only children without the necessary strength to operate caliper brakes should have a coaster brake, and they should not ride in any situation requiring quick stops or sustained braking.

If something goes wrong with your coaster brake, simply remove the entire rear wheel and take it to a bicycle shop for overhaul or replacement. It is complicated to fix, and infinitely more trouble than it is worth.

Disc brakes are heavy, but offer good stopping power under both wet and dry conditions. They are a logical choice for tandems and tricycles, but are a bit finicky to adjust and service.

Caliper brakes offer a good balance between weight and stopping power. Modern brake shoes give an at least reasonable performance under wet conditions and very good performance under dry conditions. They are relatively simple to service.

Caliper and disc systems are fairly well identical in operation and principle. All of the operations on brake levers and cables described in the section on caliper brakes below apply equally well to disc brakes. I therefore carry caliper brakes right the way through the chapter, with a section on adjustment and maintenance of disc brakes at the end.

---

* A screeching tire-smoking stop is not the quickest. When the wheel is locked, the rubber literally melts into the road, providing a *liquid* point of contact between the tire and road surface, and greatly increasing stopping distance. The quickest stops are done by slowing the wheel to the point just before locking. Skidding also means a loss of directional control and often results in a fall.

How Caliper Brakes Work

Caliper brake systems all work on the same basic principle. There is a hollow, flexible tube called a cable housing between the brake lever mount and the cable hanger:

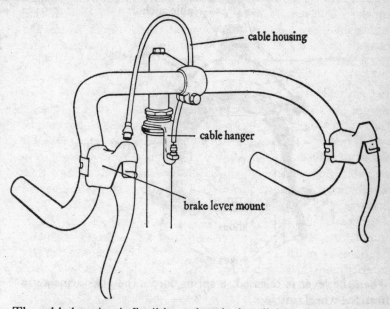

cable housing

cable hanger

brake lever mount

The cable housing is flexible so that the handlebars can turn back and forth. Through the cable housing passes a cable which is attached to the brake lever at one end:

And to the brake mechanism at the other. This is in turn attached to the bicycle frame and functions like a pair of complicated ice tongs with double pivot points. When the brake lever is operated, it pulls the cable through the cable housing and pinches together the arms (called *yokes*) of the brake mechanism, causing the two rubber brake shoes attached to the yokes to press against the wheel rim and stop the wheel:

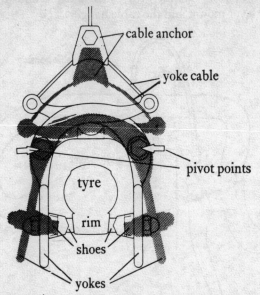

When the lever is released, a spring forces the yoke arms away from the wheel rim:

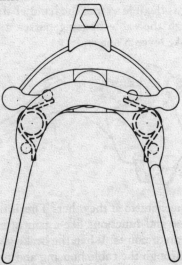

This in turn returns the brake lever to an off position, and keeps continuous tension on the entire brake assembly. This is the basic center-pull mechanism.

The side-pull brake uses only one pivot point, with the cable housing attached directly to one yoke, and the cable to the other. The effect is the same:

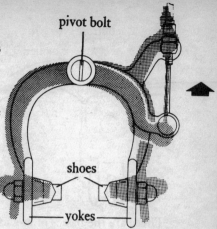

All caliper brake systems have an adjusting screw (called a *barrel adjustor*) for changing the relationship of the cable housing length of the brake cable. On the side-pull brake this is almost always found on the yoke to which the cable housing is attached (A), while on the center-pull brake it is usually at the brake lever (B) or the cable hanger (C):

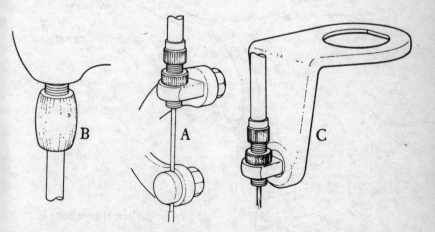

Properly adjusted brake shoes are so close to the wheel rim that the tire will not slide between them when removing the wheel. Accordingly, better grade systems have a means for creating a little extra slack in the brake cable. This us usually a small button which allows the brake lever to open more:

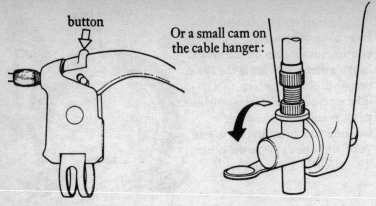

button

Or a small cam on
the cable hanger:

These are the basics of any caliper brake system: a brake lever, a brake cable and housing with adjustor barrel, a cable hanger for center-pull systems, and the brake mechanism, including yokes, springs, and brake shoes. Better systems include either a button or cam to provide extra slack in the cable when removing the wheel or servicing the brakes:

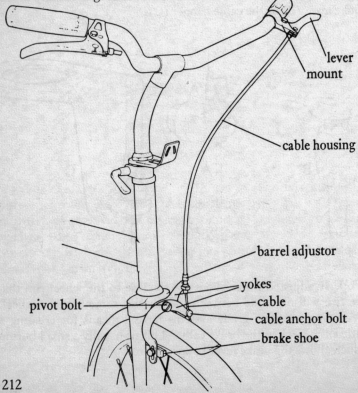

lever
mount

cable housing

barrel adjustor

yokes

cable

pivot bolt

cable anchor bolt

brake shoe

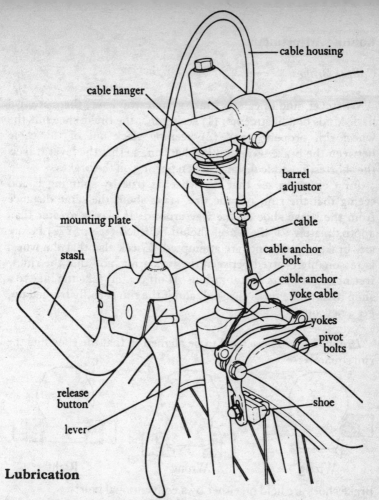

cable housing

cable hanger

barrel adjustor

mounting plate

cable

stash

cable anchor bolt

cable anchor

yoke cable

yokes

pivot bolts

release button

shoe

lever

Lubrication

Try to avoid the use of oil. At the brake levers it works out over everything and gets your hands dirty every time you ride. At the brake mechanism it dribbles down to the brake shoes, cutting braking power. A better product is a spray such as LPS-1, which displaces water and does not attract dirt. Use the little plastic nozzle which comes with the can for pin-point accuracy, and spray pivot bolts, all exposed cable (use a piece of paper or cardboard as a backstop to prevent the spray from going all over the bike), yoke cable anchor points, brake lever pivots, and inside the cable housings. Machines used once or twice a week need lubrication every two months, those in daily use, monthly. More often on tours.

Routine Adjustments

Caliper Brakes

Whatever kind of caliper brake system you have, there are two basic kinds of adjustments: (1) seeing that the brake shoe hits the wheel rim properly, and (2) keeping slack out of the cable between the brake lever and mechanism, so that the lever travels the shortest possible distance when putting on the brakes.

First check to see that the wheel is true by spinning it and seeing that the rim, not the tire, stays about the same distance from the brake shoe all the way around. If play is greater than approximately ⅛" the wheel should be trued (see p. 277) before any brake adjustments are attempted. Check also that the wheel is reasonably centred between the fork arms, and that the rim is free of major dents and abrasions. If off center, take the bike to a shop to have the forks checked, and if the rim is badly banged up, get a new one.

Brake shoes: These need to be aligned so that the shoe hits the rim squarely:

| Wrong | Wrong | Right |

Brake shoes are held on either by a conventional bolt:

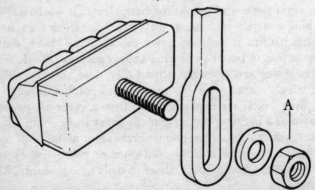

A

or an eyebolt:

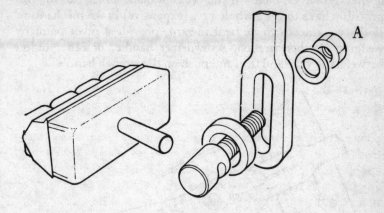

In either case, loosen nut *A*, adjust brake shoes to meet rim, and tighten. One method is to loosen nut *A* just a little bit and gently tap the shoe into the proper position with the wrench handle. With conventional bolts you'll find that the brake shoe twists to the right when you tighten the nut back down. A good trick is to set it slightly counter-clockwise so that the final tightening brings it perfectly into position. Do not use too much force. Brake bolt screws strip easily.

Eyebolt-type shoes are easy to adjust so that the face of the shoe is flush with the rim. Achieving this effect with a conventional-bolt brake shoe sometimes requires bending the yoke. Remove the brake shoe altogether and fit an adjustable end wrench snugly over the end of the yoke:

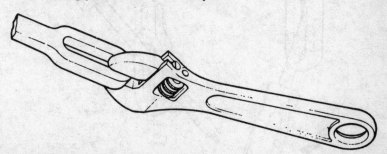

If the yoke needs to be bent outward, simply pull on the handle of the wrench. *Go Slow* – if you break or mangle the yoke you will probably have to get a whole new (expensive) brake mechanism. If the yoke needs to be bent inward, provide a pivot point by wedging another wrench, screwdriver handle, or other object between the yoke and tire, and push on the wrench handle:

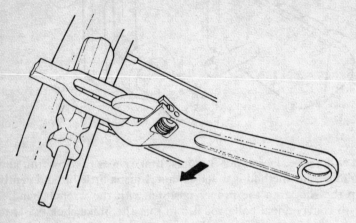

If you don't have a suitable wrench, use a screwdriver:

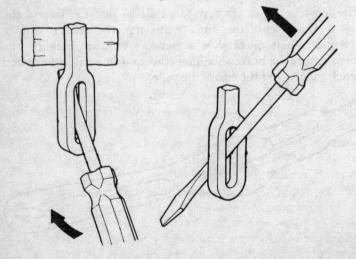

Do not be especially keen to start bending things. New brake shoes, for example, will frequently wear into correct alignment with a few days' use:

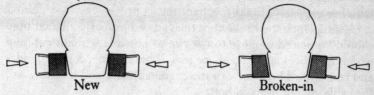

New   Broken-in

Use soft rubber racing-type brake shoes (usually colored red) rather than the hard rubber (usually black) kind typically supplied with side-pull brakes. The soft shoes wear out faster but work a lot better and cost only a few cents each. You can buy the shoes separately from the metal holder and bolt. The holder is open at one end. Slide the old shoe out and the new one in:

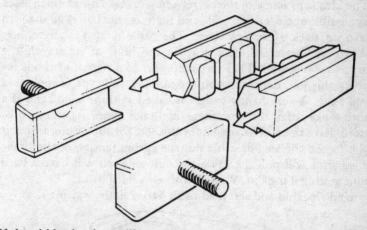

If the old brake shoe will not come out easily and you do not have access to a vise to securely grip the holder while you tap out the shoe, forget it and buy a new set of holders and shoes (about 50 cents each). Be sure to install the new units so that the closed end faces forward (the direction the bike goes), or else the shoes will slide out when the brakes are applied.

Some people consider it good practice to toe-in the fronts of the brake shoes. This is done by twisting the yoke with a wrench or screwdriver so that the front of the shoe hits the rim $1/32''$ before the back. Under hard braking however, the whole shoe is flush to the rim. If you have squealing brakes this may cure the problem. With synthetic blocks such as Kool-Stop and Mathauser a slightly greater amount of toe-in may be required, especially with less expensive brake mechanisms.

Cables: Once the brake shoes have been properly aligned they should be placed as close to the rim as possible without rubbing when the wheel is spun, ⅛″ or less. This is done, for both side- and center-pull brakes, with the barrel adjustor and locknut, and the cable anchor nut and bolt:

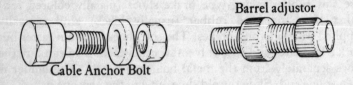

Barrel adjustor

Cable Anchor Bolt

The idea is to screw in the barrel adjustor, take up as much slack as possible at the anchor nut, and then use the barrel adjustor to take up slack every few days. The cable is always stretching. When the barrel adjustor reaches the limit of its travel, the process is repeated. There are a number of different methods for doing this job, depending on the number and type of tools that you have. A very handy gadget is called a "third hand" and is a spring-like affair for compressing brake shoes together. Bike stores have them. The reason for this tool, or substitute, is that if you loosen the anchor cable nut the spring tension of the brake yoke arms will pull the cable through and you will have a hard time getting it back in. With or without a third hand:

Undo locknut and screw adjustor barrel all the way in:

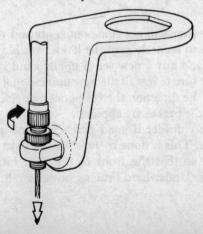

Check and see that the brake release button or cam is set for normal operation (not on all bikes). If you have a third hand, mount it. Or use a C-clamp. Or even string. If you have none of these things, squeeze the brake yoke arms together with your hand. With the other hand, pull the cable at the brake mechanism out so the brake lever is fully home, as it would be if the brakes were not on. Make sure the cable housing has not caught on the outside lip of the barrel adjustor. Now look at the amount of slack in the cable. For center-pull brakes this is the distance between the yoke cable and the cable anchor A:

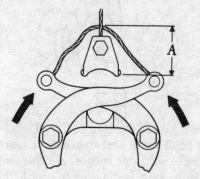

and for side-pull systems, it is the amount of new cable protruding beneath the yoke A:

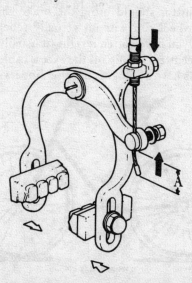

Estimate the amount of slack to be taken up with a ruler, tool handle, or finger. Disengage the yoke cable from the cable anchor (center-pulls) or the cable end from the yoke (side-pulls). Eliminate this step if you have a third hand or similar device. Use two wrenches to slacken the cable anchor nut. Avoid twisting the cable. Pass the cable the required distance through the hole in the cable anchor bolt:

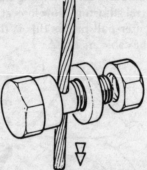

If it is sticky use a pair of pliers to pull it. Tighten cable anchor nut. If no third hand, hold brake yoke arms together again and slip yoke cable back over cable anchor, or cable back into yoke. If you have the feature, now is the time to use the brake button or cam to give you that little bit of extra slack you need. Release the second or third hand, as the case may be. Only one or two turns of the barrel adjustor should bring the brake shoes as close as possible to the wheel rim without actually touching when the wheel is spun. If you have gotten it right (it usually takes a couple of tries), use wirecutters to snip off the excess cable for a neat job. Frayed cable ends have a habit of snagging fingers and clothing.

SANGER RACER.   **AAP**

Pivot bolt adjustment
Side-pull brakes:

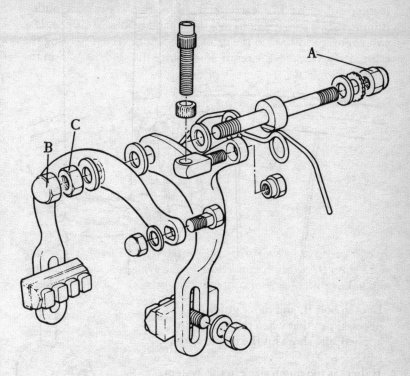

Make sure nut A is tight. Turn in locknut C one half turn while holding acorn adjusting nut B still with another wrench. Turn both B and C in flush against brake yoke arm. Back B off one half turn, hold in place and lock locknut C against it.
Center-pull brakes: see p. 235.

Roller Lever Brakes

As with caliper brakes, roller lever brake shoes must be aligned to hit the inside of the rim squarely. This is done by means of a metal guide (A) clamped to the fork blade or chainstay:

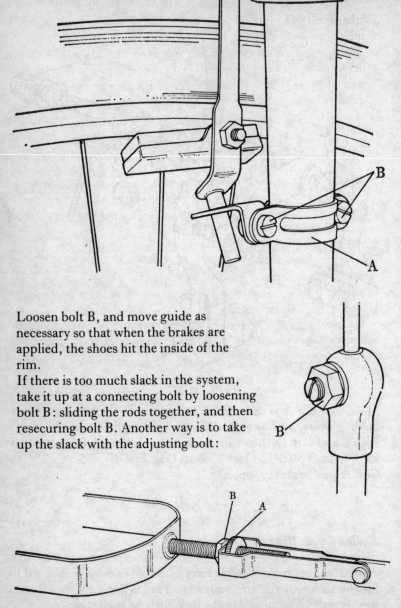

Loosen bolt B, and move guide as
necessary so that when the brakes are
applied, the shoes hit the inside of the
rim.

If there is too much slack in the system,
take it up at a connecting bolt by loosening
bolt B: sliding the rods together, and then
resecuring bolt B. Another way is to take
up the slack with the adjusting bolt:

by first undoing locknut B, and then tightening nut A.

Replacing and Disassembling Parts

Brake shoes: See p. 217.
Cables:

The frequency with which you will need to replace brake (and other) cables depends on how you use your bike. Machines consistently left out in the rain, or used hard every day, are going to need them sooner than well-cared-for or average-use machines. There is no hard and fast rule. Any obvious defect, such as a frayed cable:

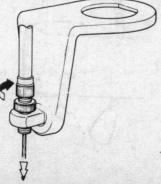

is immediate grounds for replacement, as is stickiness in the motion of the cable through the cable housing (see Trouble-shooting). It is generally good practice to replace both brake cables at the same time. They are cheap, and if one has run its course, it is likely that the other has too. The inconvenience of a broken cable is not worth the gain of a month's extra use. If you have purchased a used bike I would replace cables all around unless you know they are relatively new and obviously in good condition. Good condition means they are clean, have no kinks or frayed spots, and pass easily through the cable housings.

Unless you can specify the brand and model of brake, take your bike or old cable to the store. Cables come in different shapes, lengths, and thicknesses. It is very irritating to discover in the middle of things that you have the wrong part.

I recommend using the left hand brake lever for the rear brake. This follows standard practice, and since the rear brake is generally more favored for routine braking, leaves the right hand free for cross-traffic signals.

For any caliper brake system, first screw home the barrel adjustor:

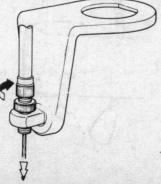

Center-pulls: push together brake yoke arms (use third hand or similar device if available) and slip yoke cable off brake anchor. Undo cable anchor bolt and nut and slide same off cable:

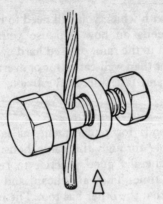

Side-pulls: One kind of side-pull brake uses a cable anchor bolt and nut at the yoke. Slack it off and pull out the cable the same way as with a center-pull. Another type of unit has a ball or nipple on the cable which slips into a slot on the brake yoke arm. You will have to replace both the cable and cable housing as a single unit. Compress brake yoke arms and release ball or nipple from yoke:

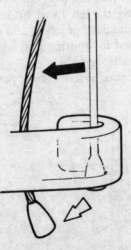

Center-pulls and Side-pulls:
Front brakes: Slide the cable housing off the cable. If yours has ferrules:

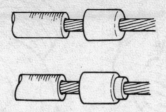

keep track of where they go.

Rear brakes: Leave the housing attached to the frame and pull the cable out of the housing. If you have a one-piece cable and housing (nipples on both ends of the cable), loosen the clamps on the frame and draw the unit through. Examine the cable housings to see if they need replacement. Are they kinked or broken?

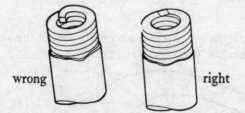

Are the ends free from burrs?

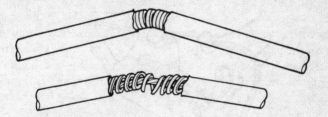

wrong   right

You can eliminate a burr by
(1) snipping off the cable housing end with a strong pair of wire cutters (pliers are not good enough);
(2) clamping the cable housing end in a vise and filing it down; or
(3) by using a tool called a taper ream, which you insert in the cable housing end and twist until the burr has gone.

If you use wire cutters be sure to get the cutting edges in between the coils of the housing or else you will mash the ends flat:

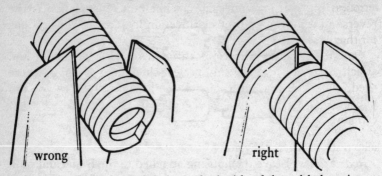

wrong   right

Use this opportunity to lubricate the inside of the cable housing.

Fully depress the brake lever. Side-pulls: move cable until it is aligned with the slot on the side of the brake handle and then slide it out sideways:

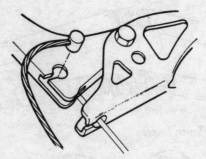

On center-pulls the process is exactly the same, or the slot may be parallel to the cable, as on the Weinmann:

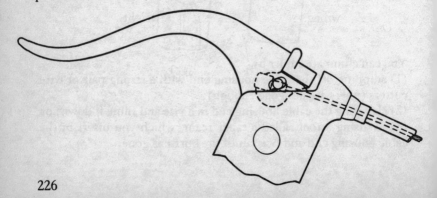

When installing the new cable, save any cutting for last. Cutting invariably frays the cable end and makes it hard to slide through the housing and cable anchor bolt. Installation is the reverse of removal, and for clarification look at the illustrations for that section.

One-nipple cable: Slip cable through brake lever mount and attach to brake lever. Front brakes: including ferrules where used, slip housing on cable. Rear brakes: slide cable into housing. Twist the cable or housing as you do this to avoid catching the cable:

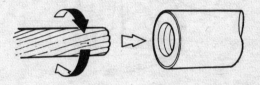

and be sure to do it in the right direction or the cable will unravel. Push free cable end through cable hanger (center-pulls), or through barrel adjustor at yoke (side-pulls), and then through cable anchor bolt hole. To adjust see pp. 218-20.

Two-nipple cable (one-piece housing and cable): Attach to brake lever. For rear brakes, slide housing through clamps on frame. Front and rear, pass cable end through barrel adjustor on brake yoke arm and fix to opposite brake yoke arm by slipping ball or nipple into slot. Take up slack with barrel adjustor. Rear brakes, tighten housing clamps on frame, and take care that they are set so clothing will not snag on the screws when riding.

Handles

   Outside bolt type:

227

To adjust, slacken A and move. To remove, take off bolt B. May have to be slid off handlebar in which case grip must be removed. If your brake lever mount has a slot in the bottom:

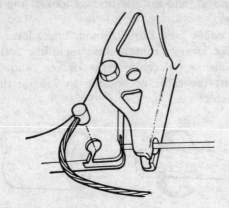

or if the cable ball or nipple will pass through the hole in the mount, then create enough slack by screwing home the barrel adjustor and clamping together the brake-shoes, and disconnect the cable from the lever. If this is not possible, then disconnect the cable anchor bolt at the brake mechanism and take the cable out altogether.

Inside bolt type:

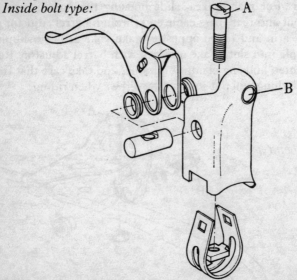

Disconnect yoke cable from cable anchor. Fully depress brake lever and use screwdriver or socket wrench on bolt A. If you are replacing the brake lever, you may need to take out the brake cable (see p. 223). On some systems such as Weinmann the cable end will pass directly through the hole B in the brake mount.

Brake Mechanism

First disconnect brake cable.
  Side-pull systems:

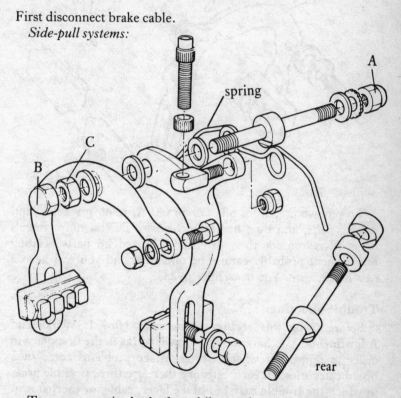

To remove entire brake from bike, undo nut A. Disassembly should be done only to replace a specific part if it won't work. Start with brake mechanism on bike. Undo the brake spring by prising it off with a screwdriver. Careful of fingers. Separate nut B from nut C, and take them both off the pivot bolt. Then the rest of the stuff. Keep the parts lined up in the order which you remove them. If you are replacing the pivot bolt, undo nut A and take off bolt. Reverse procedure for re-assembly.

Centre-pull systems:

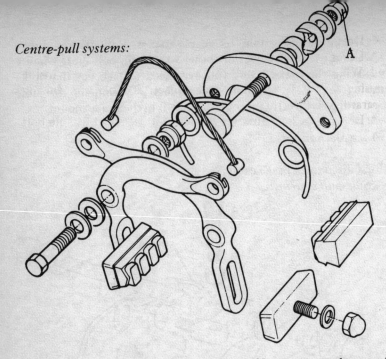

A

To remove unit from bike, undo nut A, remove washers and seating pads, and then brake mechanism. Disassembly: there's no good reason for this. Any badly busted up parts needing replacement probably cannot be obtained, and you will need a new machanism. You insist? See p. 235.

Trouble-shooting

Before using this section please read How It Works and Adjustments. You have to know how it works in the first place in order to figure out what's wrong. Brake problems come in 3 broad categories. In each category there are three possible areas in which the trouble may be: brake lever, cable, or mechanism. The first thing is to find in which of these the problem originates, and this is done by isolating and actuating each unit separately.

Category 1 – No or very weak brakes.
  * Is rim oily?
  * Are shoes hitting rim?
  * Will brake mechanism compress when you squeeze it with your hand? If no, go to Category 3, sticky brakes, below. If yes,

* Does lever move freely? Yes? Broken cable. Replace.
* Lever will not move. Disconnect cable at brake mechanism end. Will cable housing slide off cable? No? Cable is frozen inside housing. Get if off somehow and replace. If cable and housing separate easily then,
* Lever is frozen. First see if your unit has an adjustable bolt (B)

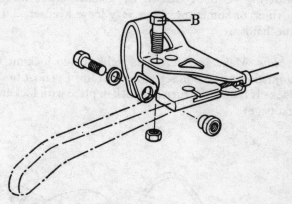

for the lever: and if so give it a try. No? A major bash may have pinched together the sides of the brake lever mount housing. Examine it carefully and bend out dented parts with a big screwdriver:

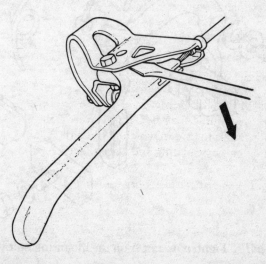

Or the lever itself may be bent. Bend it back. If the bend has been severe replace the lever or unit. Metal which has been bent a lot may look perfectly OK but it is fatigued and weak, and may well snap under pressure of an emergency stop.

Category 2 – Brakes work, but unevenly or make noises.

* Juddering. Can be caused by a loose brake mechanism, uneven rims, or sometimes by a very loose headset. To fix the brake mechanism:

Side-pulls. Make sure nut A is tight. Undo locknut C from acorn adjusting nut B and screw both in flush against brake yoke arm. Back off B one half turn and lock in place with locknut C. (see next page)

Centre-pull

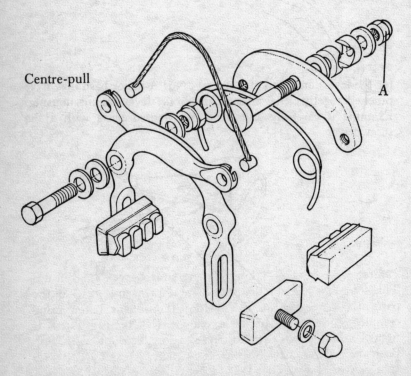

A

Centre-pulls. Tighten up nut A on the mounting bolt.

* Squealing. Brake shoes may be old and hard. Sometimes rubber from shoes has streaked rim. Clean with a strong solvent like benzene or cleaning fluid in a WELL VENTILATED AREA. Squealing brakes can sometimes be fixed by toeing in the brake shoes (see p. 217), and sometimes this problem just can't be eliminated.

Category 3 – Sticky or dragging brakes.

This is the most common problem. First determine if it is the lever, cable, or mechanism which is at fault.

* If it is the lever, see Frozen lever (p. 231).
* If it is the cable, replace it (pp. 223-227).
* Brake mechanism.

Side-pulls:

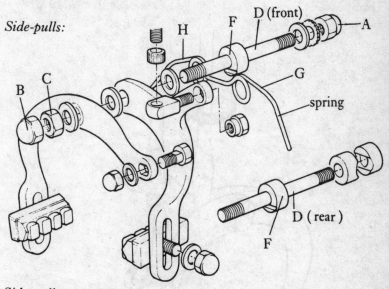

Side-pull

First make sure everything is there and properly hooked up. This sounds simple-minded, but there is a reason for each of the parts and the mechanism won't work without them. Is the spring complete and attached to both yoke arms? Make sure nut A is tight. Undo locknut C from acorn adjusting nut B and screw both flush against yoke arm. Back B off one half turn and lock it with C. Check that pivot bolt D is straight and replace if necessary. Lubricate.

If one shoe drags against rim: loosen the mounting nut A, hold brake yokes in correct position, and re-tighten. No soap? Examine brake seating pad F. If it has a slot for the spring you will have to try bending the spring. There are two ways to do this. One is to prise the spring arm off the brake yoke which is dragging and bend it outward using pliers or similar tool. The second is to take a big screwdriver and poise it against G or H, whichever is *opposite* the dragging shoe, and give it a sharp bash with a hammer. This second method is quicker, but of course a little riskier.

Still no soap? Check to see that the brake yokes are not rubbing against each other. If so, bend them apart with a screwdriver:

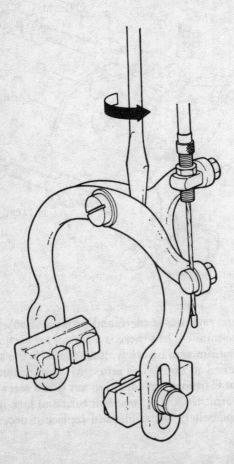

or slide in a piece of fine emery cloth (like sandpaper) and file it down.

If this is not the problem and you have tried everything else a complete disassembly (see p. 229) is necessary. Study each part to see if it obviously needs replacing (like a washer bent out of shape). It may be that the yoke cannot rotate on the pivot bolt. File down and polish the bolt, or enlarge the holes in the yokes (with a taper ream, or emery cloth wrapped around a nail). If none of these things work get a new brake mechanism.

Centre-pulls:

Centre-Pull

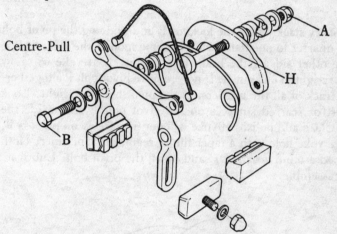

Is cable adjusted correctly?

Are all parts there? Is spring intact and properly mounted?

Is mounting nut A tight?

If one shoe is dragging against rim, slack off A, center brake mechanism, and re-tighten A.

If both shoes stick try lubricating the pivot bolts B while wiggling the yokes back and forth. No? You will have to get into the pivot bolts.

First disconnect the spring. Study the bolts to see if they are type 1, where the pivot bolt screws into the brake arm bridge H; type 2, where the pivot bolt screws into a post which comes off the brake arm bridge and on which the yoke rotates; or type 3, where the pivot bolt simply goes through the brake arm bridge and the yoke rotates on a bushing.

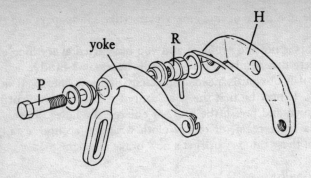

Type 1:

First try slacking off the locknut R and undoing the pivot bolt P one quarter to one half turn. On some models the locknut R is on the other side of the brake arm bridge H. If yoke will now pivot, retighten locknut R. If not, remove pivot bolt P altogether. Keep track of all the washers. Is the pivot bolt P straight? Look for dirt or scarred surfaces on the pivot bolt P and inside the yoke. Clean and polish. If yoke will not turn freely on pivot bolt, enlarge yoke hole with a taper file or ream, drill, or emery cloth wrapped around a nail. Or sand down the pivot bolt. Lubricate and reassemble.

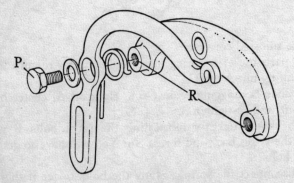

Type 2:

Undo spring and remove pivot bolt P. Remove yoke and keep track of washers. Check for grit and clean. Is post R scarred? Polish with fine sandpaper or steel wool until yoke will rotate freely on it. Lubricate and reassemble.

236

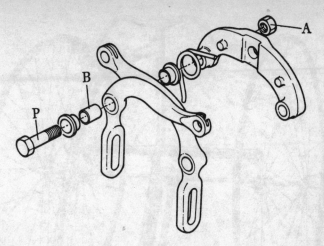

Type 3:

Undo nut A and remove pivot bolt P. Keep in track of bushings and washers. Is pivot bolt straight? Is bushing B in good condition? Check for grit and clean. If yoke still sticks, try polishing pivot bolt with steel wool. Lubricate and reassemble.

Disc Brakes

How It Works

The operation of a disc brake is very similar to that of a caliper brake. Actuating the brake lever causes a cable to pull a cam mounted brake arm which then compresses two brake shoes or pads against opposite sides of a revolving metal disc attached to the wheel.

Lubrication

Only a tiny bit of LPS spray inside the brake arm mounting point 23. Avoid at all cost oil or LPS on the disc or pads 28 and 32.

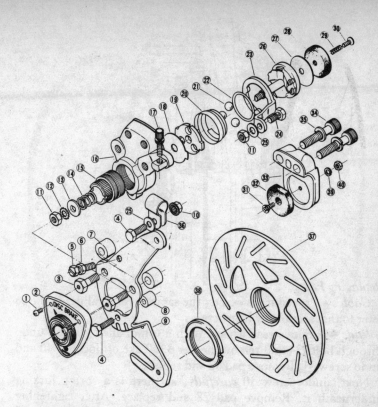

Adjustment

Unlike the caliper system, the cable adjustor bolt 17 and cable anchor bolt 24 are not used to adjust pad clearances, only to keep slack out of the brake levers.

To adjust pad clearances: Remove bracket cover 2 by undoing screws 1. Undo locknut 6 and slacken bolt 5. Use pliers to turn adjustor 15 clockwise until pads meet disc and wheel will not turn. Reverse brake adjustor counterclockwise ½ turn. Turn in setting bolt 5 until it touches holder 16 lightly and secure in place with locknut 6.

Check that the pads and disc are parallel (see over page).
If not, again slack off setting bolt 5. Slack off adjusting bolts 3, 3A, and 4. Diddle with these adjusting bolts until pad A is parallel with disc. Tighten each adjusting bolt an even number of turns until pads almost touch disc. You've done it. Turn in setting bolt 5 and lock into position. Replace cover.

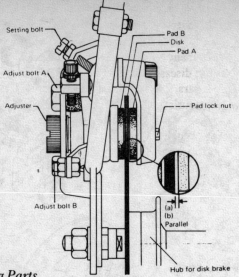

Setting bolt

Adjust bolt A

Adjuster

Adjust bolt B

Pad B
Disk
Pad A

Pad lock nut

(a)
(b)
Parallel

Hub for disk brake

Replacing Parts

Cables – Procedure is exactly the same as for a caliper brake so refer to that section for instructions.

Pads – Remove rear wheel. With a 6 mm allen wrench undo through bolts 34 and remove holder 33. Take off locknut 40 and undo screw 31. Remove pad 32 and replace.

Next, undo screw 30 *carefully*, as there is a spring lurking underneath it. Remove pad 28 and replace. After tightening down screw 30, back it off ½ turn. Restore holder 33 to mate and make sure bolts 34 are done up good. Follow procedure for adjustment, above.

Trouble-shooting

Brakes slip or are weak

Grease or oil on discs and pads. Clean disc with solvent, rub pad surfaces with No. 60 emery paper.

Brakes don't work

Pull up on brake arm lever 23. If it moves and the pads are hitting the disc it is a cable or brake problem. Turn to caliper brakes, trouble-shooting, for instructions.

If it is the unit itself that is frozen up, try removing the pads and dunking the whole unit in solvent. No? Your guess is as good as mine. Have at it and see if you can figure out what has gone wrong. If you can't, take it to your friendly bicycle dealer and see if he wants to play with it.

3. Staying Aboard

Contents

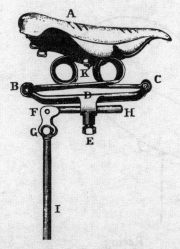

Saddle

There are two important factors in bicycle saddle design: supporting weight, and reducing friction between the legs. The mattress saddle used on bikes with level handlebars has to support all of the weight of the rider, and is therefore usually wide, and equipped with coil springs:

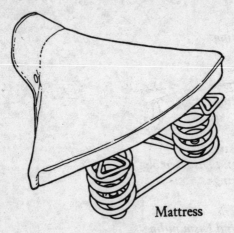

Mattress

Bikes with dropped handlebars support part of the rider's weight on the bars, and can use a long, narrow seat which minimizes friction between the legs:

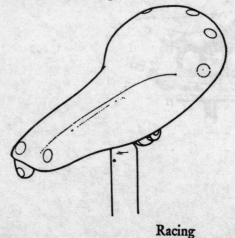

Racing

Springiness in the narrow racing saddle should be kept to a comfortable minimum as it adversely effects pedalling power. If yours is too tight or loose, adjust it by turning nut *A*:

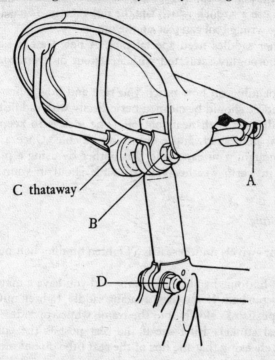

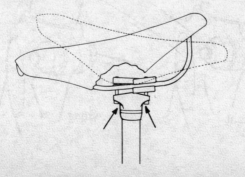

To remove the saddle from the seat post, or to adjust its position backward, forward, or to tilt it, loosen nuts *B* and *C*. This applies also to mattress saddles. Some seat posts have micro-adjusting bolts or allen screws:

Loosen bolt or screw on end to be raised, tighten bolt or screw on end to be lowered. Loosen both an identical number of turns to slide saddle forward or backward. For proper saddle position refer to Fitting, pp.100- 2.

To raise or lower the saddle, loosen the binder bolt D.

Be sure to use a wrench which fits the nut exactly. It has to be tight, and the wrong tool can tear up the nut.

Only leather saddles need special care. A new leather saddle should be thoroughly saturated with neatsfoot oil from *underneath*.

Then, depending on how much you ride and how much you sweat, the saddle should be cleaned periodically with saddle soap and lightly dressed with neatsfoot oil. The idea is to keep the leather clean, nourished, and comfortably pliable. Once a year should be enough. You can avoid this bother by using a plastic saddle, but in warm weather you will slide about in your own sweat.

Trouble-shooting

Seat tilts or swivels unnecessarily. Tighten binding bolt nuts B and C.

If the seat bottoms harshly on bumps and you have a mattress type saddle – too bad. If you have a racing saddle, tighten nut A.

The seat post sinks slowly into the frame while you ride. This can be a real stinker. First see if the seat post is the correct diameter by checking that the lips of the seat tube do not meet at the binder bolt:

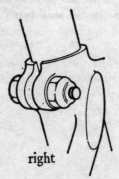
right

wrong

If the post is the right size and is greasy, try cleaning it and the inside of the seat tube thoroughly. On no account try the use of shims or abrasive material like emery paper between the seat tube and the seat post. The chances are excellent that some of the material will fall down the seat tube and get into the bottom bracket, where it will make mincemeat of your crankset bearings (thought seats were simple, hah?). The only sure-fire solution is to install a thin bolt through the seat post and tube at point P:

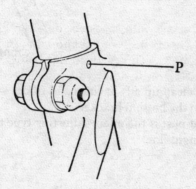

To do this you need a drill, hand or electric, a bolt, nut, and washer, and a drill bit. *Do all drilling with the bike upside down so that shavings do not fall down the seat tube into the bottom bracket.* If you are having a shop do the job make sure that they do this. Position seat at desired height. Make an initial dent with a center punch or with a hammer and sharp nail at point P. Then put a couple of drops of oil on the end of the drill bit and drill through. Go slowly to avoid heat build-up. Use single-speed electric drills in short bursts. You will want more than one saddle height position. To do this, loosen the binder bolt and rotate the seat post one eighth of a turn at the same time that you raise or lower it a little bit. Now use the already existing holes in the seat tube as a guide for drilling a new set of holes in the seat post. Repeat 3 or 4 times. The idea is to be able to make fine adjustments in saddle height without weakening the seat post. At the finish, the job should look like this:

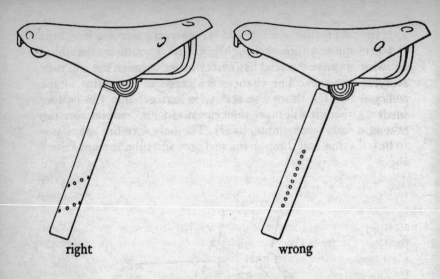

right   wrong

Be sure to clean up all shavings and filings so that they do not fall down into the bottom bracket.

If your seat post is the micro-adjusting type the holes will have to be in a straight line.

Handlebars

Adjustments

To change handlebar position loosen binder bolt *A* on stem and reset bars:

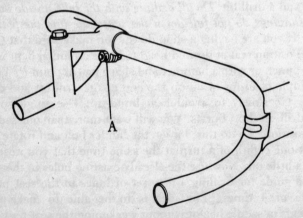

A

Height adjustments are made with the *stem* (next section).

Taping

I prefer non-adhesive tapes. Adhesive tapes gum everything up with a sticky residue which ultimately leaks out all over everything. Plastic tape is cheap and easy to clean. Cloth tape feels good but gets dirty quickly and is hard to clean. The Tape, suede finished and vinyl backed, and washable, is probably the best all around tape. See Accessories for more information.

Be sure that the brakes are in the position you want. Start about 2″ from the stem. Use a small piece of scotch tape to hold down the end of the tape where you start. Work directly from the roll to minimize confusion, and maintain a continuous light tension as you apply the tape. First take a couple of turns at the starting point and then start down the bar, overlapping ½ to ⅓ of the tape. At the bends you will have to overlap more on the inside than the outside. For a neat job, loosen the brake lever mount (see p. 227), tape underneath, and retighten:

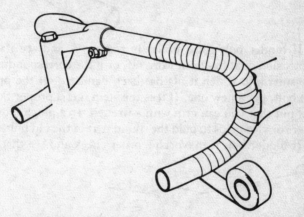

When you reach the end of the bar leave an extra 2-3″ of tape. Fold this over and push it inside the handlebar:

Finish off with a bar plug (bike stores) to hold tape securely. If plug is difficult to insert, rub some soap on and tap it in with a hammer. Bar plugs can also be made from champagne corks.

Use something – if you spill, an open bar end can make a hole in you.

Trouble-shooting

* Bar spins around on stem: tighten binder bolt *A*:

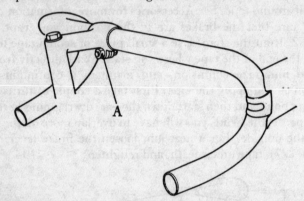

If binder bolt spins uselessly remove it and see if the little protrusion on it has been worn off, or if the corresponding slot on the stem into which it fits has been damaged. If the problem is the bolt, get a new one. If it is the stem, get a proper bolt with a hex nut that you can grip with a wrench. In a pinch, you can use pliers or vise-grips to hold the round part of the old bolt.

If binder bolt is in working order check and see that the clips

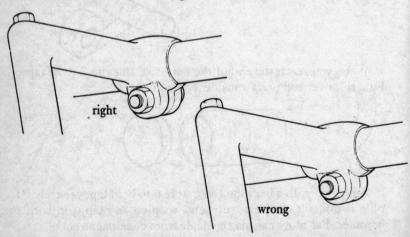

right

wrong

If they do, new bars (expensive) or a shim (cheap). Shimming: find a small piece of flat metal slightly longer than the width of the stem lips. Something that won't rust, like aluminum, is preferable (hardware stores, machine shop litter, junk lying around), but part of a tin can or a finishing nail will do. Remove binder bolt. Using a screwdriver, prise apart the lips of the stem:

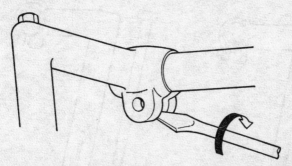

Slip the shim into the gap between the handlebar and the stem, and reinstall binder bolt.

* Bent bars: steel ones are hard to bend, alloy a lot easier. Lay the bike on its side. If the ends of the handlebars have been bent in, place your foot on the end resting on the ground (watch out for the brake lever) and pull up on the other end. If the ends have been bent out, lean your weight on the upright bar:

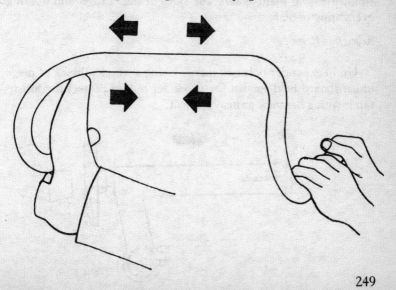

Stem

How It Works

The stem is a tube which holds the handlebar in position, and fits down inside the headset. The tube is split at the end, and down its length runs a bolt, called an expander bolt, which is attached to a wedge nut (A):

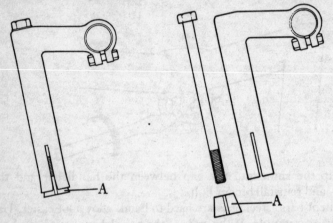

When the expander bolt is tightened, it draws the wedge nut into the tube, and this in turn forces apart the split sides of the stem, pressing them against the sides of the headset and holding everything in place.

Adjust or Remove

Undo expander bolt two turns. Using a wooden block or piece of cardboard held against the expander bolt to protect the finish, tap it with a hammer or heavy object:

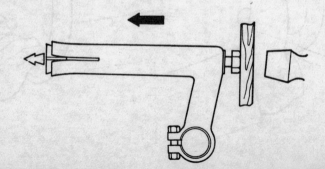

Repeat as necessary to get stem loose. Adjust height or remove. If you remove altogether and reassemble note that some wedge nuts have a dog guide which must fit into a corresponding slot on the stem:

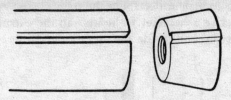

Keep at least 2½″ of the stem tube in the headset.

Retighten expander bolt so that when you stand in front of the bike with the wheel clasped between your legs you can twist the handlebar and stem in the headset. This way, if you take a spill the bars will give instead of bending or breaking.

Trouble-shooting

* Stem is loose and expander bolt comes out freely: wedge nut has come off. Take out stem, turn bike upside down, and shake wedge nut out. Reassemble.

* Stem is frozen in place and expander bolt spins uselessly: threads on wedge nut have stripped (1), or expander bolt has snapped (2).

(1) Separate expander bolt from wedge nut by grasping it with pliers or vise-grips and maintaining a continuous upward pressure while twisting it. If it is obstinate, help it along by wedging a screwdriver between the expander bolt head and the stem:

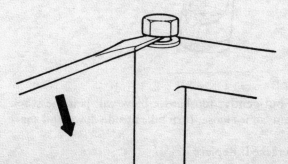

Once the expander bolt is free of wedge nut leave it inside the stem.

(2) Remove top half of snapped expander bolt. Find a rod or bolt which will fit inside stem and touch wedge nut while still protruding an inch or two above the stem.

(1) and (2): Use a hammer to lightly tap the expander bolt or rod, working the end inside the stem around the edges of the wedge nut:

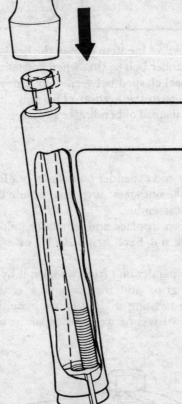

Work firmly but gently; too hard a blow will jam the whole thing. When stem comes loose, turn bike upside down and shake out wedge nut.

* Stem tube cracked. Replace it.

Headset

How It Works

The headset connects the front forks to the head tube of the bicycle frame and, through the stem, to the handlebars. The fork is held solidly to the bicycle but allowed to turn freely by using ball bearing sets at the top and bottom of the head tube. Starting at the bottom, the crown of the fork has a fork crown bearing race (A), then come the ball bearings (B),

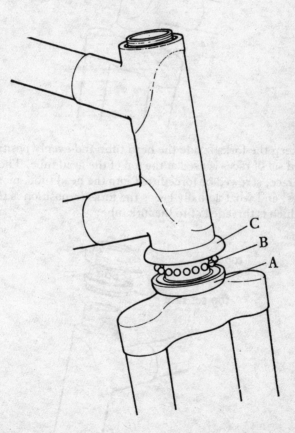

and next is the bottom set race (C), screwed or force-fitted into the head tube.

Put together, it looks like this:

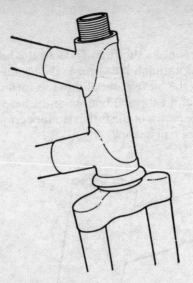

To keep the forks inside the head tube and evenly positioned, a second set of races is used at the top of the head tube. There is a top set race, screwed or force-fitted into the head tube, more ball bearings, and what actually keeps the forks in position is the top race, which is threaded onto the fork tube:

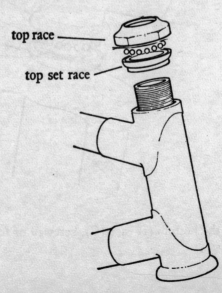

top race

top set race

This is capped by a washer, the cable hanger and/or other accessory mounts, if used, and a locknut to keep the top threaded race exactly in place:

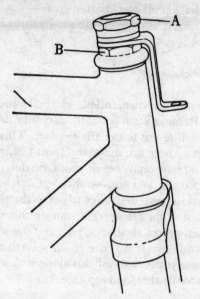

Routine Adjustments

Forks should turn freely but without excessive up and down play. A simple test for looseness is to lock the front brake and rock the bike forward and backward. A clicking noise from the headset indicates loose bearings. To adjust, loosen locknut *A* (above).

Sometimes this locknut is designed with notches. Loosen with a hammer and center punch or screwdriver:

If you are using big wrenches or pliers be careful not to bend nuts or races.

Now turn down the threaded top race B handtight against the bearings, and then back it off one quarter turn.

Snug down locknut A, being careful to keep threaded top race B in position. Check play again.

Lubrication and Disassembly

The headset should be dismantled, cleaned, and regreased about once a year. Remove stem (p. 250). Lay bike down on side with newspaper or white rag under the headset. This is to catch falling ball bearings. There are many different headsets, and no way for me to tell you how many are in yours. So don't lose any.

Undo and remove the locknut, washer, cable clamp (if you have one), and anything else necessary to get to the threaded top race. Secure the fork to the frame. You can do this with rubber bands, elastic carrier straps, shoelaces, etc., but the simplest way is to hold it with your hand. Be sure to do something, or what you do next will cause the fork to fall out along with a rain of ball bearings. Next: undo the threaded top race A:

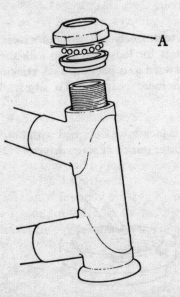

You will have loose ball bearings and are to follow instructions for (1), or bearings in a clip in which case follow (2).

(1) A few may stick to the threaded race, a few may fall on the newspaper, and most will probably stay in the top set race. Get them all together, count them, and put bearings and race into a box or jar. Next: make sure head tube is positioned over newspaper or rag. Slowly draw out fork tube. Ball bearings will fall out. Get and count them, including any that are still stuck to the bottom set race, the fork tube, or whatever, and put them in a jar.

(2) Clipped bearings: Lucky you. Remove clip, noting carefully which side goes down against the top set race, and put in a jar or box. Now draw out fork tube and lift out clip for bottom race.

Further disassembly for routine lubrication is not necessary.

(1) & (2) Soak and clean thoroughly all parts in solvent. Use a rag to clean out the top and bottom set races, and the fork crown race. Ball bearings should be smooth and unpitted. Clipped bearings should be securely in place. Races should be evenly colored all the way around where the balls run. Place them on a glass surface to see if they are bent or warped. Replace any defective parts.

Reassembly: pack fresh grease in the top and bottom set races. Just fill the grooves; excessive grease will attract dirt.

(1) Push ball bearings into grease on bottom set race. Grease will hold them in place.

(2) Put some grease inside the clip. Slip it down over the fork tube to rest on the fork crown race.

(1) & (2) Carefully insert fork tube into head tube. Keeping it snug against the bearings, check that it turns freely. Hang onto fork so that it does not fall back out.

(1) Stick ball bearings into grease of top set race.

(2) Grease and slip on clipped bearings.

(1) & (2) Screw down top threaded race. These threads are fine, so do it carefully (see General Notes for best technique). Set it hand tight, and then back it off one quarter turn. Pile on washer, cable anchor mount, etc., and locknut. Be careful to keep threaded top race in position when tightening locknut. Check for play.

Complete Disassembly

If the bike has been in a smash-up or if rust has got to the bearings, it may be necessary to do a complete disassembly.

Take fork and ball bearings out as per for lubrication. Remove crown fork race from fork. If it is stuck, pry it up *gently* with a screwdriver, working around the edges a little at a time. Be careful, it is easy to bend:

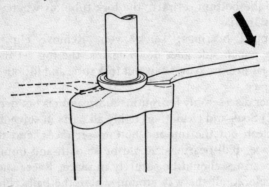

Remove top and bottom set races. You may possibly have threaded set races, in which case simply unscrew them. For force set races, insert a large screwdriver, piece of pipe, or stiff rod into the head tube and tap around the edges of the race:

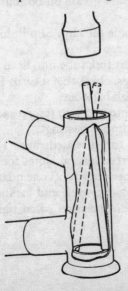

Clean all parts with solvent. Test races for uniformity by seeing if they lie flat on glass or other smooth surface.

Reassembly: screw in threaded set races. For force set races use a wooden block (to avoid denting or bending the race) and hammer:

Make sure that it is seated fully into the frame. Use a wooden block also on the fork crown race if it is balky but be very delicate, and tap evenly all the way around the race.

Trouble-shooting

* Fork tube is extremely loose in the head tube. May just need adjustment, but if things have come to this pass I suggest dismantling and checking condition of parts.

*Adjustment does not work: top threaded race or fork is stripped. Dismantle and see. It is unlikely that this is the result of excessive tightening, and likely the top threaded race was screwed down off center. When you have your new parts review General Notes, Threading, before starting.

* Fork binds or catches, or makes grating and rasping noises when you turn handlebars. Adjust as per p. 255. No go? Something is broken or bent, completely worn out, or there are too many or too few ball bearings. Review the possibilities. Has fork or headset been whacked severely lately? A couple of months ago? Did you or someone else service the headset and lose a

bearing or two, or place too many in one race and not enough in the other? Or perhaps the bike is simply ancient, and needs new races? In any case, disassemble (p. 256), clean, and check all parts. Are bearings evenly distributed (ask your bike shop how many should be in your headset), and free of dents, cracks, and pitting? Do races lie flat on a glass surface? Replace defective parts and reassemble. If you can find nothing wrong take the parts down to your bike shop and see what they say.

Forks

How They Work

The fork holds the front wheel in place and allows the bike to be steered. The fork arms are curved, giving the axle drop-outs rake or trail from a line drawn through the fork tube:

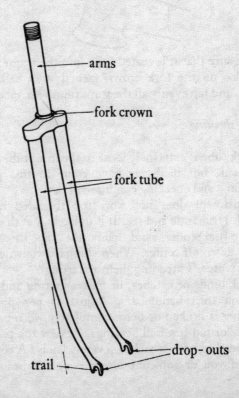

arms

fork crown

fork tube

drop-outs

trail

This rake or trail has two purposes: it makes the bike handle better, and it helps the bike to absorb bumps and other road shocks. The amount of trail varies as according to the purpose of the bike. Touring bikes have a slightly longer trail for a softer, more comfortable ride. Racing and track machines have a shorter trail for greater efficiency in transmitting rider effort to the wheels. Additionally, the forks may be solid or tubular, the latter lighter and more flexible.

Lubrication and Dismantling

Covered under Headset, p. 256

Trouble-shooting

* All problems with turning, grating noises, etc. are covered under Headset, p. 259
* Bent forks: replace them. Bending fatigues metal and makes it weak. The weakness does not show. What happens is that the fork suddenly gives up while you are tearing along at 30 m.p.h. This does not happen very often, but once is enough. Bicycle shops do have special tools for straightening bent forks and if the bend in yours is slight, you may want to try it. Be aware that you are taking a calculated risk, however small.

Tests for bent forks: the bike will ride funny. If forks are bent to one side, the bike will always want to turn to the left or right. Test by taking your hands off the handlebars. Any decently set-up bike can be ridden hands off for miles. Forks which have been bent in, usually through a head-on collision, make the bike's ride choppy and harsh, and make it feel like it wants to dive in the corners. A sure sign of bent-in forks is wrinkled paint on the upper fork arms, or at the join of the fork tube and fork crown. Forks which have been bent out (rare) manifest themselves in a sloppy, mushy ride, and curious, long arcing turns. Again, there will probably be paint wrinkles at the bend point.

4. Wheels

Contents

Wheel Removal and Replacement

Wheels need to be removed often, for a variety of reasons, and sometimes on the road. So you can and will do this with a free-standing bike, but it is much easier if it is hung up. Most 3-speeds and some 10-speeds can simply be turned upsided down on handlebars and seat, as long as cables or shift selectors are not damaged. Bikes with caliper brakes in proper adjustment should require some slacking of the brakes (see pp. 211-212) so that the tyre will pass between the brake shoes.

Front wheel, any bike

Wheel will be held to fork by hex nuts, wing nuts, or a quick-release lever:

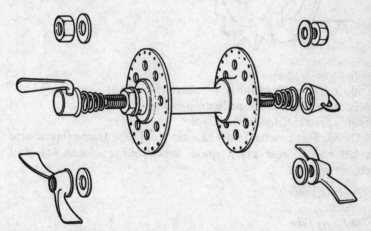

For nuts, undo both simultaneously (counter-clockwise) and unwind a turn or two. Levers, flip it. Remove wheel. Note washers go outside fork drop-outs.

Rear wheel

10-*speed bikes:*

Run chain to smallest sprocket. Undo nuts or lever as for front wheel, and push wheel down and out. If you have a free hand hold back the derailleur so that the freewheel clears it easily, otherwise just gently wiggle it by.

3-speed bikes:

Shift to 3rd gear. Disconnect shift cable at rear hub by undoing locknut A and unscrewing adjustor sleeve B from pole:

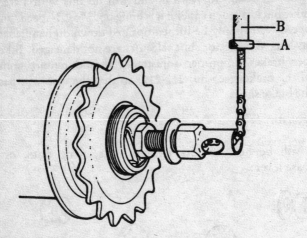

Undo nuts simultaneously (counter-clockwise). Remove wheel, and note washers are outside drop-outs.

Single-speed coaster-brake bikes:

Disconnect coaster-brake bracket from bike frame (metal arm at left end of rear axle), undo nuts (counter-clockwise), and remove wheel.

Replacing Wheels

Front, any bike

Axle with nuts: back off nuts a few turns and slip axle onto drop-outs. Washers go outside drop-outs. Set nuts finger tight and check that rim is centered between fork arms before snugging them down. Re-set caliper brakes if you have them

Levers: Slip axle onto drop-outs with lever on left side of bike. If this is difficult, hold knurled cone with one hand and unwind lever a couple of turns with the other. Slip axle on drop-outs and wind lever down just short of finger tight. Check that wheel rim is centred between fork arms, and close lever so that it points upwards and backwards. It should be firmly shut but not hysterically so. Re-set caliper brakes.

10-speed bikes:

Work axle into drop-outs, slipping chain over smallest sprocket on freewheel. Set nuts or lever for light tension. Pull wheel toward rear of bike until right end of axle hits the back of the drop-out.

Use this as a pivot point to center the rim between the chain stays, and tighten nuts or lever. Re-set caliper brake.

3- and 1-speed bikes:

Work axle into drop-outs, slipping chain over sprocket. Lightly tighten nuts (washers are outside drop-outs), and pull back wheel so chain has ½″ play up and down:

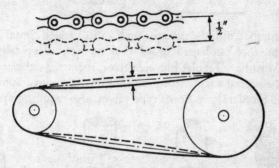

Center rim between chain stays and tighten down nuts. Check chain tension. 1-speed bikes, reconnect coaster brake bracket to frame. 3-speed bikes, with gear selector in 3rd, reconnect barrel sleeve to hub gear chain, and set locknut with cable slightly slack. Test gears and adjust if necessary (p. 307). Re-set caliper brake.

Tyres

How They Work

Any pneumatic tyre works by supporting a casing, the part touching the road, with an inside tube which is filled with air like a balloon. With tubular tyres the tube is fully encased by the casing; with wire-on tyres the tube is held in place by a combination of two wire beads which run around the outside edges of the tyre, and the rim sides:

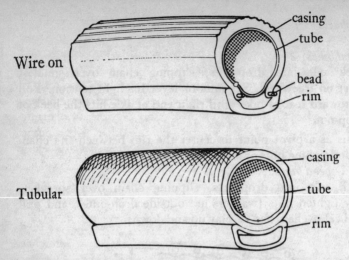

Wire on

- casing
- tube
- bead
- rim

Tubular

- casing
- tube
- rim

Air is pumped into the tube through a valve which comes in three types. Some wire-ons have Schraeder valves, the kind typically found on cars. Most have regular bicycle valves, requiring either a bicycle pump, or a special adapter for petrol station air pumps. Some wire-ons and all tubulars have Presta type valves, also requiring a pump or adapter:

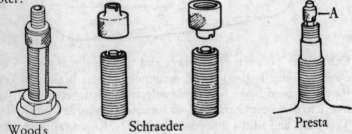

Woods   Schraeder   Presta

'Presta' valves need to have the locknut A undone in order to be pumped up.

Routine Adjustments

Tyre pressure

Use your own tyre pressure gauge (bike shops). Petrol station gauges are unreliable. When filling your tyres at a petrol station do it yourself. The proper pressure for your tyre may be as high as 100 pounds per square inch, but the total volume of air is small, and it takes only seconds to blow a tyre out. Some air pumps take a few moments to fill the tyre: others will do it instantaneously. Jab the air hose down on the valve for just a second, then release and test. Tyres should be hard enough so you can barely dent them with a finger, and bulge only very slightly when ridden.

Bicycle pump: draw hose fitting out of pump handle and fit to pump and valve. Check connections periodically and as you pump. 'Presta' valve: undo valve locknut, push pump on valve, hold firmly to tyre with one hand, and pump with the other. Keep pump perpendicular to valve. Disengage with a sharp downward knock of the hand; wiggling will lose air and possibly bend valve.

Pressure

Know the recommended pressure for your tyres. This can vary from 30 to 110 p.s.i. depending on tyre size and model. A difference of as little as 5 p.s.i. from recommended pressure can adversely effect performance.

Increase pressure for heavy riders and/or heavy touring loads. A 200 pound weight rider will need 15 to 20 p.s.i. more than a 125 pound weight rider with low to medium range 40 to 70 p.s.i. tyres, and 5 to 10 p.s.i. more with high range 90 to 100 p.s.i. tyres.

Check tyre pressure often. Under-inflated tyres are subject to greater internal friction and have less resistance to bruising. Tubular tyres in particular "breathe" air through the sides and need filling frequently, usually every day. Hot weather in the 80's and up may require that you bleed some air from the tyre to avoid over-inflation and a possible blow-out. In very slippery conditions some people reduce pressure in an effort to obtain better traction. If things are this bad it is better to just slow down.

Riding

Most tyre problems are the result of picked-up debris working into the casings as you ride. Going over rocks, through pot-holes, and on and off the curbs will cause ruptures. Cultivate an eye for these hazards, and if you are forced to go through a patch of broken glass, for example, check and see that the tyre has not picked any up. A useful gadget for tubular tyres is a nail-catcher (bike shops) which rides lightly over the tyre and brushes off particles before they can cause damage:

Keep oil away from tyres. It rots rubber. Grease, do not oil bicycle pumps. Oiled bicycle pumps can vaporize and blow oil inside the tube. Check cement on tubulars about once a week.

Care and Storage

Keep wire-on spares in a dry place. Tubular spares should be carried folded so the tread is on the outside and not folded back on itself. Under the seat is a dandy place. Secure with straps or rubber bands:

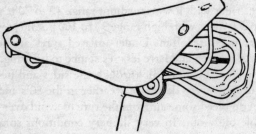

Every two weeks or so inflate a folded spare and let it stand for a while. Refold in the opposite direction.

Flats

Flats take the form of violent blow outs (rare), or punctures (common) which leak air with varying degrees of speed. Blow outs are usually terminal, doing so much damage that the tube and sometimes the tyre must be replaced. Punctures which are not gaping wounds can be repaired. There is debate as to proper policy for this and some bike shops maintain that any patching is "temporary" and prefer to install a new tube. I suggest that you patch newish tubes and throw out older ones.

You will need a tube patch kit containing patches, glue, an abrasive surface, tyres irons (the kind which hook onto spokes are handiest), and chalk.

First check valve by inflating tyre slightly and placing a drop of spit on the end of the valve stem. A leaky valve will bubble or spit back. Tighten valve if necessary with valve cap or suitable part of pressure gauge:

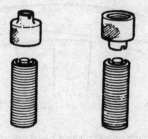

Hooray if the problem was a loose or defective valve. If not, spin the wheel and look for an obvious cause like a nail or piece of glass. Yes? Dig it out and mark the spot.

What you do next depends on circumstances. It is easier to work on a puncture with the wheel off the bike (see p. 263). However, you may not have the tools to accomplish this feat, or perhaps you know exactly where the puncture is. At any rate, the basic procedure is the same.

Deflate tyre and remove valve stem locknut if you have one. Work the tyre back and forth with your hands to get the bead free of the rim. If the tyre is a loose fit on the rim you may be able to get if off with your hands. This is best, because tyre irons may pinch the tube and cause additional punctures. To do this make sure that the bead is free of the rim all the way around. Take a healthy grip on the tyre with both hands and pull it up and off-center so that one bead comes over the rim:

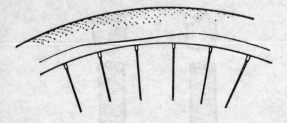

Then go around the rim working the bead completely off.

You will probably need to use tyre irons. Use tyre irons, not screwdrivers, as these are likely to cut the tube. Free bead from rim. Insert tyre iron under bead, being careful not to pinch the tube, and lever it over the side:

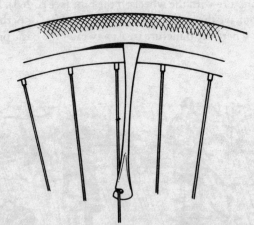

Insert second iron 2″ or 3″ away from first iron, and past where bead is over side of rim. Lever iron. For most tyres this will do the job.

270

No? A third iron. If this doesn't work, use the now free 2nd iron for a fourth attempt:

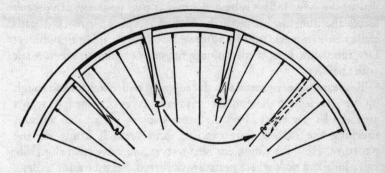

and repeat process as often as necessary.

If you don't have tyre irons which hook onto the spokes, then you will need to use elbows, knees, etc, to hold down the irons as you work away. Be careful not to inadvertently crush a spoke, and keep your face away in case something slips and tyre irons start jumping about.

If you have only two tyre irons and need a third, scrounge something up. In the country a flat rock or a stick. In the city a pencil, a beer can opener, or something from the garbage. Look around. At any hour there will be *something*. Prise up bead with a tyre iron. Insert foraged tool between bead and rim and wiggle iron out:

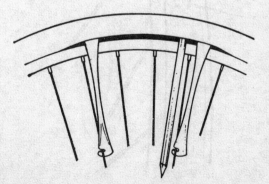

Use tyre irons to make two prises on either side of foraged tool.

Once bead is off rim. Push valve stem up into tyre, and remove tube. Use chalk or eidetic memory to make note of which way tube was in the tyre. Inflate tube and rotate it past your ear. If you can locate the puncture through the hiss of escaping air mark it with chalk. No? Immerse tube in water and look for escaping air bubbles. Dry tube with a rag while holding finger over puncture then mark with chalk.

Take sandpaper or metal abrader supplied with patch kit and rough up the area around the puncture. Spread a layer of cement over this area and let dry tacky. Peel the paper backing off a patch without touching the surface thus exposed, and press if firmly on the puncture. Hold for a moment next to tyre and valve stem alongside valve hole and note where puncture occurred. Set tube aside to dry.

If puncture was on inside of tube probably a protruding spoke caused it:

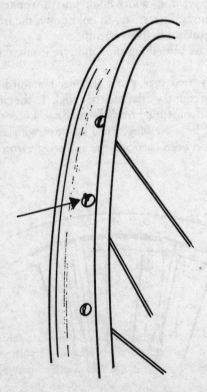

File the spoke flush with the rim. Check other spokes.

If the puncture was on the outside of the tube find what caused it by rubbing your fingers around inside the casing. Check the rest of the casing for embedded particles, and for ruptures of breaks:

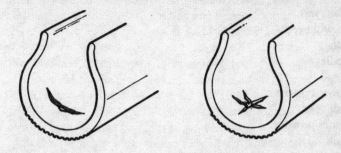

Replace the tyre at the first opportunity if it has these.

To install the tube, first inflate it slightly to prevent it from folding and pinching itself. Push the part of the tube with the valve stem into the tyre, and the valve stem through its hole on the rim. Fit valve stem locknut loosely. Stuff rest of tube into tyre being careful not to pinch or tear it. Check that valve stem is still straight.

Push valve stem partway out, and slip bead of tyre at that point back over the rim. It is important that you hold the base of the valve stem clear of the rim as you do this, or the bead may catch on it, creating a bulge in the tyre:

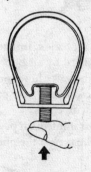

Work around the rim replacing the bead and always taking care not to pinch the tube. Ideally you can do the entire job with your hands. Check that the valve stem is still straight. The last bit will be hard.

Just keep working at it with your thumbs, first from one side, then from the other. When about 2" of bead remains give it the grand mal effort. Don't wonder if it will go over; decide that it will. If you have to use a tyre iron, be very careful not to pinch the tube.

Tubular tyres

You will need:

Patches

Needle

Thread

Rubber cement

Sandpaper

Talcum powder

Chalk

Screwdriver

Sharp knife or razor blade

Remove wheel (p. 263). Deflate tyre completely by opening lockunt A on valve and holding down:

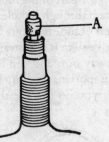

Remove tyre from rim with your hands. Inflate and immerse in water a little at a time. Do not be misled by air bubbles coming out by the valve. Since the tyre is sewn, the valve hole and puncture hole are the only places air can escape. Hold finger over puncture when located, dry tyre, and mark puncture with chalk.

With a screwdriver or similar implement pry away about 5" to 6" of the tape on the inner side of the tyre at the puncture area:

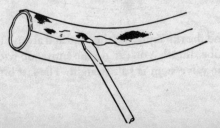

Next cut stitching about 2″ to either side of puncture. Make only two cuts to avoid numerous bits and pieces of thread, and cut upwards to miss tyre:

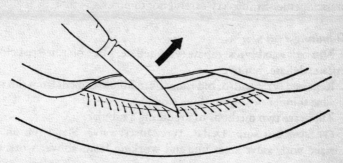

Gently remove tube and located leak. A mixture of soap and water will pin-point elusive ones. Dry tube if wet. Abrade area around puncture with sandpaper. Apply cement and let dry. Peel protective paper from patch without touching surface thus exposed and apply to puncture. Dust with talc to prevent tube from sticking to casing. Get whatever caused puncture out of casing. Insert tube, inflate, and check for leaks. Do this carefully. You are going to be mad if you get it all back together only to discover it still leaks.

Thread the needle and knots the two loose ends of thread. In a pinch 12 pound linen thread or silk fishing line will do. Using the old holes, start with an overlap of about ½″, i.e. ½″ past where thread was cut. Pinch the sides of the casing between thumb and forefinger to keep the tube out of the way:

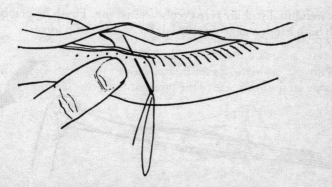

Pull stitches firm, but not so tight as to cut casing. Finish with a ½" overlap into original stitching. Layer cement on casing and inside of peeled-away tape and keep apart until dry. Position carefully and press together firmly.

Mounting a tubular

New rims and tyres: inflate tyre, deflate, place on rim (see below), inflate, deflate, remove.

Repaired tyres and/or old rims: clean off old cement from rim with shellac thinner or solvent (bike stores).

There are two methods of mounting a tubular.

(1) Slow but sure. Deflate tyre. Insert valve. Stand rim on soft surface with valve stem up, and working from above, work tyre down over rim:

Be careful to distribute tyre evenly around rim. Finish by grabbing with both hands and getting the last bit over by main force:

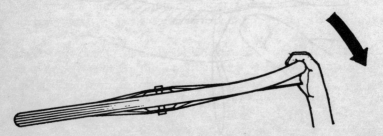

Check again that the tyre is evenly distributed and centred on rim. Roll back a portion of the tyre and brush glue on rim and lining. Repeat all the way around and from both sides. Check again for evenness. Inflate hard. Allow half a day to dry before using or tyre may creep (bunch up in spots) or simply come off the rim in a corner.

(2) Fast method. Apply glue to rim and tyre and allow to dry tacky. Wear old clothes and assemble as above.

Road repairs: use the old cement on the rim and don't lean hard into corners going home. Double-sided rim tape (bike stores) is very handy.

Rims and Spokes

How They Work

The rim which supports the tyre is laced (held) in position by the spokes, which are held fast at the hub and screw into the rim, so that they are adjustable:

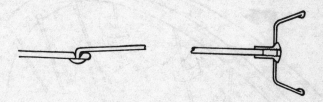

Adjustments

The tension on the spokes relative to each other determines both the strenght and position of the rim. Positioning the rim correctly, both up and down, and side to side, is a long job requiring lots of patience and skill. Most times it is much more efficient to leave this to a bike shop. If you have no alternative however, or are determined to go it alone, here's how:

Hang up the bike or placed the wheel in a jig. Spin the wheel holding a pencil or some-such at a fixed point like the fork arm or a seat stay with the point near the rim to see how bad the wobble is. If it is over ½″ pack up the entire project and take the wheel to a bike store. If they think they can save the wheel, fine, otherwise get a new wheel.

With less than ½" wobble: deflate tyre If job looks to be major, it will be easier if you just remove the tyre altogether. Pluck the spokes with your fingers – they should all "ping" – and tighten any that are slack so that they all have an even tension. Spokes are tightened by turning *counter-clockwise*. If in the course of doing this you find spokes with frozen nipples (the part which holds the spoke to the rim) they must be replaced (see below). If it is more than 3 or 4 spokes I once again suggest resorting to your friendly bike shop.

Hold a chalk or pencil at the *outer edge* of the rim while you spin the wheel so that the high spots are marked. Working one half to 1 turn at a time, tighten the spokes at the chalk mark (*counter-clockwise*) and loosen them opposite the chalk mark. Continue until wheel is round.

Hold pencil or chalk at *side* of rim so that side to side wobbles are marked. Working ½ to 1 turn at a time, and in groups of 4 to 6 spokes, tighten up the spokes opposite the chalk mark and loosen the ones next to it:

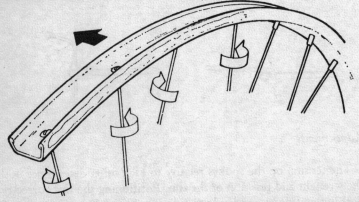

Tighten or loosen the spokes which are in the center of the chalk marks a little more than the ones at the edges of the marks. When you have finally succeeded, or compromised, run your finger around the rim and check for protruding spoke ends. File protruders down.

Replacing Spokes

Remove tire. If you are dealing with spokes on a freewheel-equipped rear wheel that go to the freewheel side of the hub the freewheel will have to be removed (p. 303). Take broken spokes out of hub and rim. Get replacements which are exactly the same; many different kinds are available.

New spokes should go into hub so that head is on opposite side of hub from adjoining spokes and spoke is pointed in opposite direction:

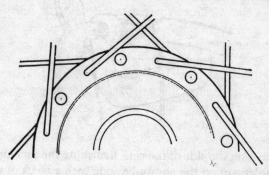

Be sure that it is correctly positioned in the hub with respect to the bevels:

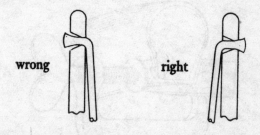

wrong   **right**

On almost all bikes the spokes touch where they cross. Weave new spokes through old as per other spokes on wheel. Place nipples on spokes and tighten. True wheel (see above), file down any protruding spokes which might puncture the tube, and remount tire.

Trouble-shooting

* For side-to-side wobbles and elliptical wheels see p. 277.
* For bulges in the rim caused by piling into curbs, stones, etc.: you will need vise-grips, channel-lock pliers, or a C-clamp.

If bulge is equal on both sides of rim place implement over bulge and squeeze *gently* until the rim is even again:

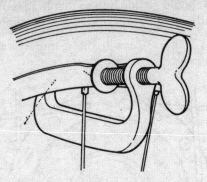

If the bulge is on the side of the rim, distribute the pinching force of your implement on the non-bulge side with a block of wood or some such:

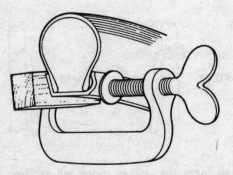

Fixing bulges almost invariably leave a slight dimple because the metal itself was stretched, but the wheel will probably be usable.

Wheel building

You may want to go the whole route and build your own wheels. This is at once straightforward, and an art. A good book on the subject is *Building Bicycle Wheels,* by Robert Wright (World Publications, P.O. Box 366, Mountain View, CA94040, $1.95).

Hubs

Excluded from this section are sealed bearing hubs. These are by definition maintenance free. When they do require servicing or repair often special tools and techniques are needed for each particular make of hub. Consult the manufacturer for instructions if you have sealed bearing hubs.

How They Work

A hub consists of an axle, two sets of bearings, and a casing. The axle is held fixed, and the casing, to which the spokes are attached, spins around it riding on the ball bearings.

Adjustments

Wheel bearings are out of adjustment if, with the axle held firmly in place, the wheel can be wiggled from side to side (usually with a clicking noise), or if the wheel will not turn easily. Wheels held with nuts or lever nuts can be adjusted while on the bike. Generally speaking however, the best procedure is to remove the wheel (p. 263). Wheels with quick-release hubs must be removed. You will need special thin hub wrenches (bike stores).

Undo locknut A from cone B:

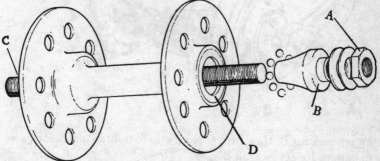

Holding axle or axle housing (quick-releases) still with wrench at locknut C (ten-speed rear wheels: if you can't get at it with a wrench use vise-grips or pliers),screw cone B fully home and then back off one quarter turn. Lock in place with locknut A. Test for side to side play. Wheel should spin freely, and on good hubs the weight of the tire valve will pull the wheel around so that the valve rests in the six o'clock position.

On a three-speed hub this adjustment is made on the side opposite the hub gear chain and sprocket:

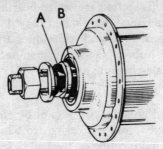

Loosen locknut A, turn cone B fully home, back off one quarter turn, reset locknut A.

On a Sturmey-Archer SC coaster hub:

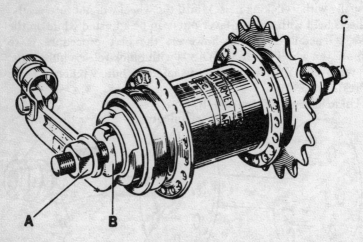

loosen locknut B, then turn C clockwise to tighten, anti-clockwise to loosen. Re-set locknut B.

Front wheel 'dynohubs' are adjusted at the left side, away from the dynamo, while rear 'dynohubs' are adjusted at the left side next to the dynamo:

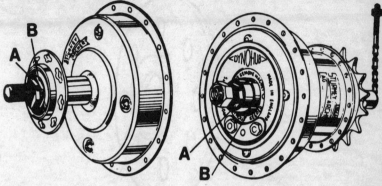

In both cases loosen locknut A, turn slotted washer B fully home, back off one quarter turn, and re-set locknut A.

Lubrication

Any front hub or 10-speed rear hub with oil clips or caps: ½ teaspoonful oil or LPS-3 a month. If a grease fitting, one or two shots of grease per month.

Multi-speed rear hubs: 1 to 2 teaspoonfuls.

Coaster brake rear hubs: if oil fitting, 2 tablespoonfuls per month; if grease fitting, two or three shots of grease.

Hubs need to be cleaned and re-greased every six months for bikes in constant year-round use, and once a year for bikes retired for the winter or used only moderately. This requires disassembly.

Disassembly and Replacement

Remove wheel from bike (p. 263). Ten-speed rear wheels, remove freewheel (p. 305). Lay wheel down on rags or newspaper to catch ball bearings. Undo locknut A from cone B and remove both while holding on to axle at C.

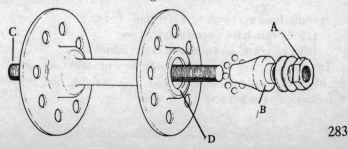

283

Remove dust cover D. To do this it may be necessary to let the axle drop in just a little way so you can pry the dust cover off with a screwdriver:

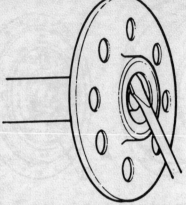

Prise out the loose or clipped ball bearings (or turn the wheel over and dump them out),count, and place in jar. Now slide axle all the way out and dump out remaining bearings. Garner and count. Undo remaining locknut and cone and remove from axle. Clean all parts in solvent. Examine bearings to see that they are not cracked or pitted. Clipped bearings should be secure in clip. Cups and cones should be even in color all around where bearings run and free of pitting. Test axle for straightness by rolling on glass surface. Replace any defective parts.

Reassembly: pack cups with grease. Not too much, excess will attract grit. Replace and lock one cone and locknut on axle. Slip dust cover on axle. Pack bearings into cup on one side of wheel. Gracefully insert axle and turn wheel over. Pack bearings into cup, replace dust cover, screw on cone and locknut, and adjust as per above.

Trouble-shooting

If something goes wrong it is usually because
    (1) the hub hasn't been serviced, or
    (2) a cone and locknut have come adrift.
In either case, if routine adjustment will not solve the problem, completely disassemble hub and replace broken or defective parts as per above.

5. Power Train

Contents

Pedals

How They Work

A pedal consists of a platform of metal or metal and rubber for the foot, an axle (called a spindle) which screws into the crank, and two sets of ball bearings on which the platform rides as it spins around the spindle.

Adjustment

If pedal can be wiggled back and forth on the spindle it needs tightening. Remove dustcap A (pry with a screwdriver if it is the wedge type):

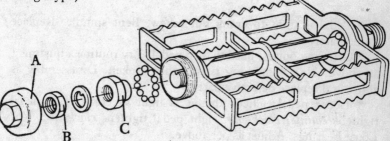

Undo locknut B from cone C. Screw cone C fully home and back off ¼ turn. Secure with locknut B. Check for play and that pedal spins easily. Replace dustcap A.

Lubrication and Disassembly

Pedals lead a hard, dissolute life and need cleaning and re-greasing every six months, more often if you ride a lot or favor wet weather. This requires disassembly. Remove pedals from crank. *Note:* right-hand pedal has a conventional right-hand thread and unscrews by turning counter-clockwise, but left-hand pedal has a left-hand thread and unscrews by turning *clockwise*. Work with pedal over newspaper or rag to catch ball bearings. Remove dust-cover A (see illustration above). Undo and remove locknut B and cone C while holding platform and spindle together with hand. Get all bearings out of dust cover end and place in jar. Remove spindle and place all bearings from crank end in jar. Clean all parts in solvent. Check ball bearings for pitting, cracks, disorderly conduct; cups and cones for uneven wear, pitting; spindle for straightness.

Reassembly: pack grease into cups on platform. Pack ball bearings into cup on crank side of platform (grease will hold them in place), and slide on spindle. Pack bearings into dust cover side cup. Screw down cone C fully home and back off one-quarter-turn. Secure with locknut B. Check for play and that pedal spins easily. Replace dustcover.

Note: When replacing pedals on bike be sure that left-side pedal, stamped "L" on end of spindle shaft, goes to the left side. It screws on *counter-clockwise.* The right-hand pedal is stamped "R" (surprise!) and screws on *clockwise.*

Trouble-shooting

* Pedal is tight to crank but askew. Bent spindle. Replace immediately.

* Grinding noises, hard to turn pedal. Try routine adjustment as above. No? Something is probably broken. Disassemble as above and replace defective parts.

* Loose pedal. Check that it is tight to crank. Left-pedal tightens *counter-clockwise,* right pedal tightens *clockwise.* No? Loose bearings. Adjust as per above.

Cranks

Cranks support the pedals and transmit pedaling power to the front sprocket(s). They are attached to a bottom bracket axle which rides on two sets of ball bearings inside the bottom bracket shell. There are three types of cranks: one-piece; cottered three-piece; and cotterless three-piece:

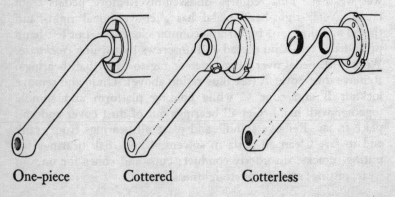

One-piece   Cottered   Cotterless

Since one-piece cranks include the bottom bracket axle, they are covered under Bottom Brackets. To test a cottered or cotterless crank for tightness, position the pedals equidistant from the ground. Press firmly on both pedals with hands and release. Rotate crankset one-half-turn and press pedals again. If something gives one of the cranks is loose.

Adjustment – Removal

Cottered Cranks

Support the crank with a block of wood which has a hole or V-notch into which the cotter pin A fits:

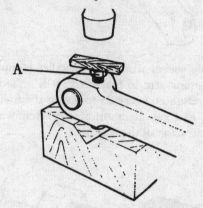

Be sure that the support block touches only the crank and is firmly in place. Otherwise what you do next will damage your bearings by driving the balls into the sides of the cup and scoring it (called Brinelling). Next: if you are tightening, give the head of the cotter pin A 2 or 3 moderate blows with a wooden mallet or hammer and wooden block combination. Then snug down nut firmly, but not with all your might or you will strip it. If you are removing, undo cotter pin 2 or 3 turns and then tap threaded end of cotter pin. Repeat if necessary. Be careful not to damage the threads as you will want to use the pin again. If you use a new pin and it does not fit, file down the flat side until it does.

Cotterless Cranks

You will need a crank installer and extractor which fits your particular brand of crank. Cotterless cranks are made of an aluminum alloy called dural and must not be tightened with the same force as steel parts. To tighten or loosen first remove the dust cover A:

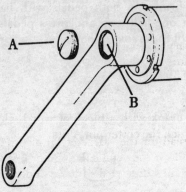

To tighten, apply socket wrench of installer to nut B and turn down, wiggling crank arm to make sure it is seated all the way. For new cranks retighten every 25 miles for the first 200 miles of use. To remove, first get chain out of way. Remove nut B. Back inner bolt A of extractor all the way out:

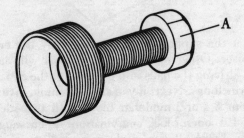

Screw extractor into crank, and then tighten down inner bolt A. *Do not do this with all of your might or you may strip the threads.* If the crank does not come loose with a firm tightening on the extractor bolt, give it 2 or 3 taps with a hammer, and tighten it one-eighth of a turn. Repeat until crank comes free. When replacing crank, be sure to wiggle it around a lot so that it is fully home before you give it the final tightening.

* There is a "click" as you bring the pedal around on the upstroke and then a momentary dead spot and another "click" as you push it down. It may be a loose pedal (p. 288), bottom bracket (p. 290), or crank. If it looks to be the crank, test and tighten if necessary as per above.

* Stripped holding bolt on a cotterless crank. Get a new bottom bracket axle. If this is impossible, a machine shop may be able to re-thread the axle to accept a larger bolt. Be sure that the head of the larger bolt is small enough so that you can still use an extractor.

* Sripped thread for the extractor on a cotterless crank. First ask your bike shop if they can solve the problem. No? You may be able to find a substitute tool which will do the job. I have one which looks like:

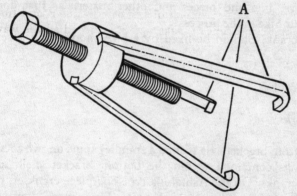

I have no idea what it is used for although I think it has something to do with plumbing. Anyway, the arms A will hook onto the crank or sprocket while the bolt passes against the bottom bracket axle.

If you can't find a substitute tool you and a machine shop may be able to manufacture a new extractor. It will be some trouble, but at upwards of £75 for fancy new cranks it is probably worth taking a stab at saving the old ones. Take your bike to a machine shop and explain that you want a steel plate or bar threaded in the center for an extractor bolt, and with holes drilled so that other bolts can be slid through and in turn be attached to metal plates which will hook behind the front sprocket:

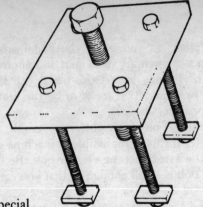

Backyard Special

If this Backyard Machine Shop Special Gizmo doesn't appeal to you, try jury-rigging your own conglomerate design of C-clamps, bolts, levers, bits and pieces and other materials. Just don't destroy your bike in the process.

* Bent crank. Should be fixed by a bike shop with a special tool for the job.

Bottom Bracket

How It Works

The bottom bracket axle (called a spindle) spins on two sets of ball bearings contained within the bottom bracket shell, and holds the cranks. On the Ashtabula type one-piece crankset, the two cranks and spindle are one unit. Three-piece cranksets (cottered and cotterless) consist of two cranks and a separate spindle. Although service techniques are fundamentally similar, we will discuss one-piece cranksets and spindles for three-piece cranksets separately.

Ashtabula one-piece crankset

Adjustment

If axle is hard to turn, or slips from side to side in bottom bracket shell, first remove chain (p. 299). Then loosen locknut A by turning it *clockwise:*

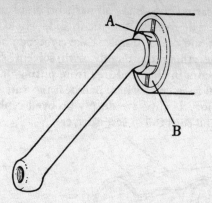

Use screwdriver in slot of cone B to turn it fully home *(counter-clockwise)*, and then back it off one-eighth turn. Resecure locknut A *(counter-clockwise)*, and check that cranks spin freely without side to side play.

Lubrication and Disassembly

Bottom bracket axles should be cleaned and re-greased once a year. This requires disassembly. Bearings for one-piece cranksets are held in clips so don't worry about losing them. Remove left pedal *(clockwise)* and chain from front sprocket (p. 299). Undo locknut A *(clockwise)*, and unscrew cone B *(clockwise)*:

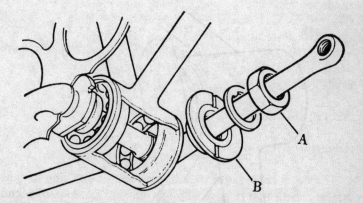

Remove ball bearing clip. Slide all parts off crank and place in a jar. Now move axle to right and tilt to slide whole unit through bottom bracket and out of frame. Take right side bearing lip off axle. Clean everything thoroughly with solvent. See that ball bearings are secure in clips and free from pitting or cracks; cups and cones are even in color where ball bearings run and free from pitting or scoring. If cups are deeply grooved replace. Remove with hammer and steel rod or screwdriver:

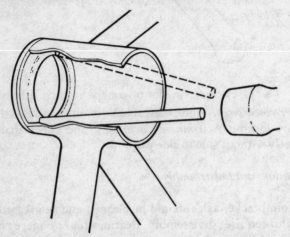

and make sure the new cups are well seated by tapping them in with a hammer and wooden block:

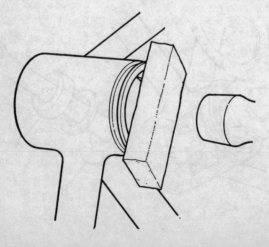

To reasemble: pack grease into bearing clips and cups. Slide one clip on axle with solid side against right cone. Gracefully insert crankset through bottom shell from right side. Slide on ball bearing clips with balls in, solid side out. Screw on cone (*counter-clockwise*), and turn it fully home, wiggling and spinning the crankset as you do this. Back off one-eighth turn and secure with locknut (tighten *counter-clockwise*). Check that crankset spins freely without side to side play. Replace pedal (*counter-clockwise*) and chain.

Three-piece Cranksets

Adjustment

Bottom bracket axle (spindle) should be free from side to side play and spin freely. To adjust, first disconnect chain from front sprocket. Loosen notched lockring C on left side of bracket with a "C" wrench (bike stores) or hammer and screwdriver combination (*counter-clockwise*):

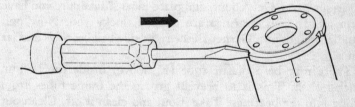

Then tighten (*clockwise*) adjustable cup D fully home with a screwdriver or center-punch inserted in hole or slot and *very light* hammer taps:

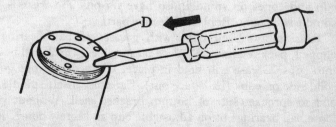

Back off one-eighth turn and secure with lockring C. Check that spindle spins freely and has no side to side play.

Lubrication and Disassembly

Bottom bracket assembly should be cleaned and re-greased once a year. This requires disassembly. Remove chain from front sprocket (p.299) and cranks (p.289). Lay bike right side down on newspaper or rags to catch loose ball bearings. Undo lockring C with "C" wrench or hammer and screwdriver combination and remove. Carefully holding axle in place against right side bearings, remove adjustable cup D:

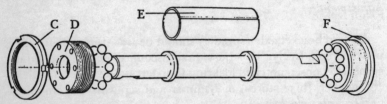

Lookout for the ball bearings! Some will fall out, others will stick to various parts. Get, count, and place in jar. Make sure you have them all. If your bearings are clipped, lucky you. Now pull spindle straight out. Garner all the right side ball bearings and jar 'em.

There may be a plastic tube (E, above) inside the bottom bracket shell. This is to prevent grit in the frame tubes from falling into the bearings. Take it out and clean it off. Clean out inside of bottom bracket shell with solvent. Examine the fixed cup F with a flash-light. If it is unpitted and wear is reasonably even, leave it alone. Otherwise unscrew and replace. Clean all other parts in solvent. See that ball bearings have no pits or cracks, and if clipped are secure in retainers; inside of adjustable cup and cones on spindle also have no pits and wear is even; spindle is straight. Replace defective parts.

Reassembly: pack cups with grease. If ball bearings are clipped, pack retainers. Replace plastic sleeve. Pack ball bearings into cups. Grease will hold in place. Clipped bearings go with solid side on cone (balls face out). Carefully insert spindle, long end to sprocket side of bottom bracket shell. Without jarring loose ball bearings fit on adjustable cup and screw home. Rotate spindle as you do this to make sure it goes in all the way. Back off one-eighth turn and secure with lockring. Be careful threading this on as it is easy to strip. Check that spindle spins easily with no side play. Replace cranks (p.289) and chain (p.301).

Trouble-shooting

 * Tight or loose crankset, grinding noises. Try adjustment as above. No? Disassemble and replace defective parts as above.
 * "Click" on pedal upstroke followed by dead spot and second "click" on downstroke. Could be a loose spindle, but more probably a loose crank or pedal (p.288).

Front Sprocket(s) (Chainwheel)

The front sprocket is the business with all the teeth attached to the right crank which pulls the chain around to deliver power to the rear wheel.

Adjustment

The only maintenance needed is to check periodically for bent or chipped teeth. Remove chain (p.299). With a strong light behind the front sprocket, rotate it, looking from the side for chipped teeth, and from above or in front for bent teeth:

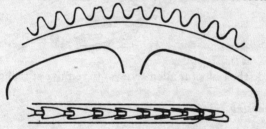

If teeth are chipped, replace sprocket (see below). If bent, take an adjustable wrench, snug it down over the bent tooth, and bend it back:

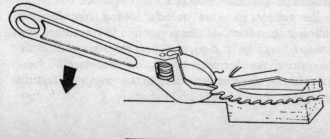

It helps a lot if you can brace the sprocket as you do this to avoid bending it.

Replacement

If it is necessary to replace your sprocket take a look at the chapter on gearing (pp205-10). You might be interested in changing the number of gear teeth.

One-speed and most 3-speed bikes have a one-piece right crank and sprocket. To remove see p.296.

Ten-speed bikes generally have a sprocket which is bolted to the right crank:

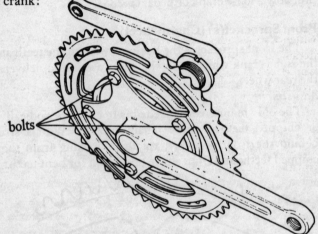

bolts

Simply undo the bolts (or allen screws) to remove sprocket.

Trouble-shooting

* There is a "clunk" every time you bring the front sprocket around. One possible cause is a bent tooth. Check by hanging bike up and slowly running sprocket. If chain suddenly jumps up where it meets the sprocket – bent tooth. Fix as above.

* Sprocket wobbles from side to side, hitting front derailleur cage or rubbing chainstays. If this is not due to incredibly loose bottom bracket bearings (p.295), the sprocket is warped. Fixing is a job requiring both great delicacy and considerable force. Techniques vary so much as according to the exact problem that I strongly suggest you leave it to a bike shop.

Chain

The chain is that innocent and simple looking business which transmits power to the rear gear(s). There are two kinds: one is used on non-derailleur bikes, is ⅛" wide, and held together with a master link:

which can be taken apart without special tools; the other for derailleur equipped bikes, is ³⁄₃₂" wide, and has no master link (it would catch in the rear gear cluster), so that a special chain riveting tool is needed to take it apart or put it together.

Removal and Replacement

Chains should be replaced every two years on bikes that see constant use, and every three years on bikes that see average service. Although the chain may look perfectly sound, the tiny bit of wear on each rivet and plate adds up to a considerable alteration in size. A worn chain will chip teeth on (expensive) gear sprockets. To test for wear, remove chain (see below) and lay on table with rollers parallel to surface. Hold chain with both hands about 4–5" apart. Push hands together, and then pull apart. If you can feel slack, replace chain.

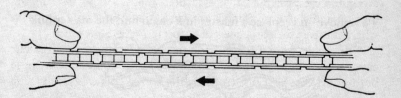

Another simple test for chain wear is to lift the chain away from the front chainring:

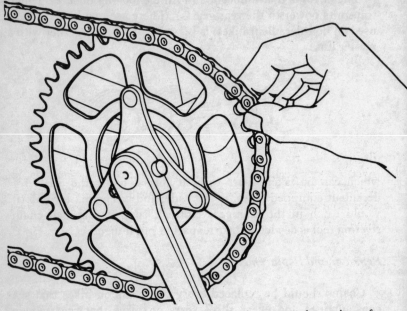

If the chain will clear the teeth it is more than time for replacement.

Test also for side to side deflection. It should not be more than 1":

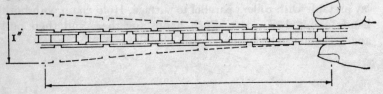

To remove and replace a master link chain find the master link

and pry it off with a screwdriver.

To remove a derailleur chain drive out a rivet with a chain tool:

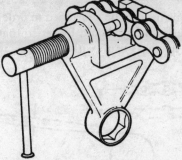

Be sure that the point of the chain tool centers exactly on the rivet. *Do not drive the rivet all the way out.* Go only as far as the outside plate. Stop frequently to check progress. Once rivet is near chain plate I like to free link by inserting a thin screwdriver and twisting gently:

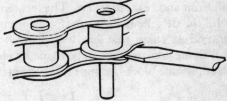

Another method is simply to twist the chain. Be careful that you do not bend the plates. To replace rivet, reverse tool:

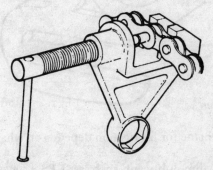

Again, be careful how far you go, or the link will jam (see Trouble-shooting to fix).

Fitting

Most new chains need to be shortened in order to fit properly. On a non-derailleur bike it should be set so that there is ½" up and down play in the chain with the rear wheel in proper position:

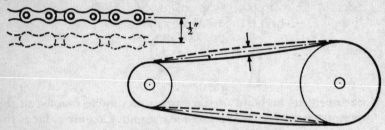

On a derailleur bike, the chain needs to be long enough to fit over the large front and back sprockets, and short enough to fit on the small front and rear sprockets. The less tension the better, but be careful the derailleur does not double up on itself. Remove links from end of chain that has two plates with no roller between them. Some adjustment can be made by changing wheel position with adjustable blocks on the rear dropouts:

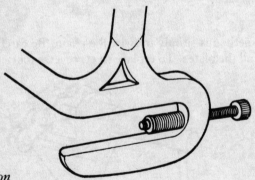

Lubrication

The scheme for lubrication depends on what kind of lubricant you use.

A dry film lubricant such as LPS-1 or (somewhat moist) LPS-3 is clean, does not attract dirt, and goes on in a flash. Apply every 1 or 2 weeks, and remove and soak chain clean in solvent every 2 or 3 months.

Oil is the common lubricant. The problem is that it attracts grit and the solution is to add more oil in the hope that it will float the grit away. Oil every link once a week, and remove and soak clean the chain in solvent once a month.

The most economical lubricant is paraffin, available in grocery stores. It is cleaner than oil. Remove and clean chain. Melt paraffin in coffee can, dip chain, and hang to dry so that drippings fall back into can. Once a month.

Trouble-shooting

* Jammed link. Use chain tool to free tight links by working the rivet back and forth a quarter-turn on the chain tool at a time. If your chain tool has a spreader slot (handy), use that:

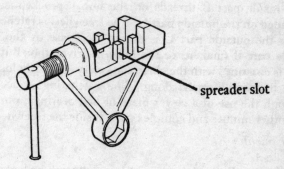

spreader slot

* "Klunk" sounds and/or chain jumping sprockets. Test chain for excessive wear as per above. May also be a bent sprocket tooth (see p.297).

Rear Sprocket

All chain drive bikes have a rear sprocket. On 1- and 3-speed bikes this is a single sprocket and is extremely simple. Derailleur equipped bikes use several sprockets (also called cogs) mounted on a freewheel.

How it Works

The freewheel is in two parts, and there are two basic designs:

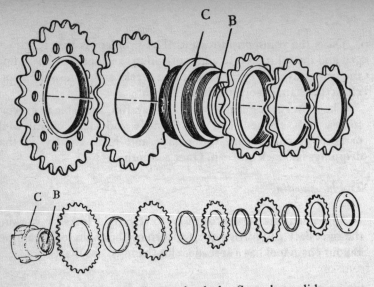

The inside part B threads on the hub. Sprockets slide or are threaded on the outside part C. The freewheel is ratcheted so that when the outside part C is driven clockwise by the chain, the inside part B (and hence the hub) is driven too. But when the bike is coasting, with the chain stationary, part C holds still while part B spins merrily along. The ratcheting is accomplished through the use of a clever maze of ball bearings, pins, springs, and other minute and complex parts inside the freewheel.

Adjustment

Periodically check for chipped or bent teeth by looking at them in profile:

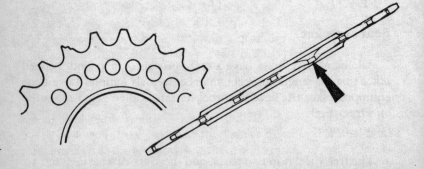

Replace cogs that have chipped or broken teeth, or an uneven U between teeth. Straighten bent teeth by removing cog (see below), gripping the bent tooth with an adjustable end wrench, and straightening:

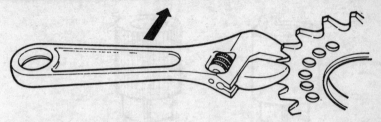

Alignment between front and back sprockets is important. Standing at the front of the bike and sighting between the two front sprockets, you should see the center cog of the back gear cluster:

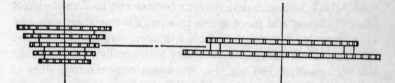

If back sprocket is too far out, so you can see the 2nd or 1st largest rear cog, the front sprocket must be moved out. This can only be done by installing a longer bottom bracket axle (p.296). If you have Ashtabula one-piece cranks (p.292) there is nothing you can do at all.

If back sprocket is too far in, so you can see the 4th to 5th largest rear cog, it must be moved out. This is done by removing the freewheel (below), installing a shim (bike stores), the freewheel again, and then possibly another shim so that the freewheel will clear the drop-outs. All this stuff usually makes it hard to get the wheel back in and may necessitate a little judicious bending. It is better to let a bike shop deal with problems of this sort.

Lubrication

A bi-weekly shot of LPS-3 is best. Remove freewheel (see below) and soak clean in solvent once a year.

Oil: a few drops once a month. Remove and soak clean in solvent every six months.

Removal and Disassembly

This requires a freewheel remover. There are two basic types, pronged and splined:

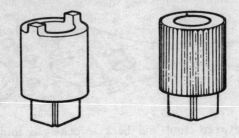

Look at your freewheel to see which kind you need. Remove wheel (p.262). Remove nut and washers from freewheel side of axle. Quick release hubs: remove conical nut and spring from shaft of skewer and place spring in a jar. Fit freewheel remover. If it won't go on you may have a spacer nut. Remove with a wrench while holding axle stationary with another wrench on the left side cone or locknut. Fit freewheel remover into slots or splines. Replace nut on axle or skewer and screw down hand-tight. Use a wrench on the freewheel remover to break the freewheel loose (counter-clockwise). This may be difficult. As soon as it comes loose, slack off the axle bolts and use the remover to spin off the freewheel by hand.

Replacing freewheel. *Note:* a new freewheel or sprockets requires a matching new chain, especially if the existing chain is more than a year old. A stretched chain will probably kick up on new sprockets. Also, if you are getting a new freewheel, read the chapter on gears. You may be interested in changing gear ratios. If you do this, be sure to check chain tension after installing freewheel (p.301). To replace a freewheel put a little grease on the threads and simply screw it on, being extremely careful not to strip the threads on the hub. Snug down with the freewheel remover secured by the axle bolt but do not bear down hard; it will tighten as you ride.

Changing cogs: For this you need a sprocket remover (bike shops) and, if you are removing all the sprockets, a freewheel vise (ditto). Incidentally, if you want a number of different gear ratios it is much simpler to have two fully set up freewheels with different gear ratios than to keep diddling with individual sprockets. However, if you are experimenting to work out the combination of cogs which is best for you ard are impatient with bike shops (they can do this job very quickly), then by all means proceed. Removing a cog is simple – it unscrews or slides off the freewheel – but tools for the job vary considerably in design. Follow the instructions given with your particular tool. If you change the small or large cog, be sure to check chain tension (p.301) after reassembly.

Dismantle freewheel. Uh-uh. This is another of those profitless jobs. If the freewheel goes, replace it.

Trouble-shooting

* A "klunk" two or three times per complete revolution of the front sprocket. May be a bent tooth on a freewheel sprocket. Check as per above.

* Freewheel won't freewheel. Try soaking in solvent to free up innards. No? Replace it.

* Freewheel turns but hub doesn't. Spin cranks while holding bike stationary and look carefully at freewheel. If both parts spin around the hub, threads on hub are stripped. New hub. If outside part of freewheel spins around inside part, freewheel is clogged up (frozen) or broken. Try soaking in solvent. No? Replace.

Gear Changer Systems

Except for the two-speed pedal-operated rear hubs, gear changer systems typically include a shift trigger, lever, or twistgrip, a cable, and the gear changing mechanism, of which there are two kinds, internal rear hub, and derailleur.

Multi-speed internally Geared Rear Hubs

These come in 2-, 3-, and 5-speed versions, with planetary or sun gears inside the hub. I consider these units too complicated to be worth disassembling, and so does any bike shop I have asked about doing such work. Here, for example, is an exploded view of a Sturmey Archer 3-speed hub and coaster brake combination:

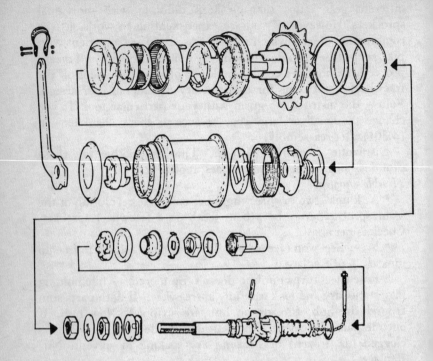

Believe me, if you run into trouble with your hub and can't solve it with routine adjustment or trouble-shooting (below), the best thing to do is remove the wheel (p.262) and take it to a bike shop. The chance of problems arising is quite small. A regularly lubricated hub should last the life of your bike.

No adjustments are possible with 2-speed pedal-controlled hubs. There are two major brands of 3-speed hubs, Sturmey Archer, and Shimano. Service techniques for both are virtually identical, and so we will concentrate on one, the Sturmey-Archer.

How They Work

Shift trigger A connects to cable B, which in turn connects to toggle chain C on hub. Position of trigger determines gear.

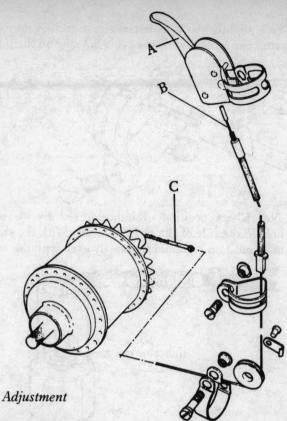

Adjustment

Three-speed hubs –

To adjust a hub first run the shift lever to 3rd or H. Then take up slack in cable by loosening locknut A and screwing down barrel sleeve adjustor B:

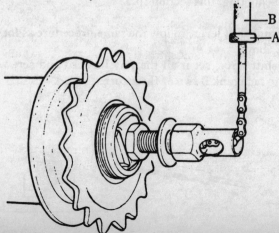

Leave cable very slightly slack. If barrel sleeve cannot do job, move the fulcrum clip which holds the cable housing on the bike frame forward:

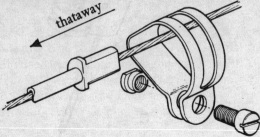

thataway

Test gears. No? Check position of indicator rod by looking through the hole in the side of the right hub nut. With the shift lever in 2nd or N position it should be exactly even with the end of the axle:

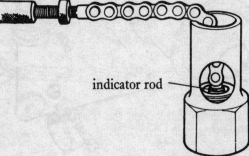

indicator rod

Adjust if necessary with barrel sleeve. Test gears. No? Remove barrel sleeve altogether. Check that indicator rod is screwed finger-tight fully into hub. Reassemble and adjust as above. No? Turn to Trouble-shooting, this section (p.314).

Five-speed hubs –

For the righthand shift lever, follow the same procedure as for the 3-speed hub, above.

For lefthand shift lever, set it all the way forward and screw cable connector to bellcrank B two or three turns:

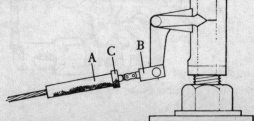

A C B

Then run shift lever all the way back, and take slack out of cable with cable connector. Secure with locknut C.

Lubrication

A tablespoon of oil inside hub once a month. I strongly recommend a quality oil such as is sold in bike and gun shops, or motorist's SAE 30 oil. Some household and other cheap oils leave behind a sticky residue when the oil evaporates. This is the last thing in the world you want. Once a month use a little LPS spray or a few drops of oil on the trigger control, cable, and inside the cable housing.

Disassembly and Replacement

Hub –

Remove wheel (p.262) and take it to a bike shop.

Cable –

Needs replacement when it becomes frayed, the housing kinked or broken, or exhibits suspicious political tendencies.

Run shift selector to 3rd or H. Disconnect barrel sleeve from indicator and loosen fulcrum clip (for illustration, see Adjustment above). To free cable from a

Trigger: shift to 1st or L, pry up holding plate A with a small screwdriver, and push cable *in* until nipple clears ratchet plate:

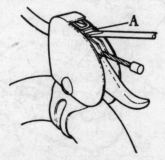

and then pull cable out. Remove entire cable and housing assembly from bike and set aside fulcrum sleeve.

Twist-grip: first take off the spring S with a screwdriver:

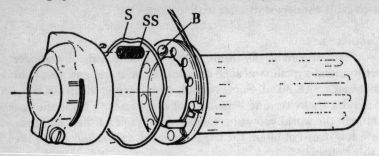

Slide the twist-grip off the handlebar and catch the ball bearing B and spring SS if they fall out. Release nipple from slot, and remove cable housing assembly from bike.

Top tube lever: undo the cable anchor bolt near the hub:

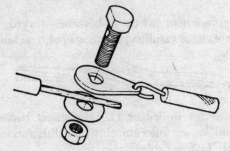

Unscrew the two shift lever halves A and B, and lift casing C away from bike:

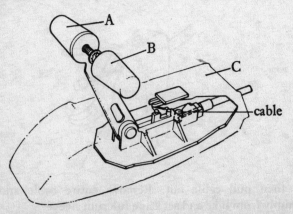

Push cable in to free nipple from slot and thread out cable.

Note: Take the old cable with you to the shop when getting replacement. This kind of cable comes in a variety of lengths. To replace a cable to a

Trigger: place the fulcrum sleeve on cable housing and thread through fulcrum clip. Pry up trigger control plate, insert cable through hole in trigger casing, and slip nipple into slot on ratchet. Run cable over pulley wheel if you have one, and attach to toggle chain. Shift to 3rd or H. Position fulcrum clip so cable is just slightly slack and tighten. Adjust if necessary as per above.

Twist-grip: insert nipple into slot. Grease and replace spring and ball bearing. Slide twist-grip on handlebar and secure with spring clip. Use a small screwdriver to work the spring clip in. Run cable over pulley wheel if you have one, and attach to toggle chain. Shift selector to 3rd or H and adjust as per above.

To tap tube lever: thread through slot until nipple catches. Replace cable housing or run cable over pulley wheel, depending on the kind of system you have. Connect cable to anchor bolt, shift to 3rd or H, and adjust as per above. Replace casing, and screw together handle halves.

If you have a bashed or recalcitrant shift control the best thing is to replace it. They are not expensive to replace.

Trigger: disconnect cable (see above) and undo bolt B:

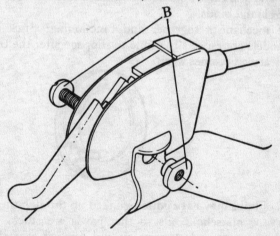

Twist-grip or top tube lever: I recommend replacing with a standard handlebar trigger, which is a much better mechanical

design and more reliable. To remove old unit disconnect cable (see above) and undo bolt B:

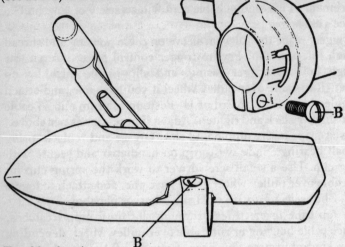

Trouble-shooting

No gear at all (pedals spin freely) or slips in and out of gear.

* Is gear in proper adjustment (p.308)?

* Is cable binding? Check by disconnecting barrel sleeve at hub (p.310) and working cable back and forth through housing. Replace (p.311) if it binds.

* Is shift mechanism together and functioning? Stick and twist-grip models are especially prone to slippage after the track for the ball bearing becomes worn:

* Insides of hubs may have gotten gunked up through the use of too heavy or household oils so that pawls are stuck. Try putting in kerosene or penetrating oil and jiggling everything around. No?

* Remove wheel (p.262) and take to a bike shop.

Derailleur Systems

A derailleur system includes a shift lever on the down tube, but also on the top tube, or the stem, or at the handlebar ends, a thin cable and (sometimes) cable housing, and a front or rear gear changer (derailleur) through which the chain passes. When the shift lever is actuated, the derailleur moves sideways and forces the chain on to a different sprocket:

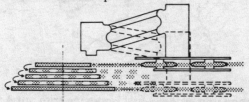

Although we are dealing here with a system, it will simplify everything to take it piece by piece first, and then deal with it as a whole.

Shift Lever

How It Works – Adjustment – Removal and Replacement

The shift lever should be set that you can move it without undue strain, but be stiff enough to hold fast against spring pressure from the derailleur. This adjustment is made with the tension screw A:

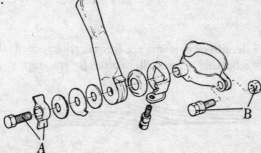

Some tension screws have a slot for a screwdriver (or coin), others have wings, and others have wire loops. All function the same way. To dismantle the lever, simply remove the tension screw. Be sure to keep all parts in order. To remove a down tube mounted lever unit undo bolt B above.

To get a top tube lever unit off remove the stem (p.250). A stem mounted unit comes off by undoing bolts A & B:

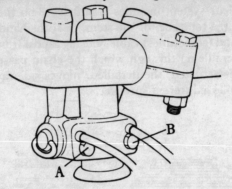

A handlebar end unit requires first removing trim nut A:

and then nut B and screw C. Then loosen Allen screw (6 mm) located at point P inside selector body, and remove unit.

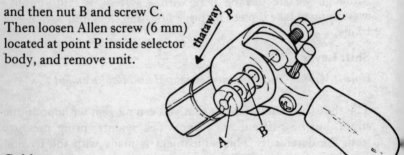

Cables
Adjustment

Cables of derailleur systems are frequently exposed, thin, and take a hell of a beating. Check them often for fraying:

Adjustment is needed when the shift lever has to be pulled all the way back to engage the large sprocket. Place the shift lever forward so that the chain is on the smallest sprocket. Some systems have a barrel adjustor, either at the derailleur or at the shift lever:

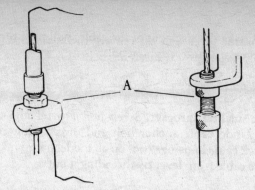

Undo the locknut A and move the barrel adjustor up until slack is removed from cable. If this will not do the job, turn barrel adjustor back down fully home, and reset cable anchor bolt.

All derailleurs, front and back, use a cable anchor bolt or screw to hold the cable. Here is the location (CB) on two representative types:

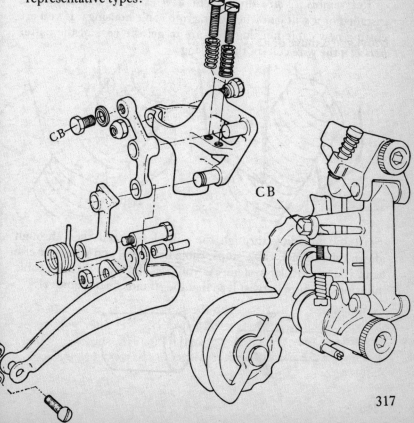

Loosen the bolt, take the slack out of the cable, pulling it through with pliers if necessary, and retighten bolt.

Removal and Replacement

Run chain to smallest sprocket. Screw home barrel adjustor, if you have one. Undo cable anchor bolt and thread cable out of derailleur. Check cable housings (not on all models) for kinks and breaks. Remove cable from lever by threading it out:

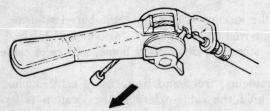

Reassembly: *Note:* do not cut new cable to size until it is installed or it will jam when going into cable housings. If you are cutting new cable housing, be sure to get the jaws of the cutter *between* the wire coils of the housing:

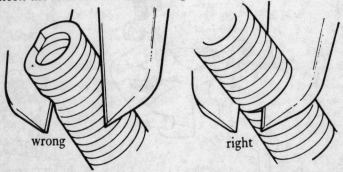

wrong   right

Start by threading through the shift lever, and then through down tube tunnel, cable stops, cable housings, and whatever else is in your particular system. As you pass the cable through cable housings, be sure to twist it so that the strands do not unravel:

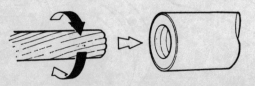

318

Finish at derailleur. Move shift lever to forward position, make sure that cable housing ferrules (if you have them) are seated properly, and attach cable to cable anchor bolt.

Trouble-shooting

Cable problems are evinced by delayed shifts, or no shifts at all. In any case, the procedure is the same: undo the cable anchor bolt and slide the cable around by hand, looking for sticky spots. Check carefully for fraying, and for kinks in the cable housing.

Derailleurs – Front

How They Work

There is a metal cage through which the chain passes as it feeds onto the front sprocket. The cage can be moved from side to side, and by pressing on the side of the chain, shifts it from sprocket to sprocket:

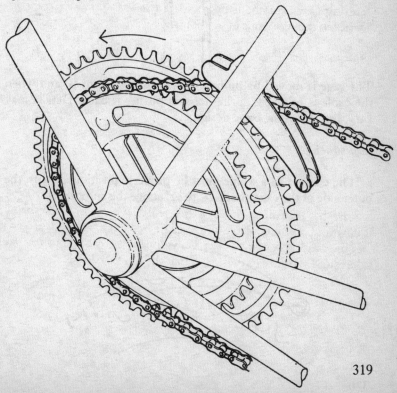

Virtually all derailleurs are built as a parallelogram. Heh. This design is used to keep the sides of the cage A straight up and down as the cage is moved from side to side on the pivot bolt P:

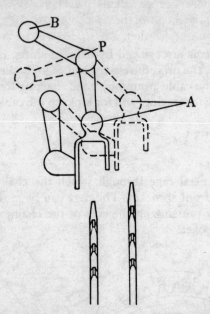

The cage is moved by pulling with a cable at point B, and when the cable is released, spring tension pushes it back. Details may vary, but this is the basic design.

Adjustment

The charger as a whole must be properly positioned, with the outer side of the cage about ¼″ to ½″ above the sprocket:

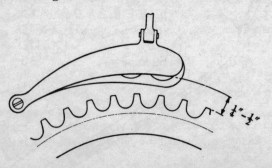

Raise or lower the unit by undoing the mounting bolt (B). The sides of the cage should follow the curvature of the sprocket. Some cages are adjustable in this respect, others (perfectly good ones) are not. Those that are usually swivel on a post between the cage and changer. Sometimes the post comes off the changer, and sometimes off the cage. Either way, there will be a locking bolt like C:

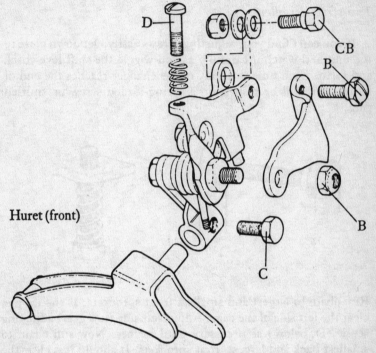

Huret (front)

Loosen, rotate cage to desired position, tighten.

Side to side travel of the cage must be set. First check that cable is properly adjusted (p.316). Front derailleurs fall into two design categories, those with two adjusting screws, and those with one.

Look at yours to determine the type.

One-screw derailleurs

Run chain to largest back and smallest front sprockets. The first adjustment is made with the cage positioning bolt C (above).

Loosen it, and move the cage so that the left side just clears the chain. Tighten. Now back off the adjusting screw D 3 or 4 turns. Run the chain to the smallest back and largest front sprockets. Using the shift lever, position the cage so that the right side just clears the chain. Turn down adjusting screw D until resistance is felt, and stop.

Two-screw derailleurs

If you can't find your adjusting screws easily, get down close to the unit and watch it carefully as you wiggle the shift lever back and forth. Each time the body of the changer reaches the end of its travel it will be resting on a spring-loaded screw or knurled ring:

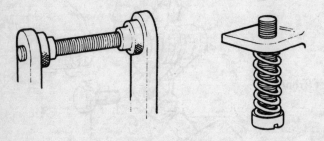

Run chain to largest and smallest front sprockets. It should just clear the left side of the cage. Adjust left side (low gear) adjusting screw (D, below) as necessary until it does. Now run chain to smallest back and largest front sprockets. It should just clear the right side of the cage. Adjust right side (high gear) adjusting screw (E, below) as necessary until it does. Test operation of gears. Sometimes it is necessary to set the high gear adjustment a little wide to get the chain to climb up on the big sprocket – but be cautious, or the chain will throw off the sprocket.

Lubrication

A little LPS or a few drops of oil on the pivot bolts once a month. If the unit becomes particularly dirty, take it off (see below) and soak it clean in kerosene or other solvent.

Remove chain (p.299). Undo cable anchor bolt and slip off cable (p.318). Now undo mounting bolt(s) B and remove unit:

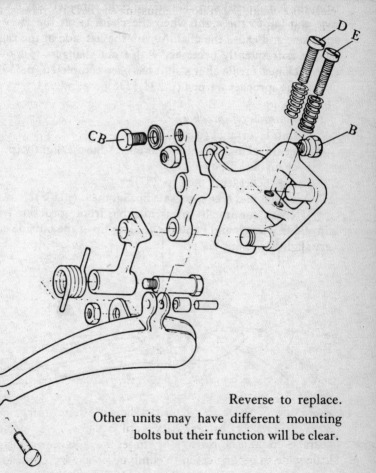

Reverse to replace. Other units may have different mounting bolts but their function will be clear.

Trouble-shooting

Most of the difficulties experienced with the front changer are actually caused by problems elsewhere in the power train. I am assuming that you have already set your changer as per Adjustment, above.

Chain rubs side of cage.
* Is shift lever tight (p.315)?
* Can you stop rubbing by diddling with shift lever? For example, the amount of right travel necessary to shift the chain from the left (small) sprocket to the right sprocket may leave the cage too far to the right when the chain is on the large back sprocket, and cause the chain to rub the left side of the cage. In fact, it is frequently necessary with front changers to move the cage back just a trifle after a shift has been completed (p.315).
* Is the sprocket warped (p.298)? Or loose (p.295)?

Chain throws off sprocket.
* Is shift lever tight (p.315)?
* Cage travel may be set too far out. Adjust it slightly (p.320).
* Is chain old? Test (p.299).
* Are sprocket teeth bent (p.297)?
* Are front and rear sprockets in alignment (p.305)?
* If chain continually over-rides big front sprocket, take an adjustable wrench and bend the leading tip of the outside cage in very slightly – about 1/16":

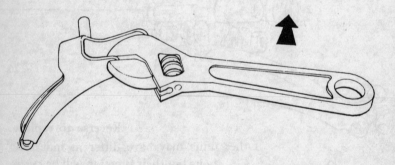

Delayed shifts or no shifts at all.
* Are pivot bolts clean? Try a little spray or oil.
* Is spring intact and in place?
* Is cable sticking or broken (p. 316)?
* If pivot bolts are adjustable, as P is on this Campagnolo unit (**opposite**) undo locknut, back P off one-eighth turn, reset locknut.

How They Work

As the chain comes back off the bottom of the front sprocket it passes through the rear derailleur on two chain rollers. The cage holding the rollers is fastened to the main body of the changer by a pivot bolt P, and is under constant spring tension so as to keep the chain taut:

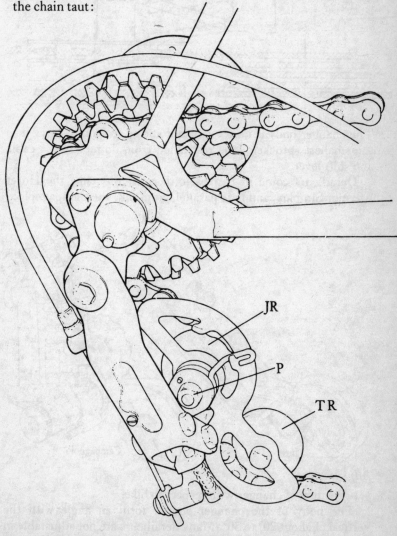

The lower roller is the tension roller (TR), the upper the jockey roller (JR). The position of the cage, and hence of the chain on the rear gear cluster, is determined by the changer body:

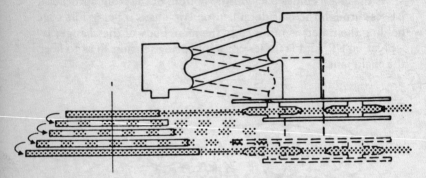

The changer body is under constant spring tension to carry it to the smallest sprocket. It is restrained from doing so by a cable and shift lever.

Derailleurs come in two basic designs, box, like the Huret Allvit or Simplex, and bare parallelogram, like the Campagnolo:

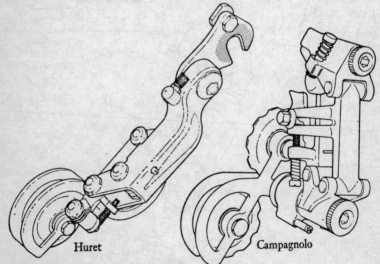

Huret   Campagnolo

Adjustment

– Position of changer with respect to bike.

The body of the changer should form an angle with the vertical of about 20° to 30°. Many derailleurs are not adjustable in this respect and are held by spring tension against a stop (Campagnolo, Simplex). Others like the Huret Allvit can be adjusted by loosening locknut A and then pivot bolt P.

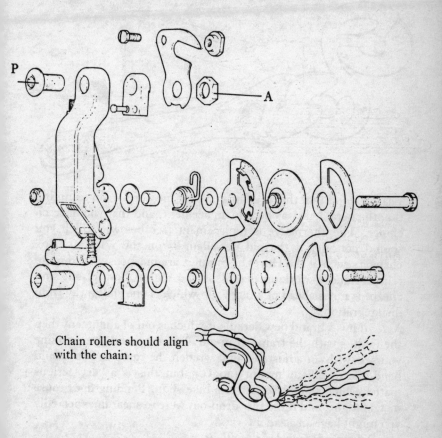

Chain rollers should align with the chain:

If your derailleur is fastened to a mounting plate, remove it (see below), clamp in a vise, and bend it with an adjustable end wrench:

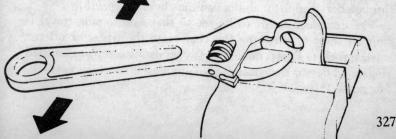

If your derailleur is bolted straight into the frame drop-out, snug wrench around the chain rollers and bend into alignment:

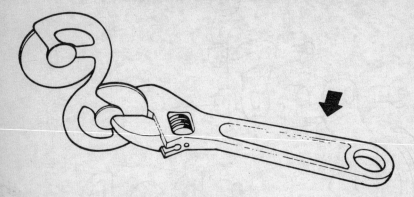

Bear in mind that this is a fairly drastic measure. I am assuming that the derailleur was bent in an accident, and that you have no choice. The alternative is replacement (see below), which you should consider if the old derailleur is on the way out. Box changers such as the Huret or Simplex are inexpensive and quite reliable, and a working derailleur, no matter how plastic and cheap, is miles ahead of a fancy job which is one shift away from disintegration.

Note: if it is a brand new derailleur which is out of alignment then the fault is with the frame drop-out. You can bend this into line yourself with an adjustable end wrench the same as you would bend the derailleur mount (above), but this is a very serious matter which should be left to a bike shop. Bending does cause metal fatigue, and if the rear drop-out were to shear unexpectedly you might have an accident.

– Side to side travel of derailleur.

First check with chain on smallest rear and biggest front sprockets, and with rear derailleur shift lever all the way forward, that there is only a little slack in the cable. Take up or give slack through barrel adjustor and/or cable anchor bolt (p.316).

The derailleur needs to be set so that side to side travel is stopped short of throwing the chain into the wheel or off the small sprocket. This is done with two adjusting screws or knurled rings, and here is their location on 4 typical units (high gear – E, low gear – D);

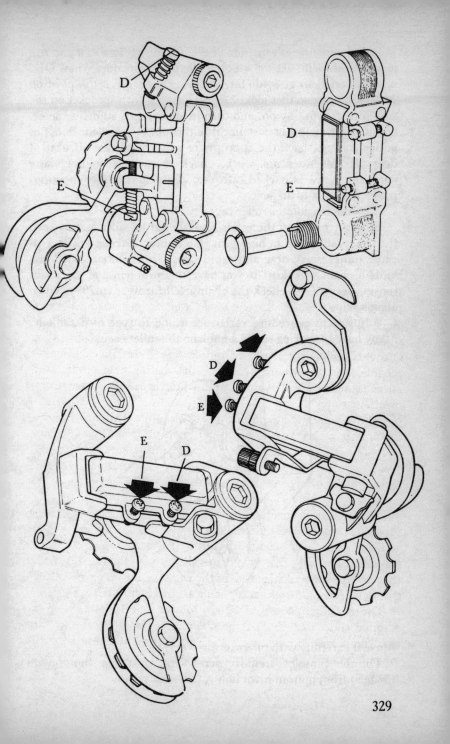

If your derailleur isn't included here, get down close to it and run it back and forth, seeing which adjusting screw does what. OK, now: if derailleur goes too far, throwing chain off, set in position with shift lever so that jockey wheel lines up with sprocket on the side you are working on, and turn in appropriate adjusting screw or knurled ring until resistance is felt. Stop. If derailleur does not go far enough, back the appropriate adjusting screw off until it does. If this does not work, check to make absolutely sure adjusting screw is backed off. Yes? Turn to Trouble-shooting, p.344, for what to do next.

    – Spring tension for roller cage.

Spring tension on the roller cage should be sufficient to keep the chain taut when in high gear. No tighter. Excess tension will cause unnecessary drag and rapid wear. On the other hand, too loose a chain will skip. If you have this problem and the chain tension seems OK, check the chain itself for wear (p.299). Worn chains skip.

Adjustment procedure varies according to type of derailleur. Many have the spring set on a hook on the roller cage:

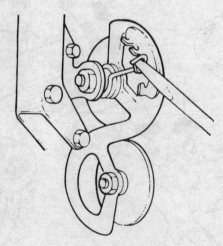

Move it carefully with pliers or screwdriver.

On the Simplex, remove screw and dust cap (not on all models) from bottom pivot bolt A (see next page).

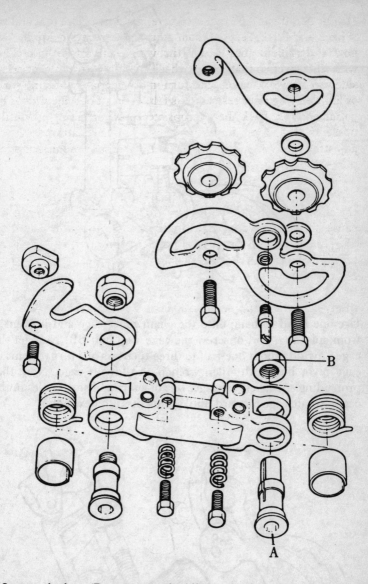

B

A

Loosen locknut B, use a metric Allen wrench to turn A clockwise for more tension, counter-clockwise for less, reset locknut.

On a Campagnolo unit, first remove wheel. Then remove tension roller by undoing bolt G:

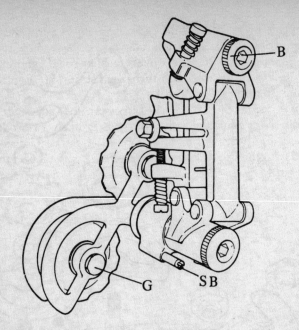

Use one hand to hang onto the chain roller cage and prevent it from spinning, and unscrew the cage stop bolt SB. Now let the cage unwind (about one-half to three-quarters of a turn). Remove cage pivot bolt with Allen wrench and lift off cage. Note that protruding spring end engages one of a series of small holes in the cage. Rotate cage forward until spring fits into next hole:

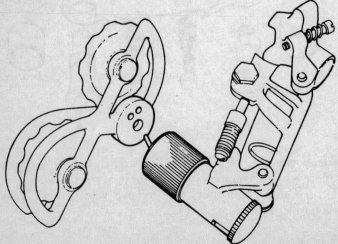

Replace pivot bolt. Wind cage back ½–¾ turn and replace cage stop bolt. Replace tension roller and go back to the races.

Shimano units: Remove wheel, tension roller, and cage stop bolt. Rotate entire cage one turn against spring. Replace cage stop bolt, tension roller, wheel.

The Maeda Sun Tour V–Luxe can be adjusted as per procedure for Shimano units, but this is likely to produce too much or too little tension. For a finer adjustment, disassemble (p.285), noting the relative position of cage with respect to spring catch setting in castlated nut. If the normal position is as A:

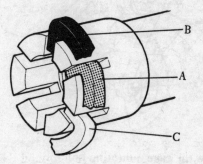

spring tension may be increased by moving spring catch to position B, and decreased by moving to position C.

Lubrication

LPS spray: once a month on the jocket and tension roller, pivot bolts, and cables. Once a year remove and soak clean in solvent.

Oil: a few drops monthly on chain rollers, pivot bolts, cables. Soak clean in solvent every six months. Regrease wheel bearings, if you have them (p.335).

Removal and Disassembly

Disconnect cable from anchor bolt (pp.317).

Remove tension roller by undoing bolt G (pp.332 and 334). Undo mounting bolt B (Campagnolo) or slacken axle nut and remove adapter screw AS (Huret Allvit) according to how your unit is mounted (p.332 and below).

Disassembly: the parts that need this regularly are the chain rollers. Otherwise do it only to replace parts. Chain rollers: get jockey roller off (tension roller is already off).

On the Campagnolo this is done by undoing the jockey roller bolt just like the bolt for the tension roller. On the Huret it is necessary to first unsnap the cage spring:

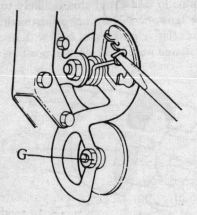

and then unscrew the cage mounting bolt CB:

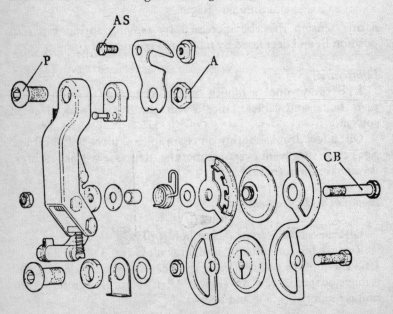

Be careful! of those shims and whatnots. Keep track of their order.

There are two kinds of chain rollers, those with washers and a metal sleeve, and those with a hub and ball bearings:

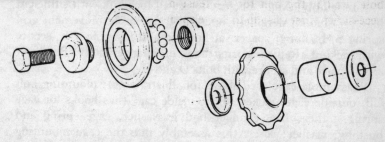

If you have the ball bearing type, disassemble the hub and remove the bearings. Both types: clean in solvent. Ball bearing type reassembly: lay one cone flat on table, place chain roller over it. Apply petroleum spray or grease. Put in ball bearings. More lubricant. Screw on second cone.

For the rest of it, the degree of disassembly possible, as well as the technique, varies somewhat from model to model. We'll do six: the Huret, Campagnolo, Simplex, Maeda Sun Tour, Shimano Crane, and Shimano Eagle.

The Huret Allvit

Undo locknut A and remove pivot bolt P with Allen wrench. Keep parts in order. Next: undo the upper lever arm bolt D: and

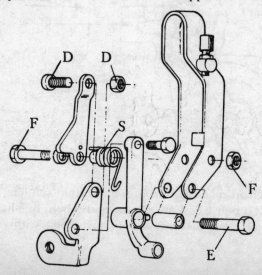

then lower lever arm bolt E. Remove lever arm, and use pliers to pry spring S off changer body. Then remove bolt F to remove spring S. Replace any parts to be replaced. Clean everything in solvent.

Reassembly: *Note:* Be sure to set all locknuts with sufficient play for smooth derailleur operation. Assemble movement arm spring S, bushing, spacer, at housing and insert bolt F, secure with locknut. Replace spring hook on changer body. Put lever arm in place and secure with bolts D and E.

Reassemble cage (see above for illustrations): mounting bolt CB, outside cage, jockey roller, inside cage (has hooks for cage spring – these face changer body), washer, cage spring and bushing, washer; screw this assembly into the cage mounting plate. Set cage spring with screwdriver. Replace pivot bolt, stop plate, mounting plate. Mount derailleur on frame. Replace tension roller. Re-engage cable. Adjust side to side play as necessary (p.329).

The Campagnolo

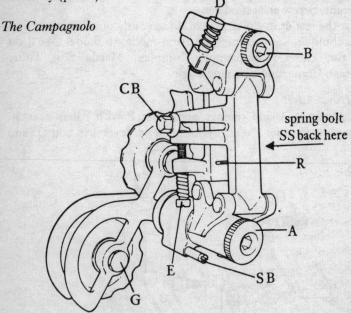

spring bolt SS back here

Hang onto chain roller cage to prevent it from spinning and remove cage stop bolt SB. Let cage unwind (about one-half to three-quarters of a turn). Remove cage pivot bolt with Allen wrench and lift off cage. Slide out pivot bolt A and spring. Back off high gear adjusting screw E to minimize changer body spring tension, and undo spring bolt SS. Replace parts, clean everything in solvent. Reassembly: screw in spring bolt SS while holding changer body spring R in position. Replace cage spring and slide in pivot bolt. Put cage on changer with two half moon sides next to changer. Put nut on pivot bolt. Rotate cage back one-half to three-quarters of a turn and screw in cage stop bolt SB. Replace jockey roller. Mount derailleur on frame. Replace tension roller, cable. Adjust side to side travel as above (p.329).

The Simplex

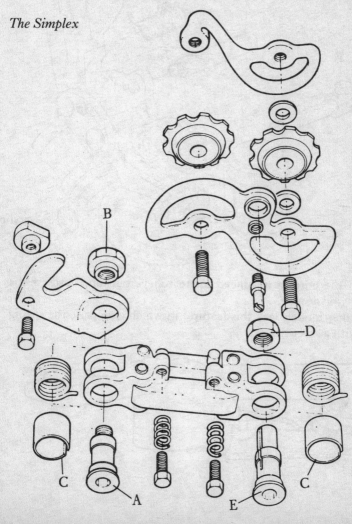

Remove dust caps from pivot bolts A and E. Spring off clips C (not all models). Undo locknut B for main arm pivot bolt A and remove bolt and spring. Ditto for locknut D and cage pivot bolt E. Some Simplex models have a circlip which can be removed so the anchor bolt F will slide out:

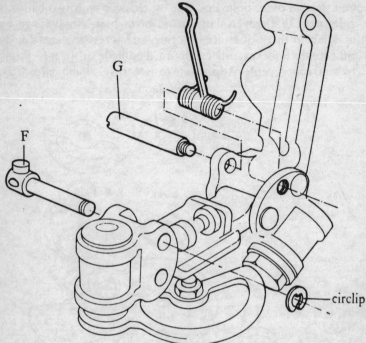

circlip

With the outer arm hinged up to relieve tension, unscrew the spring pivot pin G.

Other models lack this feature, in which case prise the spring up with a screwdriver:

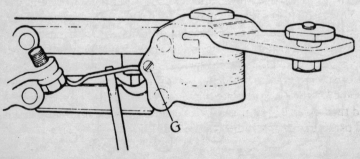

and then unscrew spring pivot pin G. Clean everything in solvent and replace defective parts.

To reassemble: Put main body spring in place and screw in spring pivot pin. Push down outer arm and secure with anchor bolt and circlip, or set spring in place with screwdriver. Put in cage pivot bolt and spring. Put on locknut and cage, and give cage pivot bolt one-half turn to right for proper spring tension before setting locknut. Repeat process for main arm pivot bolt, spring, and locknut. Fasten jockey roller to cage. Mount derailleur on frame. Mount tension roller, and then connect shift cable. Adjust side to side travel of derailleur as necessary (p.328).

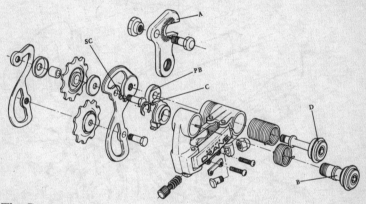

The Crane

The mounting bolt B has a spring. To get at it, prise off circlip C with a screwdriver or similar implement. It will come apart quickly. Clean parts in solvent, replacing spring if necessary, and grease. Reassemble by fitting spring, placing the head of bolt B on a hard surface, and twisting bracket A counter-clockwise while simultaneously pressing downwards. When it clicks into place, hold it firm with one finger, and with the other hand fit circlip C.

To get off the cage pivot bolt D, back it off slowly with an allen wrench, and when the cage stop catch SC clears the little bump on the frame, let the chain roller cage unwind. Finish backing off bolt D. Remove spring, plate bushing PB, and bolt D. Clean and grease, replacing parts if necessary. To reassemble, fit bolt D, spring, and plate bushing PB. Fit roller cage to bolt D and turn down 1½–2 turns. Wind cage clockwise until stop catch SC passes bump on frame, secure bolt PB.

To undo mounting bracket pivot bolt PB, slack off locknut N and then back out bolt PB.

To get off cage bolt CB, first undo cage stop screw SS and

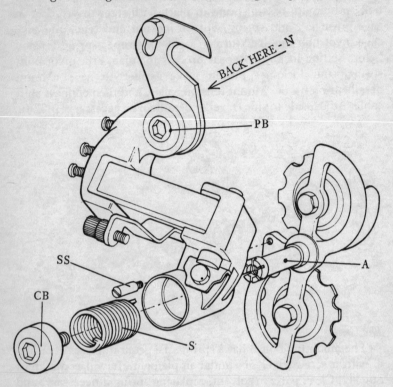

allow cage to unwind. Next, while holding cage and main body together, undo cage bolt CB and withdraw. Note position of spring S in slots of cage axle A, and of cage relative to main body. Separate cage and main body. Withdraw spring S, noting which of two holes the end catch fits into. Clean and grease, replacing parts as necessary. To reassemble: place in spring S, fitting to appropriate hole. Refit cage. If the spring tension of the cage has been weak, start from a position counter-clockwise of the original, and if it has been too strong, from a position clockwise of the original. A little diddling will get you what you want. Fit cage bolt CB. Wind cage clockwise until cage stop screw SS can be fitted.

To undo mounting bracket pivot bolt PB, remove dustcap D by twisting off or prising up with thin screwdriver, prise off circlip C, and unwind bracket gently. When reassembling, be sure that CC catch on mounting bracket plate is wound past the corresponding catch CD on the derailleur body.

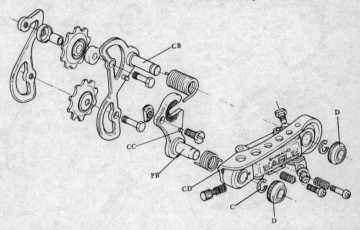

To get off the cage bolt CB do exactly the same thing as above.

The Positron

The Positron is a semi-automatic derailleur utilising a twin cable control.

Mount derailleur on dropout and axle. Move unit by hand until index pin lines up with numeral 3 on derailleur body:

Check that guide pulley is aligned with the center sprocket of the freewheel:

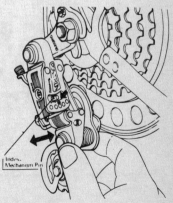

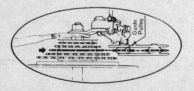

If it is not, turn the adjusting screw
in or out until the two parts align.

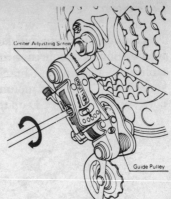

And affix the shifting lever. Loosen
the cable fixing screw on the lever:

Fit the cable end with the head
into the slot provided on the cam
plate, and the cable end with no
head through the cable adjuster:

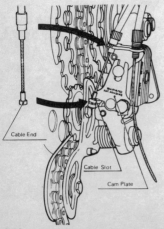

Thread cable through anchor bolt,
pull tight with pliers, and snug
down anchor bolt. Move shift
lever to 3 on lever plate and
tighten cable fixing screw. Check
operation of unit. If necessary,
adjust in or out with adjusting
screw. After about 50–100 miles
of riding, check the cables for
slack.

Cable replacement

Undo cable fixing screw and cable anchor bolt (preceding illustrations). Slide out old cable. Use the end of the new cable to poke through the hole in the side of the shift lever and move the cable fixing plate back:

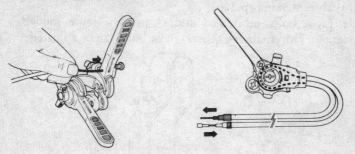

Thread cable through housings:

Fix and adjust as per instructions above.

Disassembly

Remove chain or remove tension roller by undoing bolt 14. Slack off rear wheel axle bolts, undo chapter screw and nut 11 and 12, and remove unit from bike. Undo jockey roller bolt 14.

Prise off dustcaps 1. Remove circlips 2. Pull out cage plate 15 until cage stop catch clears main body of unit and allow to unwind. Seperate. Ditto procedure for adapter 10.

Clean   parts in solvent. Be sure main body is thoroughly dry before lubricating. Assembly is reverse of above.

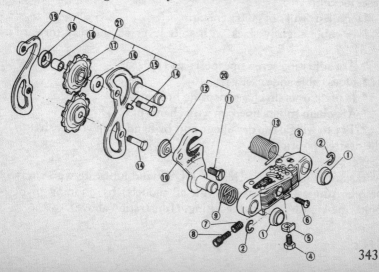

Trouble-shooting

Derailleur is sticky, won't always shift, sometimes shifts unexpectedly.

* Is shift lever working smoothly but with enough friction to hold derailleur in place (p.315)?

* Are cables sticking (p.316)?

* Are pivot bolts lubricated and clean? On some models (Campagnolo, Huret, among others) these bolts can be adjusted.

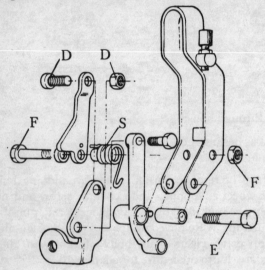

Undo locknuts for bolts D, E, and F, undo bolts one-eighth turn, reset locknuts.

Derailleur will not go far enough.

* Is cable slightly slack with shift lever all the way forward (p.317)?

* Are adjusting screws properly set (p.328)?

* Does cable slide easily (p.316)?

* Is pivot or main changer spring broken?

* Are chain rollers lined up with chain (p.327)?

* Try to wiggle the derailleur unit by hand. Can you push it to the desired position?

Yes:

works are gummed up. Clean in solvent and lubricate with spray or oil. Adjust (not possible with all models) by undoing pivot bolts one-eighth turn and resetting. (Illustration above).

No:

if it won't reach the big rear cog, remove mounting plate and bend it in a vise.

if it won't reach the little rear cog, bend mounting plate, or put in shims at the mounting bolt.

Chain throws off cogs.
* Are adjusting screws set properly (p.321)?
* Are any teeth worn or bent (p.297, 304)?
* Is chain good (p.299)?
* If chain is skipping, is spring tension for roller cage sufficient (p.330)?
* Is roller cage aligned with chain (p.327)?

Power Train – Trouble-shooting Index
Noises

First make sure that noise is coming from power train by coasting bike. If noise continues it is probably a brake (p.207) or hub (p.281) problem. If noise persists, try to determine if it comes from the front (crankset), the chain, or the rear sprocket(s). Do this by disconnecting the chain (p.300) and spinning the various parts.

Grinding noises:
Front –
* Bottom bracket bearings OK (pp. 292, 295)?
* Pedal bearings OK (p.287)?
* Chain rubbing derailleur?
* Front sprocket rubbing cage or chainstays (p.298)?
Back –
* Wheel bearings OK (p.281)?
* Freewheel OK (p.303)?

Clicks or Clunks:

One for every revolution of crankset –
* Pedal tight (p.281)?
* Crank(s) tight (p.289)?

* Bottom bracket bearings OK (pp. 292, 295)?
  * Are teeth on sprocket(s) bent (pp. 297, 304)?

Two or three for every revolution of the crankset –
  * Are teeth on rear sprocket(s) bent (p.304)?
  * Is chain worn or frozen (p.299)?
No go. Pedals and chain spin uselessly –
  Three-speeds, see p. 314.
  Ten-speeds, see p.344
Delayed shifts, no shifts, or not all gears
  Three-speeds, see p. 314.
  Ten-speeds, see p.344.
  For all other problems consult the trouble-shooting section for
the part which is malfunctioning.

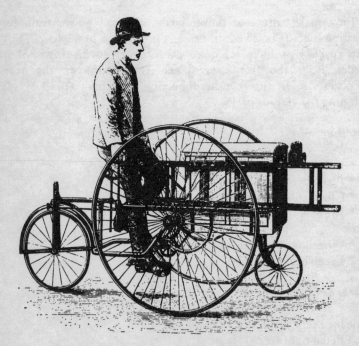

Tricycle carriers like this late 1800 s model
are what we need now.

6. Service Interval Chart

Part	Weekly	Monthly	6 months	Yearly
General	Clean with cloth and toothbrush	Nuts and bolts secure?	Wax or coat with LPS-1	Leather saddles, dress with neatsfoot oil from underneath
Tyres	Check pressure and for embedded glass			
Brakes	Check cable and shoe adjustment	Oil or LPS pivot bolt adjustment		Dismantle, clean and regrease or LPS
Rims	Check for truth and even spoke tension			
Chain	Oil, if in hard service	Check for play		
Derailleurs		Oil or LPS	Chain roller wheels – dismantle, clean and regrease or LPS	Dismantle, clean and regrease or LPS
3-speed hub		Oil		
Hubs		Oil, check adjustment	Dismantle, clean, regrease	
Bottom bracket		Oil, check adjustment	Dismantle, clean, and regrease (hard service)	Dismantle, clean, and regrease (ordinary service)
Headset		Check adjustment		
Pedals		Oil, check adjustment		
Cables		Check for fraying	Dismantle and regrease or LPS	

6 Racing

For me cycling as a sport is personal, a way of being with myself, and while an interest in going fast has necessarily involved me with competition machinery, my racing experience is limited to HPVs. Information presented here has been gleaned from books and talking to people.

The Complete Cycle Sport Guide, by Peter Konopka (£6.95, from Department RIB, *Bicycle Magazine*, 89-91 Bayham Street, London NW1) tells you everything you need to know about racing from start to finish. The author is a sports doctor and his advice on the physiological aspects of training and competition will be of interest to anyone interested in keeping fit. Selpress Books, 35 High Street, Wendover, Bucks HP22 6DU offer over half a dozen books on the subject, including *All About Bicycle Racing* and *Bicycle Track Racing*, both of which are very good. John Forester's *Effective Cycling* (Custom Cycle Fitments, 782 Allen Court, Palo Alto CA 94303 USA) offers much information of value to the racer. For the latest news on racing, obtain the monthly periodicals *Cyclist Monthly* and the *Pro News* and the weekly journal *Cycling*.

To race, you will have to belong to one or even two organizations, depending on the type of event in which you compete. There are basically four types of events: time trial, road race, track and cyclo-cross. Here are the addresses of the national organizations:

Professional Cycling Association
4 Lane Top
Queensbury
Bradford
West Yorks

Road Time Trials Council
Dellacre
Mill Road
Yarwell
Peterborough PE8 6PS

British Cycling Federation
16 Upper Woburn Place
London WC1

Irish Cycling Federation
9 Casement Park, Finlas West
Dublin 11

British Cyclo-cross Association
8 Bellham Road
Hampton Magna
Nr. Warwick

Northern Ireland Cycling Federation
9a Great Northern Street
Belfast

The appropriate national organization above will supply you with the name and address of a local club for you to join. Time-trialists need only be a member of a club affiliated to the Road Time Trials Council, but competitors in other events must also take out membership in the British Cycling Federation.

In racing you compete according to age, sex and ability, so if you are a beginner do not worry about being trounced first time out – most of the riders will be fairly evenly matched. Some of the greatest bike riders in the world are little shrimps. The less weight to lug around the better. Big people are not excluded either – on downhills they generally have the edge. What counts in the end is heart. Bike racing is an extremely rigorous sport. In skiing, running, football, and most other sports, when you are finished you drop. On a bike a lot of your weight is supported by the machine and only a small amount of energy is required to maintain balance. It is quite possible to run your body to the finish and beyond, so that when you stop you are unable to stand on your feet. Any serious racer has to keep fit with a year-round physical conditioning programme.

The three basic types of races are road, track, and cyclo-cross.

Road

Time trial

This is the premier type of event in Britain, in which each rider is timed separately over 10, 25, 30, 50 and 100 mile courses, or rides as far as possible in 12 or 24 hours. Riders are dispatched at regular intervals and must ride alone. The season is February to October, with a predominance of 10 and 25 mile events to start, then the 50 and 100 mile and 12 and 24 hour events at the height of summer, and ending with hill climbs. An advantage is that anybody can participate, racing themselves against a record. British courses are easier than those on the Continent.

Massed start

Everybody starts together, and first human over the finish line wins. The course can be 10 miles, or 2,600, as in the Tour de France. Most single day events are between 50 and 100 miles for amateurs, and 80 to 180 for professionals. Races lasting two days or more are called stage races.

In road racing riders are pitted against each other, and the resulting shenanigans are sometimes incredible. Intelligence, strategy, trickiness, and psychology play an equal role with riding ability and strength. Teams work together to launch a strong team-mate ahead of the pack to victory, and block opposition riders. In big races like the Tour de France bicycles collide and pedals jam into spokes. Bikes are of a conventional design, with freewheels and brakes.

A type of road race popular in America is the criterium. It is usually held on a closed circuit measuring less than two miles around, with sharp and narrow corners, over distances ranging from 25 to 62 miles. Very precise riding is needed to cope with the corners and the dense pack of riders created by the narrowness of the streets or road. Criterium bikes tend to have very stiff frames for quick handling, and a high bottom bracket so that pedalling can continue through the corners.

Cyclo-cross

Cross-country races from point to point or around a course, from 1 to 16 miles in length, run either as a time trial or with a massed start. These are typically through steep climbs and descents, mud, thick woods, streams and hurdles. Some sections are negotiated on foot. It is a rough sport, physically very demanding, with plenty of spills.

Track

The machine common to a wide variety of track events is the greyhound of bikes: an ultra-light frame with a short wheelbase; a fierce position with the saddle high and handlebars low; a single fixed wheel gear, with no brakes; and tyres bonded to the rims with shellac, to withstand the stresses of violent track manoeuvres. There are no quick-release hubs, gears, pumps, cables, etc., making these among the most lovely and functional of bikes.

There are many different kinds of track events. Here are a few:

THE 'BLACK SWAN:' GOING HOME—'PACEMAKER COMING ON.'

Sprint

Usually a 1000 metre course with only the last 200 metres timed. Involves all kinds of tricky tactics and scheming. There are times when racers hold their bikes stock-still while jockeying for position. *Behind* the leader and in his/her slipstream until the final sprint is the favoured winning position.

Pursuit

Two riders or teams start on opposite sides of the track and try to catch each other.

Time trials

Against the clock, as in road racing.

Devil take the hindmost

Last man over the line every 2 or 3 laps is out.

CRAWLEY : GOING DOWN.

Paced racing

Motorcycles are used as pace-setters for the riders, who stay as close as possible to the pacer's rear wheel so as to minimize wind resistance. Speeds up to 60 mph.

Madison

Teams of two riders run in relays. Events run from 50 kilometres or one hour to six-day races. Each team member runs one or two laps and then hands over to a team-mate, literally throwing them by the seat of their pants or by a hand-sling. A very spectacular form of racing.

Speedway

Run on dirt track ovals with stripped down bikes using low gearing and studded track tyres, this is a grass roots sport. Fast action, with lots of broadside skids and spills. About 100 clubs in Great Britain under

Cycle Speedway Council
9 Meadow Close
Hethersett
Norwich NR9 3DZ.

7 Accessories

Once upon a time, cycle accessories were cheap bits of decorative garb avoided by dedicated cyclists like the plague. There is still nothing quite so beautiful as a clean, no frills racing bike, but for many general functions such as commuting, touring and utility use, the right accessories can make a crucial difference in efficiency and comfort. Make sure, however, that the item you are contemplating is well made and will stand up to the job, and expect to pay for it. Proper kitting out of a rider and a touring or commuting bike can easily equal the cost of the machine.

Anti-puncture products

Punctures are the bane of the cyclist, and not a year passes without the introduction of a new product claimed to eliminate the problem. Here's a brief run-down on the merits and demerits of each type.

1. Liquid sealants. These can be used with wire-on tyres and tubulars fitted with a two-piece Presta valve. Sealant adds about two ounces to the tyre weight. The tyre is then theoretically proofed against direct punctures, as from a nail or thorn, but not against slashes or cuts, as from glass. Sometimes sealant works, and sometimes it does not. If the tyre suffers a major blow-out the sealant can create a thorough mess. It can also put paid to a tyre valve. Finally, most liquid sealants lose effectiveness after six months to a year because the solvent evaporates. In most cases, liquid sealants are more trouble than they are worth. However, if you do high mileages on littered urban streets and are plagued by punctures, and are prepared to replace the inner tube/sealant combination every six months or so, then the product may be worth a try.

2. Tuffy Tape. This is a thin ribbon of polymer plastic which is inserted inside the tyre between the casing and the inner tube. Extraordinarily tough and pliable, Tuffy Tape is effective at warding off punctures from ordinary broken glass, nails and thorns, but cannot withstand a long, needle-sharp carpet tack. In conventional $1\frac{1}{4}$ and $1^3/_8$ inch wide 55 to 75 psi tyres, Tuffy Tape has little adverse effect on performance – e.g. ride comfort, rolling

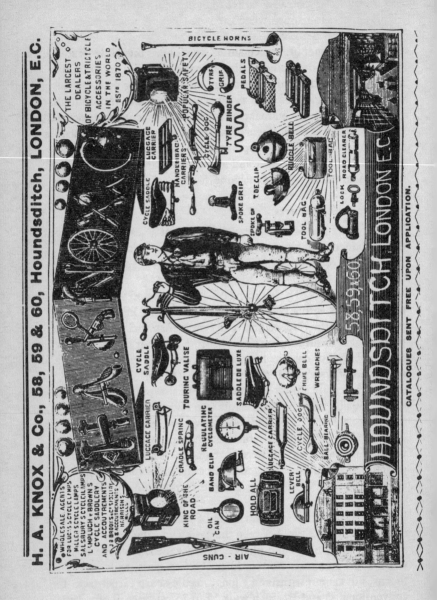
354

resistance and weight. One difficulty, however, is that in some cases Tuffy Tape can cause rather than prevent punctures.

This appears to happen when the tape changes position away from the central bead of the tyre. Some people have this difficulty and others do not, but it is a good idea to deflate the inner tube once a month or so, and ensure that the tape is correctly positioned. It is also important to use the correct size tape for a given tyre. Problems seem to arise when Tuffy Tape intended for $1\frac{1}{4}$ inch tyres is used in narrow section 1 and $1^{1}/_{8}$ inch wide 100 psi tyres. In any case, Tuffy Tape in a narrow section tyre noticeably diminishes performance – so one might as well use a heavier, more durable $1\frac{1}{4}$ inch wide tyre in the first place.

For regular riding on littered urban streets, Tuffy Tape in a stout $1\frac{1}{4}$ inch wide tyre will certainly help prevent punctures. If there is a puncture you will be able to effect a repair – a nigh impossible task when a liquid sealant has failed and deposited sticky muck all over the inner tube, tyre casing and rim. If you use Tuffy Tape, be sure to reduce tyre pressure by 5 psi as there will be less room inside the tyre.

3. Wolber Invulnerable Tyre. Available in both wire-on and tubular models, this tyre has a stainless steel mesh between the outer tread and casing that reduces punctures, on average, by 30 per cent. Ride and performance is similar to good ordinary tyres, but cost is about double. The Invulnerable is a popular alternative among performance-minded cyclists who want increased puncture protection without the prospect of product malfunction.

4. Solid inner tubes. For a brief time an American product called No-Mor Flat was offered in Britain. Although this has a pencil thin hollow core, it is in practice a solid inner tube on which nails, spikes, broken glass and even electric drills have no effect. There are two snags. Fitting the No-Mor Flat on to a rim is an event that you will remember, with pain, for the rest of your life. More fundamentally, the tube is very heavy and consequently has an extremely adverse effect on wheel performance. The ride is harsh, and the additional weight greatly magnifies the gyroscopic qualities of the wheel – meaning that it can be fatally difficult to change direction when riding the bike. (You want to turn; the bike does not.) Definitely a case of once tried, never again.

5. Solid tyres. The leading brand is Zeus. One hundred per cent puncture proof and also the stuff of a Homeric epic to mount on a rim. Once in place, it has such a rough ride that it will destroy the bike, if the rider is not shattered first. Very bad traction for cornering and braking. As one tester remarked in *Bicycle Magazine*, 'I would rather have two flats a week for life than use Zeus Airless Tyres'.

To sum up: if you are trekking through a thorn forest, liquid sealant may help, but be prepared for a mess. For very good additional protection with a sturdy $1\frac{1}{4}$ or $1^3/_8$ inch wide tyre, use Tuffy Tape. For performance with some additional protection, use the Wolber Invulnerable.

Bells and horns

Little bells and horns are forever failing or being stolen. Freon horns contribute to noise pollution. Yelling is quick, reliable, and the most expressive.

Car racks

If you possess a car, you will probably want it to carry bikes. There are two types of car rack: rear mounted and top mounted. Rear mounted versions are inexpensive, usually quick to attach, and will hold two bikes. The machines tend to scratch each other, and to collect road grit. They are also vulnerable to other cars. Top mounted versions cost more, attach easily enough, and will hold up to six bikes safely out of harm's way. The LP range of car carriers are sturdily constructed, substantial products that perform efficiently, and include a Universal model for attaching to already existing car racks. An original type of bike carrier for cars is the Zulu. This consists of pads which rest on the roof and support the bicycle, and a system of straps to hold it in place. Capacity for two bikes. The whole thing can be set up with bikes inside of four minutes, and stores into a compact bag when not in use.

Carriers

The best sort of carrier depends on your needs. Straight handlebar bikes can use the traditional wicker basket, or a wire basket, and these are surprisingly versatile and useful. Avoid the type which uses a support rack where part of the rack rests on the head tube. When the handlebars are turned the support rack scratches the head tube.

A cloth slingbag or musette can go with you on and off the bike and will manage books, papers and the odd container of milk. Most panniers are quick release and in this respect convenient, but have a zillion straps and drawstrings that are a major performance when shopping. More convenient but less commodious are the Trelock plastic ABS panniers, which have a single catch hinged lid that can be locked, simultaneously securing the pannier to the bike. The Trelock pannier will hold A4 size papers, but cannot be classed as totally waterproof. This is the claim made for the Freedom Bikepacking Commuter Panniers, which are made of Cordura and when off the bike, zip together to become a four compartment briefcase.

For around town use, a lightweight alloy spring clip carrier rack such as the Pletscher (about £5) will manage moderate loads. The steel Karrimor carrier rack (about £7) is strong and durable. Best and lightest is the Jim Blackburn alloy rack, which will leave little change from £20. Less expensive, and with many interesting design features, are the Andrew Hague alloy carrier racks.

As with many other cycle accessories, carrier rack and pannier technology is developing rapidly. It's worth popping along to a good bike shop to check out the latest models.

Catalogues

Catalogues listing cycles, components and accessories for sale by post are a good way of checking out the latest in gear, and usually contain an interesting selection of articles and a wealth of technical tips. One that I would never be without is the Freewheel catalogue (85p at newsagents or from 275 West End Lane, London NW6 1QS). More expensive but chock-a-block with hardcore equipment is *Everything Cycling* available direct from Ron Kitching, Hookstone Park, Harrogate HG2 7BZ (£4.60) or from bike shops (£3.50). Another glossy entry is the Richmond Cycles catalogue (75p from 36 Hill Street, Richmond, Surrey).

Child seats

Rear mounted moulded plastic seats will manage a child weighing up to 40 pounds, and should include a wrap-around spoke guard to prevent feet from tangling in the spokes. These seats will also neatly hold a boxful of groceries. Alternatively, a combination child seat and pannier with locking lid called the Pac 2 is available. Rear mounted seats are best used with a diamond frame bike; without the support of a crossbar (top tube) the extra weight of the child can easily cause frame whip and unstable handling.

Even on a diamond frame bike, handling can be a problem and one tidy way around this is a seat called the Easy Rider, which attaches directly to the crossbar and places the child between the adult's arms, thus creating a minimal adverse effect on bike handling.

Another route is a trailer. I've used an American type called the Bugger (my apologies for their linguistic ignorance) to cart about two hefty children, and it is a wonder. Most people recoil at the idea of placing their nearest and dearest in a 'vulnerable' trailer. I suspect that, overall, the detrimental effect on bike handling of a rear mounted carrier creates a greater danger. Further advantages of a trailer are capacity up to one-half the adult rider weight (say 70 to 80 pounds, or two kids), and quick release hitching which leaves the bike a proper bike when the trailer is not in use. It is their performance factor, plus cost, which makes a large trailer a better option than a tricycle with two side by side rear seats.

Once the child is about four, he or she can ride the back of a tandem and join the fun via a junior pedalling attachment such as the one made by Andrew Hague. Tandems, particularly good ones, can be quite expensive. However, although a child aged eight or so can ride a bike on roads in company with adults, no great distances can be contemplated, and the adults will have a full time job in the role of shepherd. Children need to be age twelve or so before they possess a sufficient attention span to be safe when cycling on roads, and the necessary strength to start dusting off the adults. Looked at as a means of family transport for eight years or so, a tandem is economically a good investment, and a lot of fun besides. Plus, if you look after it, you will be able to re-sell for a tidy sum.

Cycle bags

These are large bags designed to hold a bike with the wheels off and are a splendid way of foxing the anti-bike contingent when travelling by rail, etc. Most will *not* accept a bike with mudguards.

Fairings

At 12 mph on a bike the retarding effect of mechanical drag and air resistance is about the same. Past 20 mph overcoming increased air resistance consumes 85 to 90 per cent of pedalling effort. Put another way, in terms of air resistance 20 mph on a bike takes four times the effort required for 10 mph.

The Zipper fairing is a clear, bubble-like windscreen that mounts to the brake lever hoods in a trice, and claims a 20 per cent improvement in aerodynamic efficiency. The beneficial effect is more pronounced at higher speeds, and overall works out to allow the use of a gear ten inches higher than would otherwise be the case. On long downhills the extra turn of speed is very evident and exciting and, because of the air pressure on the screen, bike handling is actually somewhat steadier. The main drawback is vulnerability to cross-winds, and a large lorry overtaking at speed will put a Zipper equipped bike out of track by about twelve inches instead of the more usual six inches. On a very gusty day you will want to leave it off the bike.

The Zipper fairing is useful for fending off rain and snow, and helping to keep the rider warm in cold weather. The product is most effective out on the open road; aerodynamic efficiency is not of great moment in stop-and-go town riding. If you often carry your bike up and down stairs, having a Zipper aboard can make matters awkward. However, it really does mount and dismount within seconds, and on long journeys allows greater distances for noticeably less effort. (By direct mail only from Glen Brown, Zip Designs, 458 Thayer Road, Santa Cruz CA 95060 USA, price on application.)

Glasses

For urban riding a pair of glasses will spare grit in the eyes, and at speed in the country eliminate burning of the eyes by the wind. This latter seems to be personal: wind causes eye discomfort in some people, and in others, not. But if your commuting route includes heavily trafficked roads, or blustery, dirt raising weather, then glasses are a definite aid to avoiding discomfort. Plain, untinted glasses are available for those who do not want to jaundice their view of the world. Look for glasses that ride clear of the face, to help minimize condensation problems, or that embody an anti-fog element, such as the Baruffaldi (cycle shops).

Gloves
Cycling mitts are fingerless, with ventilated mesh backs and padded leather palms. The padding can help to prevent numb hands from pinched nerves, and affords some protection in the event of a spill. For cold weather there are mittens with slits cut in the palms, to give the fingers ready access for delicate tasks.

Handlebar tapes
There's quite a dazzling range of handlebar tapes available these days, and if you are at all cosmetically inclined, you should drop by a good bike shop and check out the possibilities. From the functional standpoint of comfort, if your hands numb easily, different tapes offer various degrees of padding to help insulate against road shock. Plastic and cloth tapes are generally cheap and nasty, although they are all that is required on a no-frills racing bike. The exception is Benotto tape, which comes in an outrageous range of colours, and is favoured by many top professional riders. A better grip and a subdued range of pastel colours is to be found with suede type finish tapes such as Andrew Hague Handlebar Tape and Dahltron No. 1. For more padding, Bike Ribbon micro-cell strips in a range of plain and metalized colours, and for the ultimate in comfort, foam sleeve Grab-ons. These are a popular item, and go for the real McCoy. There are a lot of imitation Grab-ons around, and most of them are distinctly inferior in performance and durability. The style minded may favour leather sleeves, which richly deserve the three full pages of instructions on getting them aboard a bike, and this explains why a handlebar and stem with leather⁻ sleeves already mounted starts at £55.

Helmet
In most fatal bicycle accidents the injury is to the head. Even a drop of two feet onto a hard surface is enough to fracture the skull. Wear a helmet whenever you cycle. It's inconvenient. So is not being able to think or talk because your head has been pounded into jelly.

A helmet must protect against impact, and simultaneously avoid frying up brain matter through lack of ventilation. Cycling is warm work, and hill climbing while wearing a helmet on even a temperate day can leave you awash in perspiration.

The classic cycling 'helmet' consists of a network of padded leather strips, and is great for ventilation but of little use when piling head first into a brick wall or parked car. The best protection is provided by hard shell helmets with a shock-absorbing liner or suspension system. Compact, inexpensive models such as the Reg 400 and Brancale offer protection, but only limited ventilation.

People who perspire easily should consider the American Skid-Lid. This has an outer shell of Lexan formed into a circular band, and four wide prongs that extend towards the top of the skull. The inner lining consists of rebound foam, and different size pads allow custom fitting. The top of the head is vulnerable to penetration by a sharp object, but the Skid-Lid is a good option for people who cycle warm, and who would otherwise not use a helmet at all.

The most satisfactory level of protection, and an adequate degree of ventilation, is to be found in the Byka helmet. This bears a close resemblance to the well proven American Bell TourLite, and consists of a hard shell with large air scoops, a lining of polystyrene, and different size pads for custom fitting.

Many people object to using a helmet while cycling. They think it looks foolish, or want to maintain freedom, simplicity and contact with fresh air. In most cycling accidents it is only the cyclist who is injured or killed. So the wearing of a helmet is largely a matter of personal choice, in which the pleasure of 'freedom' and other intangibles must be weighed against the prospect of death or disablement.

Calculating that prospect is not simple. The Department of Transport reckons that a given journey by bicycle is ten times more likely to include an accident than that same journey by motor vehicle. However, factors such as rider age and experience potential. Children cycle the fewest miles but have the greatest number of accidents, and cyclists on minor rural roads are in less danger than their urban counterparts. There is a statistical case, if one wants to make it, for saying that children, and urban and racing cyclists are well advised to wear helmets, while adult touring cyclists are at relatively little risk.

Statistics have none of the enduring imperishability of a tree or stone kerb with which your head has come into contact. They do not bleed, talk peculiarly, or spend six months in a hospital. Some of the people that this has happened to were among the most experienced cyclists around. All too often the accident was in no way their fault.

Initially, wearing a helmet is inconvenient, and can make you feel foolishly overcautious. I've used helmets for years now, and the only time I feel foolish is if I ride without one. At the VeloCity conference in Bremen in 1980, several hundred of the worlds' most experienced cyclists went on a guided tour of the city bike paths. It was about as safe and tame an affair as you could hope to find, but I still wore a helmet. I did not collect one single laugh.

There was a great billboard poster around for while. It showed a man in a wheelchair and the caption read: 'I didn't wear a seatbelt because it was inconvenient'. Wear a helmet. Always.

Kickstand
A kickstand adds a lot of weight for very little useful function. There is almost always something against which a bike can be leaned. A lightweight cure for the bike falling over because of front wheel movement is a parking brake, which can be made from a clothes pin or other handy bit, and jammed into the brake lever when required. A device specifically for this purpose is the Blackburn Brakestopper.

Lights
Adequate cycle lighting presents a whole series of problems for which there is no single perfect answer. There are three basic types of lighting systems: battery, generator, and generator with storage battery.

Generator types take power off the wheel tyre or hub, thus increasing pedalling resistance. There is more hardware, wires can snag and break, and the system is permanently attached to the bike. Underway the ligths are bright and strong, but unless a storage battery is fitted, they go out when you stop. They also have a tendency to blow out bulbs on fast downhills, although this can be cured by fitting a zener diode to bleed off excess current.

Battery lights stay on when you stop, but do not provide an overwhelming amount of incandescence to start with and progressively fade. They can be got on and off the bike easily. This is handy for map reading and roadside repairs, and for other people who happen to have need of a light – it's rare to go through a winter season on just one set of battery lights.

For riding in the dark countryside generator lights are pretty much a requirement if you want to actually see what is happening. They are also the most convenient for a bike frequently locked up on the street in that the lights are there, when you need them. Either way, generator lights are more economic to run than battery lights. A very good generator light is the Sanyo Dynapower. It is well worth complimenting a generator with a storage battery such as the Dynomight. This automatically provides battery power to keep the lights going when the bike stops. The batteries recharge off the generator when the bike is moving, and the unit includes a zener regulator to prevent blown bulbs.

If you ride mostly in town and do not want to lumber your bike with additional weight when not needed, then battery lights will probably be the most convenient. The French made WonderLites are not so great for seeing, but are readily visible to other road users, and the mounting brackets are versatile. This allows you to easily get the lights up high, where they are properly visible. The common practice of mounting lights on the fork blades and seat stays, alongside the wheels, greatly reduces visibility to other road users. A further danger is that the brackets can loosen and twist the light into the spokes. This has cause some nasty accidents.

Batteries for WonderLites are not available in rechargeable versions, and can work out expensive over a season. The standard Ever Ready battery lights use D-cells, and these can be obtained in a ni-cad rechargeable version that will save a considerable amount of money if you use lights a lot.

Any kind of lighting system is capable of failing without notice. A second back-up light of some sort is essential. The French Matex light combines a white front and red rear, weighs only five ounces, and straps to an arm or leg. Because it is moved around a lot, it is very visible. A still more eye-catching device is the Sanyo Pulseguard. This is a high intensity light which flashes 60 times a minute, and that can be attached to belt or bike. Research has shown that blinking high intensity lights are the most effective means of making a cyclist visible to motorists.

Some people object to high intensity lights. One argument is that the need for paying attention rests with the motorist. Another is that high intensity lights can startle a motorist and make them slow down!

As any study of cycling accident statistics will reveal, the problem at night is to survive. Bicycle lights are diminutive. In cities and towns they are easily lost in the welter of traffic lights, street lights and neon signs. In these circumstances not even a high intensity flasher will seriously discomfort a motorist. Along a dark back street, however, it is an attention-grabber for the many stupid, stupid motorists who drive using only their parking lights to see by. Out in the country a car coming up from behind may be doing 70 mph to your 10 mph. That's an 88 feet per second speed differential, and if the visible range of your rear lights is 300 feet or less, it is under the distance required for a car to stop (315 feet). In short, if the motorist blinks and rubs an eye, or turns for a casual quick glance at a passenger, you can be wiped out A high intensity flasher light may indeed make a motorist slow down, and this is exactly what you want.

One way to understand the situation, and to silence the clods who think that a seat stay mounted rear light ought to be sufficient, is to realise that the risk of a fatal accident is nearly four times greater under conditions of darkness. Furthermore, of all accidents, 85 per cent happen in urban areas, with 30 per cent of these entailing 'grave consequences' for the cyclist; of the remaining 15 per cent of accidents which happen in rural areas, fully half result in serious injuries or death for the cyclist.* Why? In most instances it was because the motorist did not see the cyclist.

Fred DeLong, technical editor of the American magazine *Bicycling*, took the trouble to replicate a series of accidents. He used the actual vehicles, equipment and clothing involved in the original accident, or duplicates in identical condition, at the same locations and times of day. In nearly every instance, and despite the use of regulation cycle lights in some cases, the problem was that the motorist could not see the cyclist, *even knowing that the cyclist was there*.

Cycling at night is dangerous. The only sensible way to do it is looking like a Christmas tree gone berserk. See also the reflectors entry in this chapter for more information.

Locks
See chapter 4.

Mudguards
A requirement for tourists and people living in rain forests or at the end of muddy tracks. They do add a lot of air resistance through, and if you want to go like the clappers and doen't mind a strip of dirt up your spine once in a while, then leave them off. The short models are completely useless. Full length plastic mudguards are light, and easy to get on and off the bike (weekend racers, note), but eventually warp and fail. Much better are the ESGE and Bluemels chromoplastic models, which will stand years of abuse. Stainless steel and aluminium mudguards are durable, and offer a mounting point for lights and other gear, but tend to be noisy. This can be cured with undersealing paint (motor accessory shops).

*Keller, H., *The position of cycling accidents within the entire accident pattern*, Documentation, 1st International Bicycle Congress, Velo/City 80, Bremen, p.238.

Nail pullers or flint-catchers
These are small half-loops of wire that ride just above the tyre
and brush off shards of broken glass, pebbles and other nasty
things. Most effective with tubular and narrow section HP
tyres, and a significant challenge to fit if you use mudguards.

Odometer
In the economy version these are a little gizmo that works off
the spokes and tells how far you have gone. This is a function
also usually included in electronic speedometer/computers (see
separate entry).

Pumps
I long ago tired of fending off little urchins who filch
equipment, of seeing an expensive aluminium barrel pump
dented and therefore made useless, and of pumps constantly
falling about the place while carrying a bike up and down stairs.
I keep a large workshop pump at home, which inflates tyres
with magnificent efficiency, and carry a short pocket pump that
will serve for emergencies. For touring, however, you will need
a decent pump. One of the very best is the Zefal Preset, with a
self contained pressure regulator.

A workshop pump will include a pressure gauge, but its
readout is likely to have only a passing affinity with reality. For
accurate work with modern high pressure tyres – essential for
peak performance – use a separate tyre pressure gauge.

You may also want to possess a tiny Presta/Schrader adaptor,
which allows a Presta tyre valve to be inflated with a garage air
line. If you use this be very careful; cycle tyre pressures are
high, but the volume of air is small, and only a moments
inattention is required for the whole thing to blow to
smithereens. Personally, I frequently have the opposite
problem, i.e., a Schrader valve and only a Presta type
pump...

Raingear
The classic cycling cape drags over the shoulders, back and
handlebars, allowing air to circulate up from underneath. Also
circulated is road spray from your own tyres, and from other
vehicles. This kind of garment is as outmoded as the Dodo bird,

although for reasons of simple economy capes still have many adherents.

The problem when cycling in the rain is to keep away wet from both without and within. Conventional waterproofs that seal out the rain also seal in body perspiration, and of the two types of drenching the former is preferable. The difficulty has been resolved by a new material called Gore-tex. This is a stretched out membrane of P.T.F.E.
with billions of microscopic holes. These are of a size which keeps large molecules of liquid water out, but allows free passage and evaporation of the smaller molecules of the water vapour generated by the body. Gore-tex fabric is also extremely windproof.

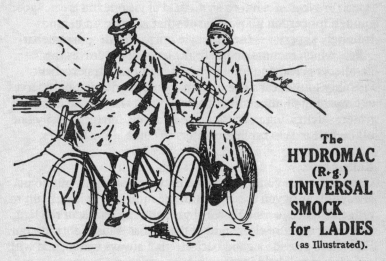

The
HYDROMAC
(R·g.)
**UNIVERSAL
SMOCK
for LADIES**
(as Illustrated).

A very nice thing about Gore-tex rainwear is that it is available in a range of styles to suit different tastes. My Berghaus Mistral Alpen jacket (it is alas no longer produced, although there is talk of a similar new model) is a prized garment that looks equally good over a pullover, or a business suit. At the other end of the specturm the shapeless Berghaus Mistral works entirely to function, and will withstand with ease a full Dartmoor gale.

The Caldo range of Gore-tex clothing is designed for cycling and is probably the most stylish currently available. Several models feature the useful refinement of underarm zips for ventilation control. A well shaped optional hood will zip to any of the Caldo jackets. This is important. A large hood such as on a jacket designed for hiking is a serious impediment to vision when cycling.

A good line of value for money Gore-tex clothing comes from Been Bag, which in style takes after orthodox cycling garments. Top value has to be the Greenspot nomad Gore-tex jacket (optional trousers available) in any colour you like so long as it is royal red or blue. By post only, check issues of *Bicycle Magazine* for current price.

Rear view mirror
The small mirrors which mount to the back of the wrist or attach to eyeglasses have a small field of vision, and are not good enough for certain knowledge of what is going on behind. Infinitely superior is the Mirrcyle mirror for drop handlebar bikes, which mounts on the brake lever hood, leaves the handlebars clear and unobstructed, and provides excellent visibility to the rear. The information provided not only serves as a warning of impending danger, but is also a great aid to faster, safer riding in traffic. The Mirrycle mirror is easily one of the best aids to cycling comfort to come along in years.

Reflectors
Good lights are your main defense system at night, but do not always identify you as a cyclist to the motorist. It is difficult to judge distance to a single rear light, and the dazzle of the light itself may obscure clear sight of the cyclist. Plus, lights can fail. Reflectors provide a good back-up that always works, and with proper use will help identify you as a cyclist.

A red rear reflector, usually mounted on the mudguard, is a legal requirement. Wheel and pedal reflectors will also sooner or later be a legal requirement. Wheel reflectors are not very useful, as they ordinarily become visible only when the cyclist is already broadside on to the motorist. The exception is when wheel reflectors are mounted to return illumination fore and aft; they then have a stroboscopic intensity which is very effective. Pedal reflectors are very good. Their low position is readily picked up by headlights, and their attention getting distinctive pattern of movement readily identifies the presence of a cyclist.

Most reflectors are limited in mechanical effectiveness. Far better are retro-reflective materials, which will reflect light back to a source regardless of the angel of incidence. An excellent product when made of retro-reflective material is the Sam Brown belt, which immediately signifies a two-wheeled vehicle to other road users. Another good item are retro-reflective trouser/arm bands which, like pedal reflectors, are very eye catching.

Panniers, jackets, gloves and so on can all be highlighted with retro-reflective tape, dots and stickers. These all help to tell the motorist who and what you are in time enough to take the appropriate action for your safety. At the minimum you should have at least one set of moving reflectors for catching the attention of motorists, and one item such as a Sam Brown belt or reflectorized jacket to identify you as a cyclist.

Shoes, toe clips and cleats

Ordinary street shoes do not provide sufficient support for the foot unless used with rubber or metal platform pedals. Cycling shoes have a steel or fiberglass shank in the sole to distribute the impact of the thin edges of the commonly used cage type pedals.

Shoes for racing have no heels, and are not intended for walking. Shoes for touring have heels, and in the steel shanked leather soled versions will stand casual walking about. Dual purpose shoes with partially stiffened soles are designed for both cycling and walking, and for many people, excel at both functions. You can now have a cycling shoe which can stand a 2000 mile tour and yet looks perfectly in order with formal clothes. Brands to check out are Madison, Bata, Adidas, Sidi and Rivat.

Toe-clips nearly double pedalling efficiency, and ensure that your feet will remain on the pedals in the event of a mis-shifted gear or unexpected bump. Many ordinary shoes and most cycling/walking shoes have soles with sufficient texture to grip the pedals when snugged down with straps, but can be slipped out with ease when required.

Cleats attach to the sole of the shoe and then in turn lock to pedal. They give tremendous get up and go and are a must for racing and fast riding, but can be inconvenient on a tour when you want to stop and stoll around (you'll have to change shoes or go barefoot), and downright dangerous in traffic.

For winter riding lined cycling boots are available, and for wet weather there are slip on booties that will go over regular shoes. One can also fit toe warmers over the toe clips.

Speedometer
Tyre drive models are generally inaccurate and increase drag. Electronic models offer many other functions, such as elapsed time, journey distance, average speed, maximum speed reached, cadence rate and so on, according to make. Setting one of these up to be accurate can be chore. However, they can be a very useful training aid when practicing for competition or riding for fitness.

Spoke guard
This is a thin plate mounted on the rear wheel that prevents the rear derailleur from catching in the spokes. With a properly adjusted derailleur this should never happen, but should the derailleur malfunction or break (as has happened to me), then down you go, and with the back of the bike twisted into spaghetti.

Trailers
Trailers are absolutely super for hauling around groceries, laundry, children and all manner of heavy gear. Most models attach and detach from the bike in seconds and can free you of the need for racks and panniers – very nice if you are running a high performance machine.

One simple, versatile and relatively inexpensive trailer is the Bike-Hod, which comes complete with a roomy waterproof bag that can be detached when not required. The Bike-Hod trailer frame itself will manage an extraordinary assortment of things, including a full size cello or 4 x 8 foot sheet of plywood. I'm very fond of the rather expensive American Cannodale Bugger, which is designed to carry two children, and that will also manage a wide variety of other items. Trailer technology is very much on the move these days; pop along to a bike shop to check out the latest models.

When using a trailer do not exceed a total weight greater than one half rider body weight, and be cautious when descending hills and over rough ground. It is difficult to overturn a properly designed and loaded trailer, but it can be done.

Tub pouches and toolkits
If you are travelling light – no mudguards, racks or panniers –
a tub pouch or toolkit can be useful for carrying a spare tyre,
tools, additional clothing, a bit of money or whatever. Most of
these fasten unobrusively underneath the saddle, and many
have quick on-off Velcro fittings.

Turn signals
These are silly on a bike. There is not enough distance between
the blinkers to clearly indicate that a change of direction is
proposed. A hand signal is much more definite.

Water bottle
These can be surprisingly useful. Vigorous cycling dehydrates
the body, and a drink may not be readily to hand unless carried
on the bike. There are any number of patent concoctions
available that variously contain gluclose and/or salts.
Personally, I find that a little honey in plain water is just the
ticket for a lift when nearing the end of a long ride. Thermal
bottles are also available for a warm (or cool) drink of soup.

Summary
The right selection of accessories can make a vital difference
to your cycling efficiency, comfort and safety. Do not be afraid
to spend a healthy wad of money, as the return on investment
will probably be excellent. But be aware also that there are
many people who have climbed aboard some beat-up old bike
outfitted catch-as-catch-can, and traversed entire continents.
You can always improvise; the virtue of purpose designed
equipment is usually that it is very much better.

8   Dream – Ramode – Sunfighter – Dream – Birthright

Everybody has dreams and here is one of mine: cars exist only in memory. Cycles are used for local personal transport and light goods carriage, and mass transit systems for long journeys and bulk loads.

The efficiency of such an arrangement in terms of money and energy expenditure is tremendous. A cycle factory is a low-technology operation that is far easier to initiate and maintain than an automobile factory. Cycle production and use does not necessitate vast support industries in petroleum, metals, rubbers, plastics and textiles. Road requirements are minimal. There is no need for traffic regulation, licensing, courts, solicitors and expensive insurance. There are no hundreds of thousands of maimed people requiring expensive hospitalization, emergency and other medical services.

A dream? In China, there are 22,535 people for each motor vehicle, as against 3 people per motor vehicle in Britain. (Heilman, Gail, *Bicycling!*, June 1977). People cycle or use public transportation. A direct comparison would of course be misguided. China is culturally very different, and is a developing country that is austere by Western standards. Much work is done by hand, including crop irrigation, waste disposal and movement of goods up to several hundredweight. A bicycle can cost up to two years' wages, and is obtainable only with a government permit. Money alone is not enough. But bicycle production is steadily increasing to meet demand and in terms of sheer transportation efficiency China is headed down the right road.

In Britain, providing for cyclists is a popular topic for conversation. The government has at last gone so far as to say that cycles ought to be a recognized feature of the general transportation system. Some of the prospective schemes are appealing in concept as, for example, a nationwide network of cyclepaths built on disused railways.

But the main transportation situation in Britain is quite unchanged. British Rail is headed the way of the Dodo bird. Route closures have been a steady feature for many years and continue apace. In turn, motor vehicles and roads are proliferating, and one prediction is that the end of the century will find 27 million cars in use. (Bendixson, T., *Instead of Cars*, Penguin Books, 1977). Until there is a viable mass transport system for people and goods, cyclists and pedestrians will have to slug it out with motor vehicles.

'Planning' is a very relative term with a scope that depends on where you start your thinking. At one level, providing for cyclists may mean creating a cycle lane along a road, or even an entirely segregated cycle path without so much as the smell of a motor vehicle. At another level, the approach can be to eliminate the problem altogether. Most people have to travel to work; but one way of changing this is to rearrange matters so that people live and work in the same area. This is not a small task.

Little more than a decade ago, cycles were not an important part of the scheme of things in Britain. 'Whatever can you say about bicycles?' laughed one friend on learning that I was writing a book on the subject. On participating in my first London cycle demo I was amazed to find that my 'Cars kill' and 'Rights for cyclists' placards were unique. Nowadays matters are very different. You can actually earn a living working in the area of cycling (and with far healthier long-term prospects than in the automotive industry), and cycle planning and activism is intense at many levels.

Take for example the conversation of disused railways into cycle paths. This scheme has origins which the Bristol Cycle group Cyclebag, who in the summer of 1979 built a bike path along 8 kilometres of disused railway between Bath and Bitton, using limestone grit rolled over the existing railway ballast. The route passes through pretty countryside, was originally graded for trains and is therefore easy to cycle, and immediately found a high level of use by both cyclists and pedestrians. The success sparked more work by Cyclebag and other groups, and helped the commissioning by the Department of Transport of John Grimshaw & Associates, to produce *Study of Disused Railways in England and Wales – Potential Cycle Routes* (£11.50, HMSO).

Very briefly, it turns out that over 11,000 kilometres of railway has become disused in England and Wales since 1923, and a good proportion of this is readily convertible into bike paths without major expense. In fact, at 1983 prices over 600 miles of railway cycle paths can be had for £7 million – less than the cost of 3 miles of motorway. Construction is labour-intesive, giving local employment and demand for materials. The study gives full details on construction and technical details, costs and methods for promoting paths. Also now available is a map of potential cycle routes and 33 annexes to the original study, examining a range of 33 possible routes in detail. These include a full schedule of costs (map £2.95, annexes £2.70 each, from

John Grimshaw Associates, 35 King Street, Bristol BS1 4D). Railway cycle paths are commercially viable, useful to everybody and a long way on from running around the place with placards.

A railway cyclepath is only one type among many. The classic example of building an entire town with provision for cyclists is Stevenage, the first of the New Towns and largerly the responsibility of a one-of-a-kind genius, now retired Chief Engineer Eric Claxton. Stevenage has a population density greater than that of Central London, and yet there is not one single traffic, cycle, or pedestrian stoplight or sign in the entire town. The flow of traffic even at rush hour is so smooth that there does not appear to be anybody around.

The Stevenage system succeeds because it is a *total* transportation system. Roads for pedestrians, cycles, mopeds, and motor vehicles are separate and never conflict. It is possible to drive a motor car throughout the town without once encountering a cycle or pedestrian. As a result the average speed of rush-hour traffic is 20 mph, double the average of other cities, and better still than the average in major metropolitan regions such as London.

If you are cycling it is also possible to go anywhere you wish in town via the cycleways or footpaths (on which pedestrians, cycles, and mopeds have mingled freely and almost without incident for over 20 years), and never encounter a motor car. The official cycleway system is 25 miles long, and is shared by all types of cycles, mopeds up to 50cc capacity and pedestrians. The cycleways frequently run alongside main roads but are separated by grass verges and trees from both the roads and footpaths. There are in addition a number of crosstown cycleway links which run independently of roads. Some were originally country lanes from which vehicular traffic has been withdrawn. Additionally, cycles make free use of over 100 miles of footpaths so that most cycle journeys are door-to-door. There are no rules or regulations (and hence no need for the police to concern themselves with traffic regulation) governing the use of the cycleways and footpaths, no 'cycles must or must not'. Cyclists are free to use the vehicle carriageways if they prefer. The existing cycleway system is so attractive, however, that only the odd racer in training buzzing along at 25-mph-plus chooses to mix with the cars.

The different types of roads are kept separate through the generous use of underpasses. These are a study in sensitive design and architecture. An overpass for cycles must rise at least 16 feet over the road, necessitating either a long or steep gradient. An underpass for cycles only requires 7 ft 6 in of headroom; and by excavating to a depth of only 6 feet, using the excavation material to gently raise the road 3 feet, the differences in gradient are still further minimized. The cycleways are normally 12 feet wide and carry two-way traffic. Construction is similar to a footpath, with minimal lighting and drainage. The main costs derive from the earthworks and concrete underpasses needed at intersections to keep cycleways and motor roads apart.

The benefits of a system such as Stevenage's are often intangible and not easily reckoned on a balance sheet. What is the worth of never ever having an obstruction or aggravation in travelling? That whole series of abrasions, conflicts, and problems for which most of us armour up each day just doesn't exist in Stevenage. What price a mother's peace of mind, knowing that her children can walk or cycle anywhere – and never encounter a motor vehicle? Sixty per cent of the workers in town go home for lunch. How do you measure the value and effect of this increased home life? These are alterations in the quality of life, perhaps describable as similar to the relaxed pastoral peacefulness of a 'primitive' society – but with full technological benefits! The worth of this sort of thing can only be determined by each individual.

CYCLES TO MEND! TYRES TO ME—END!

Other benefits are more tangible:

The cycleways serve the interests of a large segment of the population aged 6 to 16 who cannot drive cars. More than 8% of children cycle daily to school. This figure is low, because Stevenage's primary schools are located within easy walking distance of home. Of secondary school children, 17.4% cycle to school.

Such few accidents as do occur on the cycleways are minor. Pedestrians, cyclists, and moped riders are all equally vulnerable and take equal pains to avoid each other. Stevenage's safety record is 4 casualties per 1,000 population per year as against a national average which is more than 50% greater. The direct saving in medical service costs is considerable, to say nothing of life and limb.

By encouraging cycling and walking, the Stevenage system promotes mild exercise. There are more than 4,000 regular cyclists, about 11 per cent of the people working in Stevenage, and at least 10,000 recreational and shopping cyclists. This health benefit may seem minor, but for many people it is the only exercise they get, and as such may extend their longevity by up to five years.

An immense amount of time is saved. There is a high car ownership rate per household but people walk and cycle because it works better than using cars.

Looking over Stevenage as an exercise in the benefits of providing for cyclists is fun, but does not hold much relevance for already existing communities. There are many methods for helping to integrate cyclists into the scheme of things, and no space here for a full discourse on the subject. The starting point for anyone with an interest in cycle planning is *The Bicycle Planning Book*, by Mike Hudson (85p, Friends of the Earth). Mike Hudson is also the lead author of *Bicycle Planning: Policy and Practice* (£39.50, Architectural Press). The book is good but not fully up to date, and grossly overpriced at £39.50 purchase price. Go to your local library to look it over. A general survey of the government politics for cycle planning is *On Our Bikes?* by Caren Levy (£2.95, Friends of the Earth). The broad view is put by Don Mathew in *The Bike is Back* (60p, Friends of the Earth).

There's one bit of business that I cannot resist sharing with you, however, which is contained in the tri-lingual (including English) *Woonerf* (no price available, published by the ANWB, Wassenaarsweg 220, Postbus 93200, 2509BA, the Hague, Holland). A Dutch woonerf is a residential precinct designed primarily for people, and only grudgingly for cars. The latter can gain access, but slowly and not in great numbers.

Landspace in a woonerf belongs to the people, and is safe for children to play in. Such an arrangement gives a far wider dimension to the concept of 'home'. It is definitely the sort of thing that we should head towards. A woonerf demonstrates a key concept in planning for people – territory. In many communities people are secondary to the routing of motor vehicle traffic. For example, zebra pedestrian crossings are often provided only after a certain number of people die at the location. How crazy can you get? The life of a child is worth more than the convenience of a bunch of commuters.

If we really are to enjoy urban living, then we have to get rid of cars and heavy goods lorries. Four out of ten vehicles will someday kill or maim a human being. I used to live in New York City, a town active with muggers. I liked it very much. I saw nothing unusual in always being careful, and sometimes carrying a sword. When I came to England the more benevolent social climate was at first unnerving, and then very relaxing. Civilization. In the same fashion, life without cars and carnage will prove infinitely more pleasant and liberating.

Technologically, the prospects look bright. HPV development is concentrating on road going vehicles for everyday use. These will probably be fitted with small electric motors to assist acceleration and hill climbing. Recent legislation allows the use of such a vehicle without licensing or tax requirements. The motors can be arranged to engage only when a certain amount of pressure is applied to the pedals, e.g. your comfortable working rate. One limitation of electric assist is that more power capacity brings more weight, as in the case of heavy and ponderous milk float. Personal transport HPVs will favour overall light weight and pedal rather than electric power.

Economically, HPVs have got it all over cars, and anyone with a grain of sense will want one. But the change that will truly get rid of cars will have to take place at a basic social level, and be reflected in planning with fundamentally different priorities than those which got us into this pickle. Human life, human contact, loving relationships, worthwhile work and clean premises are the things to go after, not faster production of a refrigerator or television set. As a consumer commodity cars have played a tremendous role in shaping our society. They will be shifted out only with a great deal of work and change.

Promoting and supporting cycling will help in this direction, and

also gains you and yours immediate benefit. If you are interested in this sort of thing, contact one of the groups listed below.

Cycle campaign groups have been established in many towns and cities. For details of your nearest group, contact the Cycle Campaign Network, c/o London Cycling Campaign, Tress House, 3 Stamford Street, London SE1.

The Cyclists' Touring Club has recently appointed a Rights Officer to deal with planning and campaigning issues, who can be contacted at Cotterell House, 69 Meadrow, Godalming, Surrey GU7 3HS. Friends of the Earth run a bicycles campaign from their London office, 377 City Road, London EC1V 1NA, and many local FoE groups are involved in local bike campaigns.

So long!

Index

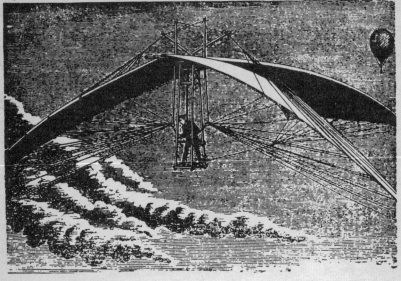

Belgiers de Groof 1874

The author

Richard Ballantine rates education an exercise in frustration tolerance
levels and refuses to divulge his breaking point. He has engaged in a
gamut of occupations and is the co-author, with John Cohen, of *Africa
Addio* (1966), and with Joel Griffiths, of *Silent Slaughter* (1972). He is
the founding editor of *Bicycle Magazine*, has a monthly column in
Bicycle Action Magazine, and is a contributor to *The Bicycle Buyers'
Bible*.